EXPLORERS AND THE NEW WORLD

OTHER BOOKS BY THE AUTHOR

The March of the Teutons
America and the War of 1812
Opening of the Civil War
America and the Monroe Years
Adams vs. Jackson

EXPLORERS AND THE NEW WORLD

EUGENE M. WAIT

Nova Science Publishers, Inc.
New York

Senior Editors: Susan Boriotti and Donna Dennis
Coordinating Editor: Tatiana Shohov
Office Manager: Annette Hellinger
Graphics: Wanda Serrano
Book Production: Matthew Kozlowski, Jonathan Rose and Jennifer Vogt
Circulation: Raymond Davis, Cathy DeGregory, Ave Maria Gonzalez and Raheem Miller
Communications and Acquisitions: Serge P. Shohov

Library of Congress Cataloging-in-Publication Data
Available upon request.

Includes bibliographical references and index.
ISBN 1-56072-964-3

Copyright © 2002 by Nova Science Publishers, Inc.
227 Main Street, Suite 100
Huntington, New York 11743
Tele. 631-424-6682 5 Fax 631-425-5933
e-mail: Novascience@earthlink.net
Web Site: http://www.nexusworld.com/nova

Printed in the United States of America

Dedication

To My Parents:

Eugene Wait
Virginia Rice Wait

CONTENTS

PREFACE

This book on the New World is the tenth published volume of my combined works of 36 books finished and in the process of being prepared for printing. The first book came out in 1972 and the second in 1999. The others followed and are following in short order. All are of the highest quality. So far there are four of my nine volumes on the Age of Lincoln, one of my four books on the Civil War (with more than four planned), two volumes on Imperialism from 1896 to 1906 (five wars in detail), and my Reformation book.

The first is a book entitled *The March of the Teutons* on the Germanic peoples from before Christ to Jamestown, a volume now rare and which has been called a near-classic. The second is *America and the War of 1812*. The third is *Opening of the Civil War* from Lincoln's election day to mid-June of 1861. The fourth is *America and the Monroe Years*. The next is a book tentatively entitled "Zenith of Imperialism," followed by "Adams vs. Jackson," "The Jackson Years," "Great Challenges of Reformation Europe," and this book.

At the time of this writing, I am typing a book "Bull Run and Beyond" and a general concise history of the Civil War in total. Ready to be typed are five more books, following the first Jackson book and a sequel to Bull Run. Then there are many books from the caveman to Jackson. I am expanding my Roosevelt series, my Truman series, and my West series.

You will find all of these of the highest quality in five million words. Read one and you will want to read all.

For this book, I want to thank especially my parents, siblings, Willeen Gray of the Butt-Holdsworth Library, and Librarian Evelyn Jaegelli, formerly of this library. The thanks I have for other people for other books are in my other prefaces.

And thanks to editor-publisher Frank Columbus who believes that talent will win in the publishing industry. My talent is now free to fly, but I will leave it to you to assess my standing among historians. Thank you for reading my works.

Eugene M. Wait
Kerrville, Texas
December 4, 1999

ABOUT THE AUTHOR

Eugene Meredith Wait was born on July 13, 1936, in Longview, Texas. At age eight, he started working with door to door selling. At age seventeen, he joined the Army Reserves. He shortly graduated from Kerrville's Tivy High School. At age nineteen he got an AA from Schreiner College. At age twenty-one he got a BA in history from the University of Texas-Austin. At age twenty-two he began his two years active duty in the Signal Corps. At age twenty-five he received an MA from Texas in Latin American history. In the next years he got all of a Ph.D. from Texas except the orals. Sickness ended that at age twenty-nine. Meanwhile he had worked at the Latin American Collection for Dr. Nettie Lee Benson, who recognized his great talent. The library is now named the Nettie Lee Benson Latin American Collection. When he left he had a scholarship for library science in the specialty of Latin America.

In the next many years he worked at various jobs from manager to dishwasher and did civil service, cared for aged parents, and researched and wrote at a pace of 100 hour weeks for most of the 39 years from 1961 to present. He received rejection slips enough to fill a large box. His talent was generally recognized only by a few until Frank Columbus discovered him in 1998. One year later his second book came out and Columbus told the author that he wanted to publish all books by Eugene Meredith Wait. Wait plans at this time to write more.

Besides his books, he has two scholarly articles, three scholarly book reviews, and 24 minor articles. He owes his success, he says, to his parents and their allowing him to work at age eight at his request. He says that obstacles are meant to be overcome. Religion is the most important thing in his life and work is the most fun. Wait says he was born to write history.

Chapter I

PRINCE HENRY THE NAVIGATOR

In ancient times, the Carthaginians had established a colony at Ceuta, on the north coast of Morocco, making it the southern post of the Straits of Hercules or Gibraltar. The position fell to the Romans; then in succession, over the centuries, to the Vandals, Byzantines under Justinian I, Visigoths, and Arabs. Under the latter it was repeatedly captured by rival Arabs and Moors. It was an early trading center and, in the fifteenth century, it was noted for it's brassware manufactures, ivory, gold, and trading in slaves.

The city was coveted by the Portuguese and the monarch John I captured it in August of 1415 with the battlefield help of Prince Henry the Navigator and two of his brothers. They were knighted on the next day in the mosque, dedicated to the Christian victors. It was a crusading objective, but there were economic reasons for the capture. The city was rich and was the terminal point for the trans-Sahara trade. The Portuguese were to learn about this trade. Also, they learned about the African Negro lands of the Upper Niger and Senegal rivers. In time, they were to desire these blacks for slaves, their lands and their gold, slaves, and ivory which would make a relatively poor country such as Portugal rich.

At this point, the Portuguese were to become more and more interested in the fabulous Christian kingdom of Prester John. This man was legendary long before this time, but he was originally a patriarch of Christians in India where St. Thomas was supposed to have spread Christianity in the first century. There was the report that he had come to Rome in 1122 from India, and had told of the miracles of the shrine of St. Thomas. Nearly one quarter of a century later, his supposed position was increased. Now, he was a Christian conqueror and potentate who rules over vast dominions in the Far East.

Next, in a later chronicle, a bishop from Jibal in Syria told of the Nestorian Prester John who had made war against the Persians and captured the city of the Persians, the city of Ecbatana. According to this account, he advanced to fight for the Church at Jerusalem, but had to turn around at the Tigris and return home. The bishop who told this was at the papal court in 1145. An added choice bit of information was to the effect that he was of the ancient race of the Magi, who had visited Jesus at his birth, according to the Gospels.

About 1165, there was presented to Christendom from Prester John a forged letter addressed to Emperor Manuel I, Cominus of the Byzantinian Empire. According to this letter, Prester John claimed he was the greatest monarch in the world and a devout Christian. Most of these spurious letters dealt with the wonders of his empire. His wish, he said, was to visit the Holy Sepulcher and subdue the enemies of the Cross.

The legend was growing. He had seventy-two kings under him. There were tales of monstrous creatures found in current legend and Amazons of other strange races. Also, one could find the Fountain of Youth and other marvels. In later centuries, before the search was undertaken for him, the locale of this great Christian ruler gradually shifted to Ethiopia or Abyssinia, especially since in 1402 and later, a few Ethiopian monks and envoys came through Jerusalem to Europe from the isolated Christian Coptic kingdoms in northeast Africa. The Portuguese felt that this king of Ethiopia would be an ideal ally against the Moors. One of these Ethiopians reached Lisbon thirty-seven years after the fall of Ceuta to John I's army.

An interested Prince Henry the Navigator talked much with those who had made voyages to various ports of the world. He conversed with Moors from Fez and Morocco. They told him about the Azenegues near the Negroes of Jalof. He opened his mind to the conjectures of learned men and the fables of chivalry. He may have heard about the knowledge of Arabic geographers and may have known about what the Arabs discovered. Planning to explore a passage somewhere to the south, a curving away of the continent of Africa, he settled on the promontory of Sagres on the edge of Portugal. After a dream of promise, he awoke one morning in 1418 to send forth suddenly two ships under the command of Johan Gonzalez Zarco and Tristan Vaz to sail down the Barbary Coast to discover what was beyond. These two captains were young men searching for employment after the end of the Ceuta campaign.

Their object was to undertake the general molestation of the Moors and discoveries beyond Cape Nam, that had not been passed as it allegedly was the place of no return. The two captains did not go beyond that point on this occasion. A storm blew them off course and they found refuge in an unknown island they named Porto Santo. They returned to a delighted Henry and reported that "they found there a race of people living in no settled polity, but not altogether barbarous or savage, and possessing a kindly and most fertile soil."

Perseverance had been Henry's forte thus far and he needed some more in the face of such popular feeling that was felt also by his crews and even his captains. For a while, they had been content with Moorish plunder and the voyages of discovery were stalled. He had some doubts for awhile. He took aside his man Gil Eannes, who had been on one fruitless voyage, and consulted this man that he could not "meet with such peril that the hope of your reward shall not be much greater." He was not to allow public opinion to sway him, but should undertake the passing of the Cape. The resolve Gil Eannes took with him was sufficient and he passed the terrible Cape Bajador. He brought back foreign plants in a barrel of the newfound earth. Henry was most grateful. This passage preceded a lull in discovery down the coast, which lasted from 1434 to 1441, but the Azores remained to be discovered.

Prince Henry collected his maps and noted the existence of the St. Bredan Islands and sent ships to re-discover them for Portugal. In 1431, Goncalo Velho looked and found nothing but the Formigas Rocks in the sea. Another voyage in 1432 by the explorer discovered Santa Maria and then, other islands. These Islands were the Azores. Prince Henry promptly stocked Santa Maria with cattle. On July 2, 1439, King Alfonso gave his Uncle Henry the privilege of settling the ten major islands. At the time, several were to be considered worth colonizing. Many of the colonists were Flemings who traded and fished as well as farmed.

During the lull, Henry the Navigator was involved in affairs of state. In 1437, he went on the expedition to Tangier. There, his brother Ferdinand was captured to die in slavery to the Moors. In 1438, King Duarte died and Henry had the regency to attend to. In 1441, he sent out his master of the robes, Antonio Goncalvez, with an object to kill and load up the skins of "sea wolves;" some of which had been seen on a former voyage, in the mouth of a river one hundred and fifty miles beyond Cape Bojador. Antonio went and captured some Azeneghi Moors. Before he returned, he was met by another sea captain called Nuno Tristan who also captured some Moors. All returned to Portugal.

Also, in 1441, Prince Henry appealed to Pope Eugenius IV for a grant of possession to Portugal for all the lands they should discover and conquer from the Cape of Bojador to the Indies. He wished also for plenary indulgence for those who would die in these efforts. The pope granted this during a period when he was engaged in uniting the Orthodox and Catholic Churches, which failed, as did a Crusade against the Turks. In the battle, he was defeated at Varno.

Meanwhile, the recently captured Moors promised to give black slaves in ransom for themselves. Henry agreed because the Negroes could be corrected, whereas the Muslims could not. Goncalvez took them back and received ten black slaves, some gold dust, a target of buffalo hides and some ostriches' eggs for two Moors, exciting the Portuguese, who had seen no blacks before.

Information that there was gold further south and that Goncalvez had obtained gold changed minds quickly. If there was gold to be gained, the climate may not have been so bad after all. The gold awakened enough covetousness to supply sailors. On the heels of this changed opinion, Nuno Tristan made further progress down the African coast. Off Adaget, one of the Arguim Islands, he captured Azenegues, non-black natives. When he returned to Portugal, there was an onrush of favor for the explorations of Prince Henry the Navigator. There were slaves and other commodities to bring back. Former wars had meant suffering for the soldiers had no gain for the nation. These conflicts on the African coast required little fighting for substantial and greater gains.

Henry authorized a company in 1444 to form at Lagos that would undertake discovery and a slaving expedition. The first act of this company was to attack the people of the islands of Nar and Tider. The expedition brought back about two hundred slaves. Prince Henry rewarded one of the leaders, and took his own fifth, some forty slaves. Thus, Portugal undertook another step in the slave trade which was to grow.

In 1445, the princely promoter fitted out an expedition and gave the command to Gonslava de Cintra. He failed in his attack on the natives they found near Cape Blanco and was killed. Others on the expedition, including some more principals also lost their lives. Later that year, Henry sent out three other ships. The regent of Portugal ordered these captains to enter the river d'Oro, and to convert the natives to Christianity, and whether successful of not, to make a peaceful alliance with them. They tried, but succeeded in neither. This expedition returned with a single Negro gained in ransom. A Moor who wished to see Portugal was also taken abroad.

Dinis Dyaz or Dinis Fernandez wanted to find employment with the regent and command a vessel. This was done. A bold man, the explorer pushed down the coast and passed the Senegal River. This river divided the Moors from the Negroes, who were astonished to see the ship. They paddled out in their hollowed logs until they saw men in it. Wisely, they fled but Dixie captured four of them and sailed on to discover Cape Verde. He returned to receive the honor of favor he deserved.

Meanwhile, in 1453, the Turkish sultan, Muhammad II took Constantinople and was well settled in that corner of Europe and therefore there was no surprise. In subsequent years, the Turks moved the Mamluks of Egypt and Syria, and the Persian Empire, but for the time, there was a European Christian alliance and peace. This call for a holy crusade was never followed and the Turks were allowed to expand step by step into Europe. The next impact of Turkish expansion was met by the Balkan kingdoms and the countries of the Danubean basin and did not immediately concern the more western nations of Europe.

There were three papal bulls that pertained to Portuguese imperial aims in the sixth decade of the fifteenth century. The scholar Pope Nicholas V provided the first two of the bulls and the noble born Pope Callistus III provided the third. Nicholas had tried to arouse a crusade against the Turks and Callistus had done likewise. Both were concerned about the incursions of the Moslems, and it is in this light, that these bulls should be studied. The first bull was issued on June 18, 1452, and it authorized the Portuguese king to subdue the Saracens, pagans, and other unbelievers, and to capture their goods and lands, enslave them, and transfer their property to themselves. The unbelievers included all of the people of the littoral and the Negroes of the interior.

The second dealt with the Portuguese imperial drive and begins in eloquent terms and praised about the work of Henry the Navigator since 1419. The popes liked his colonial and religious zeal. It was issued on January 8, 1454, and Nicholas knew his intentions to circumnavigate Africa, make contact with the peoples of India and use them to attack the Moslems. He saw hope in the work of conversion and gave to the Portuguese a monopoly on trade and conquest south along the western coast of Africa and to India.

On January 8, 1454, Pope Nicholas V issued this decree that in consideration for his paternal care of all nations of the world and his wish for the salvation of it's peoples provided authority for the Portuguese king to bring into the faith other peoples. The sheep the kings were to bring into the fold of the triune God would gain for them "the reward of eternal happiness and win pardon for their souls." For the glory of God, "with deserved favors and special aid," these kings and princes were not only to repress Saracen ferocity and infidel enmity, but conquer remote lands "and without sparing effort or cost, bring them under their dominions." These rulers had promised to undertake this project, "if relieved of certain outlays and handicaps."

Nicholas had learned that Henry the Navigator and Alfonso of Portugal and the Algarnes had followed in the footsteps of John with a zeal for the savings of souls and ardency in the Christian faith, to spread the domain of Christianity. The pope noted the taking of Ceuta in Africa and other campaigns, and the settlement of groups of the faithful in lovely islands, the building of churches, and the baptism of pagans there. The idea of these explorations and conquests was to go to India and outflank the Moslems with the aid of the people of India. At this point, Nicholas wrote about the progress of the search as far as Senegal, beyond the lands of Guinea. Evidently the pope sanctioned slavery by exchange or lawful contract of sale, which led many of the slaves to become Christians.

Alfonso and Henry asked the assistance of the papacy because of the heavy risks, labors, and costs of the voyages of exploration, and the dangers which would beset the Portuguese if regulations were not provided and enforced. According to the bull, natives of discovered Africa had been lost in the conquests. The Portuguese are "a so lawful rulers who with the help of the natives have marched through such extensive provinces" and conquered such areas, fearing "that others may in cupidity be led to sail into those regions and spoil the good and laudable work or usurp it's fruits, or at least impede their success." Seeking profit or trouble foreigners might bring forth weapons and other dangerous objects or teach the natives the arts of navigation that would slow or stop progress.

A young Venetian by the name of Cada Mosto was abroad a Venetian galley, learning his trade, when it was detained by contrary winds at Cape St. Vincent in 1454. Prince Henry the Navigator took an interest in the ship and sent his secretary and the Venetian consul abroad. The two men gained an ardent interest in Cada Mosto and the other Venetian there by showing some articles from the new territories such as Madeira sugars gained under the seafaring genius of the prince. There were gains of 700-1000 percent they said. Cada Mosto was interested and learned the terms: that an adventurer pay for his own ship and goods and give the prince one fourth of the produce or use a Portuguese ship dividing evenly. In the case of allure of this last, the prince bore the whole loss. Henry was desirous of seeing Venetians take a role; they paid, because of their experience in such commodities that the Portuguese were seeking.

When Cada Mosto saw the prince, he was impressed and immediately came to terms. He moved his merchandise on board the Portuguese ship on the way to the African coast. He learned and wrote of whatever he saw. The Portuguese factory at Arquim was busy. Merchandise flowed in from the south and was traded for gold and slaves. The Moors were the middle men and traded their Barbary horses to the chiefs of the Negro tribes and returned with from ten to eighteen slaves for each horse. They also gave silks from Granada and Tunis and silver to the chiefs for slaves and gold. Slaves numbering between seven and eight hundred were sent from Arguim to Portugal, for a chief trade. The king of Portugal by this time would allow his countrymen to seize no more Moors for the slave trade.

By this time, Prince Henry had died on the 13th of November, 1460, his explorers had reached such a difficult and dangerous stretch of coast that there seemed to be no prospect of improvement, because the North Star was too low on the horizon, that they would not soon see it to guide them further. In addition, there was a certain contentment: the merchants enjoyed a modest trade at the Senegal and the Gambia and the Crown was unwilling to finance further exploration. Henry had left a load of debt. Exploration had proved expensive, but there was a successful voyage commanded by Pedro de Cintra, which attained one advance in 1462. He discovered Sierra Leone, a mountain of roaring thunder, and reached Cape Mensurado. Alfonso V was interested in a crusade in Morocco and so seven years passed without advances down the coast.

In 1469, the Portuguese king leased further exploration rights to Fernao Gomes on condition that Gomes pay an annual rent and that the energetic man explore one additional three hundred miles of coast for each year of his lease. It lasted for five years, and he more then kept his obligations and made a fortune to boot. He also fought for the king of Morocco and was knighted. Before he was finished, he reached Benin. All in all, he explored nearly two thousand miles of the West African coast, passing the equator by two degrees. Because of the ensuing war with Castile in 1475, Gomes did not wish to renew the contract, and the king turned over the business of Guinea to his son John. Two years later, Gomes escorted the fleet home as an officer of the Portuguese Crown. Subsequent explorers brought discovery down to 13 degrees south, past the Congo, by Diego Cao's first voyage of 1483-84 and down to 22 degrees south by his second voyage of 1485-87, against the Berguela current and the southeast trade winds. Cao had covered 1,450 miles of coastline.

Recognized heir to the throne of Castile after her half brother Henry IV, the fair and moral Isabella was most sought after in the marriage market. She herself preferred her second cousin Ferdinand of Aragon. There were many reasons for such a happy event, both political and personal. The chief advantage would be the union of the two reigns or Aragon and

Castile, that would benefit all concerned. People in the two kingdoms came from a common stock and spoke one language. Institutions and historical conditioning were most similar. Not only were characters more alike, the geographical position of each on the same peninsular seemed made for a union that the marriage of Ferdinand and Isabella would bring. Personally, their moral character was suited to each other. Good looking in appearance, the prince had shown a chivalrous valor from boyhood, and was from manhood, a mature person. Ferdinand was superior in terms of personal merit and personality.

However, there were those opposed to this match. Headed by the family of Mendoza, a party honored the cause of Henry's "illegitimate daughter" Joanna. The marquis of Villent tried to get Joanna married to the son who was the heir of Alfonso of Portugal, which would strengthen her position and give her partisans additional strength for the elevation of Joanna to succeed Henry in Castile. Also, Alfonso was invited to press his suit for Isabella's hand, but the future queen refused. A powerful marquis threatened Isabella because she did not follow his wishes. Only the anger of the people of Ocana, where she was residing, kept Villene from imprisoning Isabella in Madrid, because he was not moved by the princess' tears or entreaties. The common people supported the Aragonese match.

Fortunately, Isabella was encouraged by her friend the archbishop of Toledo and she determined to conclude the negotiations herself. The primate arranged the support of the nobility including Don Frederick Henriquez, Admiral of Castile and father of Ferdinand's mother. Isabella sent the Aragonese envoy home with word that she would marry their prince. Ferdinand and his father were overjoyed, and on January 7, 1469, the marriage articles were signed.

On December 11, 1474, Henry IV of Castile died from a long lingering disease without making a will or settling his succession. Fortunately, Villene had died a few months before at the height of his power over king and nation. The weak monarch had lost his dominating adviser and his wits, and now, his life. His dissolute reign marred the nation with immorality, wasted resources, poor justice, and favoritism.

When Isabella learned of her half brother's death, she signified to the people of Segovia that she desired to be elaborately proclaimed queen in that city where she was then living. They were eager for this, and escorted her under a canopy of rich brocade to the castle, where the nobles, clergy and public magistrates were waiting. She rode in splendor on a Spanish jannet, with two civic officials holding the bridle, preceded by an officer of her court with the naked sword symbolizing sovereignty. He was on horseback. Alighting from her palfrey and ascending the platform, she went through the ceremonies, and then all repaired to the cathedral for services. A crowned Isabella received news of the adherence of the largest and wealthiest cities in her kingdom, one after another. Joined by her husband, she, he, and the archbishop worked out an agreement on the sharing of power with her idea that their interests were indivisible, and that his will would be hers.

Called upon by several Spanish nobles to secure the throne for his niece Joanna, Alfonso V of Portugal entered Castile in May of 1475 with an army. The plans were for him to marry the princess and therefore gain Castile for Portugal. He sent a messenger to Pope Sixtus VI in Rome for a dispensation for the marriage to Joanna because of the consanguinity of the parties, and approved the two of undeclared sovereigns of Castile. Because Alfonso debated marching into the undefended territories, Ferdinand and Isabella were given time to prepare. In July, the Portuguese king marched his troops again. Toro was surrendered to him, but a woman led the resistance in the fortress, valiantly delaying Alfonso some more. Meanwhile,

Zanora submitted. Ferdinand tried to engage Alfonso, but failed and had to retreat because of supply troubles and lack of besieging equipment.

The Archbishop of Toledo, for some time disgruntled, joined the cause of Alfonso, but the Catholic monarchs were beginning to have some success. Spaniards would not fight for a Portuguese king, and Ferdinand and Isabella's forces were soon raiding Portugal. In August, she convened an assembly of the states and was talked into borrowing half of the amount of plate in churches to raise funds for the defense of Castile. Alfonso remained in Toro while Isabella was raising, equipping, and training a suitable army in Spain.

In order to protect his communication lines, Alfonso had his son Prince John come to relieve Zamora in Portuguese hands from a threat from Ferdinand and all his army. The son came to Toro on February 14, 1476. Alfonso then marched to Zamora, but he chose an unsuitable position. Still the Spaniards were caught between the citadel and Alfonso's army. Isabella's squadron of light cavalry cut off supplies to the Portuguese. Next, Alfonso heard that additional troops were on the way to aid Ferdinand. A swollen river kept him from fighting, and his troops were affected by the cutoff of supplies. Alfonso marched his army anyway.

Ferdinand followed Alfonso and passed through a defile into a wide plain to discover that the Portuguese had turned and were forming in order of battle. The Spaniards prepared for battle. He forced Alfonso in the center. The Duke of Alva on Ferdinand's left faced the Archbishop of Toledo. The Portuguese retreated and the invasion and the war was over.

Chapter II

CHRISTOPHER COLUMBUS

Ferdinand and Isabella restored internal tranquillity and established good government for it's time. Once well situated, the Catholic monarchs returned to the idea of conquering the Moorish nation to the south in Spain. The Moorish ruler provided the pretext for the war. Muley Abul Hacen was the aggressive and proud son of the amiable Abdn Ismail, who had died in 1466. Greatly involved in domestic troubles, Abul Hacen could only nurse hopes of marching against the Spanish. On December 26, 1481, the garrison of Zahara on the frontiers of Andalucia was surprised by a force under the Moor that scaled the walls of the fortified town in a storm. Every guard who resisted was murdered and the men, women, and children were enslaved in Granada.

The mortified Christian Sovereigns strengthened the frontiers and sought a retaliatory measure. A captain of scales by the name of Juan de Oretega proposed a daring raid upon the Alahama deep in the Moorish Kingdom of Granada. This proposal was approved and carried out and succeeded. They sacked the Alahama. Ferdinand and Isabella were overjoyed and felt this victory was an auspicious omen for their planned war on Granada. A general war followed.

There had been an English connection in the later fifteenth century with lords to the west of Europe and it was reported that an island lay west of Ireland, called "Brazil." This was nothing new because maps from 1325 presented it in different locations in the northern Atlantic, but a voyage was made in 1480 to find the land. A certain John Jay partly owned a ship with which he sailed westward seeking the island. Thomas Floyd was master. The English left Bristol on July 15, 1480, to search west of Ireland for the famed island, but were beset by bad weather and were unable to find the island of Brazil. They returned by the eighteenth of September. Lost in the midst of June to the bases for this island to be on the maps, but in 1325 many people in the northern colonies knew about the existence of Greenland. Perhaps Brazil and Greenland were the same or fishermen had long found the fishing banks of North America that early.

Another search was undertaken during the succeeding year. One of the collectors of customs for Bristol, Thomas Corft, took an interest in unknown lands to the west. A partially owner of the two ships, the George and the Trinity, he victualled, then and in early July of 1481, they sailed out of port. Nothing is known of the results of this voyage, but there were other trips in the years ahead out of the port of Bristol and England almost preceded Spain in the discovery of America.

Meanwhile, Sultan Muhammad II invaded Italy in 1480, and took Otranto in Italy, where he placed a market for Christian slaves that flourished. The long peninsula of Italy possibly escaped a longer campaign by Turks, when the sultan died in 1481. By this time, the Turks had a successful navy that the Venetians had met by establishing a peace in order to retain trading privileges at the island of Crete. A clash between Turkish and European navies was delayed for another time. For the time, the Turks used the navy to defeat the Mamluks, and extend their rule around the Levantine shores of Syria, Palestine, and Egypt.

Christopher Columbus grew up to be a tall man, ruddy, and red haired with obvious Teutonic ancestors among the Latin. He was conscious of being Genoese origin, in which lands his family had lived for at least three generations. Steadfast in his Catholic faith and loyal to the Genoese state, he never became a naturalized Spaniard, but wished his heirs to maintain a house in Genoa for some member of the family in need. He wished them to work for Genoa's honor, welfare, and the promotion of the other members of the family.

Giovanni Colombo was a weaver of woolen cloth as was Christopher's father, Domencio, prominent enough to be caretaker of a gate in the city wall. Weaving cloth was family tradition. The explorer's mother was a daughter of a weaver. Her name was Susana Fontarossa from the valley of the Bisagno River. Towards the end of 1451, or according to another account, in 1436, Christopher was born in the city of Genoa, a place where people were proud of their state. Growing up in the business, Christopher and his brother were wood carders, and moved to Savona where the eldest son was known as a hard working, steady going lad who was more secure, than Domencio who was an easy going man, not always attending to business or making his promises or branching out. During his youth, he gained some experience as a sailor.

There were not too many years at sea, but Columbus later claimed that he served Rene dAnjou on a material mission of importance, which would mean he was not a common sailor long, but had become a captain. It is possible that he served the French at sea against the newly-wed Isabella and Ferdinand. At the time, there were Genoese vessels, but this got into a ruckus with the fleet, all but destroyed, so if Columbus was involved, he was serving with the Franco-Portuguese fleet at the Battle of Cape St. Vincent in 1476. Columbus swam ashore in Portugal. As soon as he recovered, he sailed to England and for the northern seas to reach Iceland and beyond. He probably learned of the existence of Greenland on that voyage. Next, he returned to Portugal and visited Madeira in 1478.

The progress of Portugal appealed to Columbus and he readily made residence in Lisbon. He earned a livelihood by making land maps and charts for vessels to be used at sea. It was there that Christopher met a lady whose father had just died, and since both were Italian, they had common origins, which bound them together in a growing friendship. The father had been in the service of Portugal's king, and although they did not belong to the nobility, the family had a relatively high standing. The father was Bartholomew Perestrello, heading affairs of the island of Porto Santo near Madeira, and his lady was Felipa Moniz Peretrello. They were married, and Columbus by this union, and his residence, became a citizen of Portugal. A door was opened to the new husband, when the bride's mother, with whom they resided, brought to him the maps and data her late husband, Perestrello had accumulated. This increased the future explorer's' knowledge and by events unfolding, he made contacts through his wife's family.

Next, Columbus joined in expeditions to Africa's Atlantic coast and gained experience in ocean travel. Because his wife had property on the newly discovered island of Porto Santo in the Madeiras, the pair made residence there on the seven mile island and it was there that a son was born. They named him Diego. These were exciting times in the Madeiras, and there were reports of lands to the west of the Azores. Bodies of two men were washed up upon one of the islands and of a race unknown to Europeans. Artificially carved wood was also found on the beaches brought ashore by a west wind. In a letter to this son, later written, he noted the trade Englishmen from Bristol had with the people of Ireland. He might have read at one time or another of the discovery of Vineland found in the writing of Adam of Bremen, and known in the north country by sailors, but he did not wish to find land in this cold country, if indeed he knew about those lands.

The Genoese sailor was well prepared for his great discoveries beginning his youth as a sailor and navigator and then later as a map and chart maker, becoming expert at each step of the way. Many active men were involved in geographical and navigational studies, and much was known, but this was not always readily available of the common man. The chief motivation for private shipping was commercial ambition. Knowledge was the key to successful shipping in the many skills required for navigation. Although they might undertake trips within the Mediterranean for money, they held a greater dream to cut the middleman and trade directly with India. The indirect oriental trades made many merchants rich, but mankind is a greedy species and greater wealth was desired. Increased supplies of silks and spices could be sold because of the great demand. In the search for a direct route, the Portuguese had sailed forth down the coast of Africa and Columbus was close to what was happening.

Sometime between the end of 1483 and the summer of 1485, Columbus gained an audience with the Portuguese king, John, proposing to discover "great islands to the south, islands and mainland, very fertile, and rich in gold, silver and pearls, precious stones, and inhabited with considerable population; and by this route, he claimed he would arrive at the land of India, the great island of Cipangu, and three realms of the Great Khan."

Columbus wanted three caravels, small vessels of the times with three or four masts, with provisions for one year for this voyage and merchandise to barter with the savages, which he would encounter. He made greater demands for himself. The future explorer wanted to be made a knight, and to be made admiral and viceroy and perpetual governor of those lands he would discover, plus, receive one tenth of the products he obtained. These were great demands. The king gave him over to a committee of a bishop, a physician, a cosmographer, and the king's physician. Columbus could not convince these men, but King John did secretly send a ship to do what Christopher suggested without having to reward him with his high demands. Columbus soon fled Portugal for Spain. The Portuguese voyage failed without him.

In 1485, Columbus sailed from Portuguese Lisbon to Spanish Palos and Moquer. Because he left Lisbon secretly, Christopher had no possessions, but fortunately he stopped off at a Franciscan monastery, La Rabida. The monks gave his young son some bread and water, and Columbus and Brother Juan Perez began talking about the Grand Khan. The monk was interested in such things, and had connections with the Spanish Court, having been the Queen's substitute father confessor. At the same monastery was a good cosmographer, Antonio de Marchena. The monks advised him to see the duke of Medina-Sidonia, don Enrique de Gusman, and the duke of Medina-Celi, don Luys de la Cerda. Leaving his young son in the good care of the monks, and with money for travel and food, Columbus went to Gusman who was in a serious dispute with the marquis of Codiz, and who was not interested. Cerda sent him to the queen of Castile.

In April or May of 1486, Columbus had an audience with the sovereigns. They were preoccupied, but made him a member of their suite. For five years, he lived off their largesse or pension. Meanwhile, he was making overtures to other countries in particular, through his brother Bartholomew, who sought the support of the newly crowned Henry VII of England. After almost five years in Spain before the Court, his ideas were rejected, because they were busy with war in Granada.

Columbus had come to the Spanish Court at an inappropriate time, because all of the resources of the Crown were tied to the military effort. In addition, Columbus was unfortunate in the channels, which were presented. His early friend, Fray Antonio de Marchena, guardian of the convent of La Rabida in Andalucia, due to deep interest in the project, gave him an introduction to the pedantic Fernando de Talavera, prior of Prado and confessor to the queen. Should Talavera be interested, Columbus would get the interest of the court, because this moral and benevolent religious man was high in the royal confidence. Although Talavera's learning was based upon the conservative views of his class, and he was subject to superstition and ancient beliefs, he had relayed Columbus' ideas to Ferdinand and Isabella, and they had the confessor select a council to consider the matter. It was composed of eminent scholars, chiefly churchmen. This council took time. Meanwhile, there were other crusades afoot in the Christian world.

Although he was weak willed, and a partisan and tool of Cardinal Giuliano Della Rovere, later Julius II, Genoan Giovanni Bathista Cibo was as interested in meeting the Turkish threat as Innocent VIII, and made a couple of efforts in 1484 and 1490 to rally the Christian rulers to undertake the crusade. On November 21, 1484, Innocent VIII addressed all European powers to warn them of the great danger against the Church and western civilization, from the Turkish advance, and to summon them to act. The situation was so serious that delay would be fatal. This call was not heeded. Spain was unable to act, because the Spanish people were busy with their own crusade and indeed the campaign against Malaga was at a critical point. This stronghold blocked further Spanish advances. The siege of this barrier was to last for a few more years.

Ferdinand and Isabella undertook a diplomatic effort at this time to gain a papal bull for royal patronage in conquered lands. The first step was taken when Isabella had the Conde de Tendilla, request from the pope, an exact copy of a former grant of patronage to Isabella's predecessors of Castile. Innocent replied with a copy of the grant sent by Eugene IV, on August 9, 1436, to King John of Castile for his use as a right of patronage in lands recovered in his crusade. This earlier bull spoke of John as a celebrated champion for Christ with his splendid victories and deserving graces to evangelize and encourage John and his successors to continue their campaigns. Alfonso VI had already received patents to churches or oratories, which in the case of John, Eugene gave for the struggle. Eugene IV ordered that John and his dynasty would receive many dignitaries, be able to bestow other ecclesiastical benefits and patronage in reward. He broadened patronage to include lords, mosques, and holy places taken from the Saracens.

On December 13, 1486, Innocent sent the Bull of Granada, which expressed to the Spanish monarchs, papal concern and commission for the propagation of the orthodox faith and its interest, assistance, and favor. He would reward their crusade by making them "rulers, guardians, and keepers of the lords they conquered, and the people their resident."

King Dom John II of Portugal learned that there had arrived one day in 1484, a Negro whom he believed to be king of Benin, a distant lord. Others were to say he was not a king, but a mere ambassador, although it was possible that he was a deposed or fugitive king from a decided culture. The Portuguese did not know where his land was, and were told it was twenty months journey west of Abyssinia. Mixed up in their geography, they thought this must be near India, which was east and not west of the land of Abyssinia. Indeed, their confusion was tied with legend and a lack of a clear mind. All of wonder after all was to the east and so, the man must have come from the wonderland. That was what they sought, the fabulous east.

Benin was a land on the westcoast of Africa, and at one time very extensive, with many subject tribes in the general position that we call now Nigeria. Their rivers are the Niger and Benin with their interlocked courses and tributaries. Pure black were the people of this land with a well organized and powerful government. This was not known to the Portuguese in 1484, although they were to discover it by accident in the second year in their course down the West African coast.

With the Negro came many of his people and they settled in Portugal where John directed questions about India. They told the Portuguese king what he so obviously wished to know. He wanted to learn that the Christian, Prester John, lord of great riches, ruled over India. An impressed John desired to know more. He secretly sent two of his equerries to seek out far lands. The two men, Canarian Gonzallo de Pavia and Pero de Couilhan, went from Portugal to Jerusalem, but did not venture forth to Abyssinia with monks of their land, because they knew not Arabic. The monks were Friar Anthony of Lisbon and Peter of Montaroyos, who had a knowledge of many languages.

Christopher Columbus, as we have seen, made his first proposal to reach Asia to the Portuguese Crown, when the idea of exploration was a popular one in Portugal. Although the Portuguese preferred to continue their southward trek around Africa instead of going across the vast oceans, they found nothing startling about such an idea. Indeed, several authors had written about such a possibility in western Europe, but the ways of the west were set. No political explorer had undertaken such a plan. Then, several travel authors, who suggested the idea, included that most popular travel author of the latter day medieval period, Sir John Mandeville. In theory, if the earth was round, which it was believed to be, one only needed sail far enough with the right current and wind to reach Japan and China. There were many theories about how far one would have to travel, and Columbus had his.

Obviously, John of Portugal believed that Columbus was correct, because he sought the advantage for the Portuguese. John sent out the Azorean Portuguese, Fernor Dulmo in the following year to find the islands without giving Columbus the rights the native of Genoa wished. Dulmo was to see out lands, including one known in fable as the isles of the seven cities. The chosen route with prevailing winds in the latitude of the Azores that was taken was the wrong one, and he failed.

Still, there were left other possibilities, but these seemed crushed by Cao's return without results and John reopened negotiations with Columbus. When Diaz returned with his rounded Cape of Africa, Portugal already had a route to the eastern sphere and Columbus was no longer needed. Columbus went to France and England with his ideas. These were fruitless missions and Christopher turned to Castile, where there were fewer vested interests as we have seen.

Since gold and slaves could be taken from the West Coast in large amounts and numbers, King John II was rich enough to finance a search for Prester John. At the time of the mid-eighties, the Portuguese had believed that his kingdom was somewhere beyond the Nile

River, and they believed that the West African rivers were tributaries or branches of the Nile itself. They were disillusioned when their contacts did not agree. The natives of Africa knew nothing of a back door to Prester John.

An encouraged king had put his efforts into sending Bartholomew Diaz on a voyage around the African Cape. Diaz set sail from Lisbon with three ships on August 1, 1487. Southward bound, he lost sight of the coast and sailed eastward into the Indian Ocean unknowingly. Upon regaining land, he wanted to sail forward to India, but his men would not let him. He turned back, and found the Cape of Good Hope, and explored unknown coastlands to the West African littoral. Upon reaching Lisbon in 1488, he reported his discoveries.

Meanwhile, overland traveler Pero de Couilhan followed local paths and succeeded in reaching western India in 1488 by land. On the way back, this Arabic speaking land explorer visited the Persian Gulf, and traveled down eastern Africa for a long way, before reaching the developed Jwahili lands. On the way back to Portugal, he stopped at Cairo, where he followed orders awaiting him there to go to the highlands of Abyssinia to discover Prester John. The Emperor of Abyssinia or Ethiopia received him well, but would not allow him to leave. He gave Pero a wife and lands and Couilhan lived there for thirty years until his death.

After the long years of fruitless endeavor, Columbus decided in 1491 to leave Spain for France and take his visionary ideas to the French king, who had earlier sent him a letter of encouragement. First, however, Christopher would visit his friend Perez and the Convent of La Rabida. Juan Perez greeted him warmly and listened gladly to his tale of efforts. When Columbus told him that he was headed for France, Perez was aghast, and persuaded the explorer to wait there while the guardian would to himself to the court to use his influence. A new ally, Martin-Alonio Pinzon provided the money, and Columbus found the mule for Perez' trip.

Once he reached the newly established city of Santa Fe, north of Moorish Granada, Perez was granted an audience, and was so earnest and reasonable that he exercised great influence with is discourses in favor of the Colombian plan. In addition, several other eminent persons buttressed his arguments. With the Moorish war almost over, Ferdinand and Isabella invited Columbus to come to Santa Fe and sent money enough for his trip. Christopher came promptly and arrived in camp in time to witness the surrender of Granada.

The queen set up a commission to consider Columbus' proposals. He demanded the same rewards that he had before, that is, to be viceroy and have the hereditary rank of Admiral of the Ocean. He also asked for a tenth of all that was bought and exchanged, found or acquired, in the lands to the west. These were hard requests!

Columbus stood firm on his conditions of employment for his great project, and a cold Ferdinand would not agree. However, his wife was most favorable to the enterprise. Besides, the suggested hope, of the glories and wealth reported by Marco Polo was there and the explorer appealed to the principle of extending the Crossover great numbers of heathen. Also, profits could be used for a new crusade to recover the Holy Sepulcher. His ideas affected the religious nature of Isabella, and the plan would have been immediately approved except for the high demands of the Genoan Columbus.

His friends once more stepped into the breach and Louis de St Angel frankly told the queen, that if Columbus succeeded, the great demands would be well deserved, and if he failed, nothing was lost. Christopher required nothing for his project except the cost of the voyage. Isabella agreed and offered to pawn her jewels for the enterprise, but this was not necessary, for St Angel, the receiver, advanced the funds that he held. Aragon would not pay the costs and would not benefit from the great wealth the queen believed would be brought back.

On April 17, 1492, a definite arrangement was drawn up. Isabella agreed that Columbus would be their admiral, viceroy, and governor-general of all he should discover in the western ocean. The new admiral would have the privilege of nominating three candidates for each territorial governor, from which the Crown would select one. The monarchs granted Columbus commercial jurisdiction. The Queen promised that he would be entitled to all of this forever, and receive one tenth of the products and profits within the limits of his discoveries. All of his descendants would have the privilege of being entitled "Don."

Despite his royal order, Columbus had difficulties in getting together a crew. Sailors were concerned over the difficulties of the journey, particularly it's dangers. Finally he received his help from Martin-Alfonso Pinzon, who found ships suitable for the journey, and by his example urged his kin and friends to ship out on Columbus' ship. Once others saw that the Pinzons were going, they got aboard too, because the Pinzon name carried great weight in the port of Palos.

Chapter III

SAILING WEST

Columbus and his men set out for the bar of Saltes on board their three small ships. The bar was at the entrance of a bay at the junction of the Rio Tinto and Rio Odiel. In the town of Palos, three miles upstream of the Tinto, the two monarchs saw the admiral off. The area of the junction provided about two thirds of the sailors on board the ships, including the three Pinzons. They set forth for the Canaries. It was eight o'clock on the morning of Friday, August 3, 1492. On the sixth day out, trouble with the Pinta's rudder, which jumped out of gear, developed. One day later, it gave trouble again, and was again repaired. Still, there was no real resolution of the problem, until they reached Tenerife, one of the Canary Islands, where permanent repairs were made in the rudder.

The Spaniards on the isle of Hierra and Gomera, which the fleet had reached, swore that they had seen land to the west. Columbus remembered, when he heard this, that he was in Portugal in 1484, when a man came to Portugal from the island of Madeira who had asked the Portuguese king to allow him to bring a ship to go to land he saw every year, and always in the same way. In addition, the admiral recalled hearing the same tales from men in the islands of the Azores. Surely, there was something out there, and Columbus felt that it must be the Grand East. All these people were in agreement about the direction, appearance and size. Taking on water, wood, and meat in the islands, the admiral and his captains set out in the ships once again, for the unknown, watchful for three Portuguese caravels, he had heard, were cruising to take him on orders of the Portuguese king. It was Tuesday, the sixth of September.

Subject to an occasional calm sea and an occasional heavy sea that sent "much sea over the hours," Columbus secretly recording the correct distance and giving the men a lesser figure "in order that the crews might to become discontented and alarmed, if the voyage was lengthy." He rebuked the sailors who were steering badly, but with sufficient success. On the eleventh, they saw a large piece of a ship's mast floating in the water. The leagues went by. In one twenty-four hour period, he made sixty leagues. On the thirteenth, the currents were against them. The next day, those in the Nina reported seeing a fern, and tropical bird, which was known to stay well within twenty-five leagues of land. A large meteorite was seen and some rain fell. Next, the sailors saw green seaweed. Surely there was land nearby. Columbus believed the mainland was further away. Time passed and they saw land.

On Friday, October 12, 1492, the day after the discovery, the Spaniards saw naked people on shore and Columbus took possession of the island. Observing the land's green trees, water, and fruit, he gave gifts of red caps and glass beads to the Indians, who had come forth to see the strange people from the seas. The gifts brought Columbus the friendship of the pleased Indians. "Afterwards," as Columbus wrote in his journal, "they came swimming to the ship's boats, where we were, and brought us parrots and cotton threads in balls, and spears and many other things, such as small glass beads and hawk's bells, which we gave to them. In fact, they took all, and gave such as they had with goodwill, but it seemed to me that they were a people deficient in everything."

Men, women, and children were all naked. Well built, they had handsome bodies, very good faces, short coarse hair and cut short, and brown skins. They were variously painted. Not knowing weapons, they cut themselves handling the swords they were shown. Native spears were reeds locking in iron heads, with fish tooth and different sharpened points. The natives indicated that they often had to defend themselves from attacks of nearby peoples. Columbus thought that they would make good and adequate servants, and could easily be made Christians since they had no creed as far as he could tell.

At dawn on Sunday, Columbus set his ships out to explore the coast of the island and saw other Indians who thought the Spaniards had come from Heaven. The admiral saw two or three villages with their swarming natives on the shore, "calling us and giving thanks to God. Some brought us water, others various eatables, others when they saw that I was not inclined to land, threw themselves into the sea, and came swimming, and we understood that they asked us, if we had come from Heaven." Because of a great reef of rocks, he saw around the island, he would not try to land, but he noted deep water and a large harbor with a very narrow entrance. He was to write that this island was flat, and that there were more than the one like it, some of which the admiral and his men explored and were told of gold, to be found elsewhere.

Word went out that these Spaniards were good and powerful men and when they came upon an island, people in canoes came alongside with water and what they had. The Spaniards gave small beads, glass, brass thimbles, and leather thongs, which were received with great thankfulness. Once again, there was the possibility of gold and gold mines nearby. The Indians told Columbus that Samoet, wherever that was, was an island or city where there was gold. Columbus searched diligently for this land. The natives had scant cotton cloths to wear, the water was clear, and there were marvels of trees and fish. Parrots and lizards made up the only land animals on the islands.

All of the people of the island Columbus called Fernandina were like those already seen, just as nearly naked. Columbus noticed "that some of his boys from the ships had exchanged some little pieces of broken dishes and glass for their spears." Those Spaniards, who had gone for water saw inside the native houses and told their admiral that the interiors were swept and clean, and that nets of cotton were used for their beds and coverings. The houses were high and peaked, and the so called chimneys were cornices or thatch roofs and the various villages contained no more than fifteen houses. They found that married women and girls of eighteen or so wore cotton drawers. There were also large and small dogs.

Columbus sailed in the area as best they could with various contrary winds and much rain. On the nineteenth, they discovered a land which the natives with Columbus called Samoet, the gold island, and which Christopher renamed Isabella. The island later became Crooked Island. He reached a cape as it seemed to him, which we see now as the southern tip of Fortune Island. There was much exploring to do and along the way, the natives in the ship spoke of a king living inland, who wore much gold. The admiral did not "put much trust in what they said, both because, I do not understand them well and because they are so poor in gold, that any small amount which this king may wear would seem to be much to them."

On the twentieth, Columbus was still around Crooked and Fortune Islands. Columbus landed again on the following day and found an empty house with all it's household goods. Again, he commented about all the greenery, woods, and lagoons. Singing birds were joyous to Spanish ears, and there were immense parrots that darkened the skies overhead. Columbus remembered about the unusual bird and trees and a snake they had killed trying to escape into the water. Contact was made with a village of Indians who had earlier fled. Since Columbus would allow none of his men to take anything, and they gave glass beads for water, the natives become quite friendly. They talked of Cuba that Columbus thought must be Japan, and another large island that was later to be called Santo Domingo or Hispaniola. He also hoped to reach the mainland shortly, and give letters from the Catholic king and queen to the Grand Khan.

Columbus waited awhile to see if the kings of the place brought any gold. Meanwhile, his men traded with the Indians. Some of the painted Indians had pieces of gold hanging from their nose, and they traded these gold ornaments for hawk's bells and glass beads, not realizing the imbalance of the trade, since these novelties seemed valuable to the natives.

On the twenty-third of October, Columbus set out to discover Japan, as the thought, and followed a west-south-west direction, so the Indians said he must, for the great island. They said there were gold and spices there and great merchants, so it seemed to the primitive Indians. Five days later, they entered a lovely river and discovered a fine island with greenery and mountains. He wrote in his journal of the lands he saw.

Sending forth two men with two Indians to explore, Columbus hoped to learn more about the interior. One of the men was Rodrigo de Jerz of Ayamonte, and the other was Luis de Torres, who sent because he knew Hebrew and Chaldean and some Arabic and thought that he could talk to the Orientals better than any person with lesser knowledge. The Indians told of gold and pearls. Meanwhile, the Spanish cleaned the bottoms of the ships on a fine beach. In a few days, the Spanish explorers returned and described an Indian town and the fertile land. Some of the Indians thought the Spaniards came from Heaven, and the Spaniards were not attacked. They were told of the Caribs who were cannibals. In subsequent explorations, he had trouble with contrary winds and fearful Indians. He sailed to many islands and named many capes. His exploration extended into December and Columbus heard much about the cannibal that he did not believe.

Meanwhile, the Indians were all ready saying that gold lay ahead at another place. Before returning to Spain, the admiral had a fortress built and a number of men left in the West Indies in a place he called La Navidad. Early in 1493, he returned across the ocean for Spain.

Having been forced by the weather to find refuge in the Portuguese river of the Tagus, Columbus sent word overland concerning his success and received a most honorable reception from John of Portugal. There were those in Lisbon who wished to cripple the endeavor by killing the now haughty Columbus, but the God fearing Portuguese king forbade this and showed the Spanish admiral honor and much favor.

Sailing forth to the south, Columbus crossed the bar of Slates and entered the harbor of Palos about noon on March 15, 1493. Ever happy to make the arrival, the people spied the ship bearing wellknown features and flags, and knew that Columbus and his men had returned from a watery grave. Their fears were assuaged and they awaited news of their relatives and friends who had been aboard the ships. Some of the people were to be crushed by the losses of men. The populace swarmed to the shore and greeted the arrival. Word spread, and more came to the harbor.

When they learned about the voyage's success, the people cheered Columbus. They accompanied the admiral, his crew, and the captured natives to the principal church. There, a solemn thanksgiving was celebrated and prayers were offered up for the return of the sailors and their leader. Bells rung, and the people were transformed into joy. They listened intently to the tale of the voyage and the descriptions of the lands found in the west, and the reunion of sailors and subjects.

Columbus was delayed only briefly at Palos. He wanted to report to their magistrates who were then in Barcelona. Going overland, his trip became as great procession. The people of the country were gladden, everyone wanted to see the discovers, and learn what the Indians were like. Taking the natives who were wearing their simple costumes, and decorated with golden ornaments of plants, birds, and mammals which could be found no where in Europe, the admiral set out. Multitudes turned out along the route. In Seville, the large population turned out and every window, balcony as well as the housetops were filled with people. This slowed them down and it as not until mid-April that they arrived in Barcelona.

The court nobility and cavaliers joined the municipal authorities of Barcelona in welcoming Columbus at the gates and escorting him to the court. Ferdinand, Isabella, and Prince John were waiting under the royal canopy. When the admiral came up to the royal throne, they arose, extended their hands, and showed him the greatest mark by having him be seated and tell of his voyage. It was a proud moment for Christopher, for only the greatest magnates were allowed to sit in the presence of a sitting king. Columbus told of his adventures, what he found, and the opportunities that lay before them. Describing the islands, their great climate and soil, and the precious metals found there, he said that the natives were suitable for conversion, being untouched by idolatry.

Everyone gave thanks on their knees when Columbus had finished and the choir of the royal chapel sang the Te Deum. In the days ahead, the Spanish monarchs made honorable distinctions, and the admiral was with Ferdinand wherever he rode outside the palace, but Columbus' thoughts were already on his second voyage.

As soon as the Catholic Majesties at Barcelona had learned of the return of Columbus, and of his discoveries, and before he arrived to make a personal report, the rulers of Spain applied to the pope for his confirmation of their right to the new territories. They wanted to prevent the Portuguese from taking any action to claim or seize what the Spaniards had discovered. Papal bulls of four different popes had granted Portuguese rights to lands to the south and beyond, "and there was a general impression that their claims under these bulls extended as far at the Indies."

Further, because of the lack of geographic knowledge, there were doubts about where the lands found by Columbus were located in relation to the known world and in relation to the lands granted to the Portuguese by the popes. Ferdinand and Isabella thought it necessary to notify Rome of their pretensions. They could be confident that Alexander VI supported their claims because he was of Valencian birth, and owed them money and favors for their working on his behalf. He acted and gave the Spaniards exclusive rights and possession of the new lands. Columbus was later to urge that a demarcation line was advisable; the rulers requested it; and Alexander responded favorably. The line originated with Columbus, that clear-mind and good heart.

It was perhaps fortunate that Columbus erred in his belief about the length of a degree. Had he known the exact distance westward from Europe to Asia, he might have been unable to command his men to go such a distance. As it was, he had to hide the exact distance he had gone from his men. The fearful sailors were hesitant to go even as far as they thought they were going. Columbus believed that the length of a degree to be 56 2/3 Italian miles, the commonplace idea of medieval geography originating in the ninth century. The astronomers of the Caliph-Al-Mamun had determined this length. Columbus himself, figured the length of a degree to be such following the accepted practice of the late fifteenth century. He already knew what the result would be, and what he did to verify this. Finding the degree to be correct, Columbus thought that the circumference was 20,400 miles on the equator, which he believed to be at the port of El Mira, when it actually was 26,000 miles.

In his navigational notes, Columbus wrote that according to Holy Scripture, the dry part of the earth was six parts to water, seventh part, that for every parts dry, there was one part wet. He read the Book of Esdras for this information. He wrote that "the world is not so large as the common crowd says it is, and that a degree on the equator is fifty six miles and two thirds. This is a fact that one can touch with one's own fingers," In addition, Christopher believed that the number of degrees in the known was 283, or the degrees of 77 for the Atlantic Ocean from Europe to Asia, and estimate of substantially 45 degrees more than his contemporaries, believing the world to be smaller. This was based on Marinas of Tyre as corrected by Ptolemy.

Columbus followed the parallel of the Canary Islands, deviating from it only twice. First, he did in late September search for islands and again, he deviated in the final days of the fist voyage to follow the land signs in the southwest. He took the route he did in order to take advantage of winds and currents, a good trip, as it was on these, following Seneca. The currents and winds that passed the Azores, came from the west and that parallel was avoided as was the area between the two island chains, where calms prevailed. Columbus needed more in the shortest time possible, so he took advantage of all benefits of ocean travel. He also chose well on his return to Spain, discovering by art both of the great sailing routes in the North Atlantic, one westward, and the other eastward. Los Casos wrote that "Christopher Columbus in the art of navigation exceeded without any doubt, all others who lived in his day."

There were several days to gain great wealth. First, from inheritance or family grants or by seizure. Secondly, from trade or manufacture. Thirdly, from trade in spices, slaves, and gold. And fourthly, wealth could be obtained from seizure of gold and slaves by conquistadors. The world of Columbus used all of these methods.

In addition, in the field of religion, which was also foremost among the Europeans, was the spread of their religion--Roman Catholic Christianity. There were two methods that were usually combined, one could convert by force or persuasion. Even when religion was expanded by force, it was necessary to educate the natives as to the tenets of Catholicism. Parry noted that there were two obvious universal and admitted motives propelling the Spanish and Portuguese, and other Europeans to venture overseas. These were to acquire wealth and converts, in that order.

Despite all of the gold and spices to be obtained, land with the laborers to plough, sow, and harvest was the principal source of great wealth. Someone must obtain the land and the diligent and docile peasantry to make it fertile and fruitful. The quickest way to become newly rich was to seize the land in warfare and to hold it by a grant given by the king. The

Spanish were used to doing that in their reconquest of Spain from the Moors in the medieval period. Successful warfare provided new lands over the centuries, but the Crown was more powerful by the time of Columbus and the kings and great noblemen got the lion's share of the territory in the successful war with Granada. But now, Columbus had returned to tell of new dominions and lesser men would have the opportunity to acquire land by conquest outside of Europe.

One could, and did, grab unoccupied lands and force out tribes that did not utilize the land they were encamped upon. These could be colonized by farmers and herders from Spain and Portugal. Later, the English could drive away or kill natives for desired lands in the north of Hispanic American lands. Men could escape feudal tenure by putting such lands with the small amounts of advanced capital from the crown or nobles of their homelands. Islands such as the Canaries were subject to this brand of endeavor. These brought in revenue for the needs of Prince Henry of Portugal and others in subsequent decades to his activities. This fashion lasted more than two hundred years.

Now that both Spain and Portugal were reaching toward India and China, there was danger of conflict between the nations. Pope Alexander VI thought it a wise thing to divide the world between them. Portugal would have access and control of the trade by the eastern route to lands of the Orient. Spain could go by the west to the eastern lands. The divisions reached the other side of the globe, and because it's dimensions were not yet clearly known, it could not be determined where the eastern dividing line would cut. Alexander was in the dark, but it was avoided, the demarcation line would be a success. It did not work out this way. The papal chancery had advised the pope to act in this manner and Alexander for once in his life did a benevolent act with good intentions.

Later, when the Portuguese king objected, that the line would not give his ships room to travel in the Atlantic, the pope extended the line westward two hundred and seventy leagues halfway between the Azores and the land and the land just touched on by Columbus. On September 25, 1493, a papal bull settled the matter and a troubled Alexander dealt with other matters. This pope had a corrupt record, being descended from Borgia on his mother's side. He had advanced in the Church rapidly, unlimited by his greed for gold, land, and women. His children were to cause him difficulties and he was reprimanded by Pius II for his worldliness, but Alexander was to gain the papacy through large scale bribery, and appeared victorious in this world.

Gold was the prime motivation for the Spanish. They went westward to find gold directly or to gain it by trade and conquest. India and China would be theirs; new lands with a rich measure of possibility. When Columbus wrote his journals, he shrewdly mentioned gold constantly, which he thought would attract those who would be sought to support his endeavor. He was doubtless intent upon enriching himself, but he did not need the lure of gold to entice himself, although he expected to gain riches and power for his work. Already determined, Columbus would not require such inducement, but all those he dealt with in all the layers of society did. It was a dangerous undertaking and only the thought of gold would keep his various fleets on their way.

Sailors going to the ends of the earth were concerned over their safety but greed kept them going. The key requirement was the support of monarchs who seized the lure of gold and financed him. They were all agreed, no matter what was their station in life, on the gaining of riches that they believed was so abundant in the Indies and easily taken. So ran the desire of the Spaniard that Columbus catered to, and in which Columbus probably shared.

He wrote at the time of his third voyage that "it was needful also to speak of the temporal gain therein, foreshadowed in writings of so many wisemen, worthy of credence who wrote histories and related how in these ports there are great riches." At the time there was no immediate "caravels laden with gold." Later, he was to disclaim a motive of gain, honor, or wealth. He sought, he said, to serve as ambassador and met the Grand Khan of China when Marco Polo had written about. He claimed in 1502 to be instrumental in spreading the Gospel to China and financing the conquest of Jerusalem. Religion was a great motivation for the historic Columbus, but when he discovered the first island, he sought eagerly "to discover more lands and to probe their secrets." This was the intellectual nationalism for Columbus.

On May 29, 1493, Ferdinand and Isabella expressed their wishes for the good treatment of the Indians. Religious Spanish monarchs had a great interest in native welfare, but although they consistently worked for the protection of the Indians, rough and unkind colonials treated the native badly. In this directive, before Columbus' second voyage, the admiral Christopher Columbus was instructed and promote and spread the Catholic faith, and convert the natives of the new found land.

The monarchs were pleased that the Indians were ready for a new faith, having nothing in laws or customs that would hinder this conversion. They wished Columbus to see that the religious he was taking with him would, "when they reached the Indies, use all their talents and zeal to acquaint the natives with the fruits of our own holy faith." These religious should teach the Indians Spanish in order that they should come to know the Christian religion and would be treated with considerate attention. Spain's monarchs insisted that the Spanish give no offense, be liberal, give presents, and show much honor. They granted the admiral the power to chastise any of his men who mistreated the Indians.

Chapter IV

VASCO DA GAMA

The Spanish monarchs were eager for the admiral to return to the Indies and for Columbus to set upon settlements on the fringe of what they considered Asia. When Columbus set out on his second voyage from Cadiz on September 25, 1493, he carried with him in seventeen sail, men and cargo for colonization. He had with him twelve hundred people including farmers, priests, gentlemen soldiers, and artisans. There were tools for the farmers and artisans and animals for farming. Their goal was the settlement of the island of Hispaniola, of a farming and mining colony which would raise its own food, and mine and collect gold to send to Spain. From there, they could go to Japan and China. One could undertake exploration of the lands and seas to the west. The chief problem was insufficient food to last until the next year's harvest.

The Columbian landfall on this trip was the wild Caribbean Island of Dominica, having traveled on a much more favorable southern route. He passed through the Lesser Antilles, Virgin Islands, past Puerto Rico to northern Hispaniola. From there, he explored the southern coast of Cuba and saw Jamaica. The men wanted to search for gold and slaves and made enemies of the natives. They did not want to clear the forests, build houses, and plant crops. Columbus did not have the personality and temperament of a colonial governor with these troublesome people. The great explorer stayed in the Indies until 1496.

Before returning to Spain, Bartholomew, the discoverer's brother, persuaded some of the settlers to start building the city of Santo Domingo on the southern coast. Christopher was no governor, and a poor viceroy; his suit was sailing and especially discovering. The Spaniards in the New World were a disorderly bunch in the days of Columbus. It was a very difficult to command these greedy Spaniards, all seeking a sign of distinction and to be Don's and to live off the labors of others, so that it required a strong hand and a smooth rein.

At Hispaniola, Columbus sought the tiny colony at La Navidad to find it totally destroyed. The native chieftain, Guacanagarí told Columbus what happened, that the Spaniards had quarreled among themselves and each tried to seize as much gold and as many women as possible. They straggled over the countryside, and then, when weak and dispersed were killed by the neighboring Indian Chief, Canabo. He burned the town and killed the rest. Not to be deterred, and with large numbers of men, Columbus and his men were intent upon building another fort elsewhere in Hispaniola, and called it Isabella. Columbus learned about the mines of Cibao and sent some messengers to find out where they were. The Indians they met gave gold to these men, and they returned with the good news, and the admiral decided to build a colony at Cibao.

At this point, Columbus sent a letter back home to the Catholic monarchs in which he told of the discoveries he had made. He sent the gold he had obtained from the Indians and gave reasons why there was not more. His people had been ill and guards were necessary to guard against the Indians, so that there was no one available to gather more gold. The monarchs approved. Next, he suggested building a fort near the source of the gold. He asked for more provisions and complained that the casks of wine were leaky. The monarchs ordered provisioning and for Juan de Fonseca to find out who had sold the crown the casks so that they could reimburse the crown and see that nothing like this happened again.

Some Indians from the Cannibal Islands were seized and sent to Spain to become slaves. These Caribs were to be baptized and taught Castillian to serve as interpreters in the work of conversion. The natives of Hispaniola feared that cannibal Caribs and would be impressed that these would remain slaves. In the margin, the royal decision was written that "this is all well, and so it must be done; but let the admiral see whether it could not be managed there that they should be brought to our Holy Catholic Faith, and the same thing with the Indians of those island where he is." Columbus suggested that the cargoes of livestock and other needs of the colonists should be brought. Columbus also suggested that the cargoes of livestock should be paid for in slaves.

While the messenger was on the way, Columbus' colony suffered greatly. There were too many men and too little provisions. Food and medicine were insufficient and the health of the many men began to fail. It was a shock to the lesser nobility, to the people of the Court and the priests to have to labor in the field. They had to expect to find gold on the seashores and now they had to labor manually under strict regulations. They never forgave Columbus for this indignity to their pride. They did hear of the gold mines and saw specimens of ore gained from them, and this cheered them. Admiral Columbus went and founded the Fort of St. Thomas in the Cibao gold country.

In order to stake their claim more fully, it was a duty upon Columbus to sail forth to look for the spice islands and the shores of India and China. The admiral named his brother, Diego Columbus to be president of the governmental council and Pedro Margarite to be captain general and set sail on April 24, 1494, on a voyage for more discoveries. On this voyage, he rediscovered Jamaica and suffered from a pestilential drowsiness. Because of this illness, Columbus' voyage was shortened, and he was back at Isabella on September 29, 1494. Upon their arrival, he was cheered to see his brother Bartholomew newly arrived. It was a good visit between Christopher and Bartholomew for the admiral was very much a family man.

He found a state of disorganization and war between the Spaniards and Indians. Margarite had gone on his ordered march, but the harshness of the commander and soldiers had turned the natives against their guest from Spain. He was to treat the Indians kindly, but instead, they swaggered over the country consuming Indian provisions, raped, and created havoc with their waste, injury, and insult. They pillaged and the Indians passed from terror to despair, and took their revenge upon the Spaniard wherever they could. The Spaniards almost went the way of their brethren of La Navidad.

Canoabo was still at large on the island of Hispaniola and was a sore threat to the invaders. He threatened St. Thomas. Guatiguana was hostile and besieged the fort at Magdalena at Isabella. The latter cacique or chieftain had killed eight Spanish soldiers and had burned down the house in which forty ill Spaniards were housed. Columbus led an army against Guatiguana's force and routed it completely. He enslaved a large part and reduced to obedience his Macoriz.

In February of 1495, the admiral sent back four ships laden with slaves. Ferdinand and Isabella had wished for some other way to Christianize the Indians rather than through slavery. Next, Columbus met on the field of battle, Canoabo with his mass of Indians. On the broad plains of the Vegal Real, Christopher led one force and Bartholomew another, which attacked the natives from different quarters, and very quickly defeated the out-classed Indian force of superior numbers. The Indians were vulnerable with their slight arms and exposed bodies against firearms, steelclad men on horseback and fierce dogs. After the battle, there were more slaves for the Spaniards and Canoabo was still free before St. Thomas. Ojeda took the chieftain by treachery at a supposedly friendly meeting. Using fetters as a gift, Ojeda put them on the Indian and evading pursuit, took him to Columbus. He was sent to Spain and his forces were defeated by Ojeda.

With his control of Hispaniola settled, Columbus levied a tribute upon every Indian over fourteen years of age. In the next year, he extracted service from the Indians who had no gold to pay. However, the Indians tried to starve out the Spanish by planting no crops. This reacted against the natives and many of them died of hunger, sickness, and misery. Those who complained against Columbus were not interested in this, but in their own past grievances, and Columbus had to return to Spain in 1496 to face his accusers. He was well received by Ferdinand and Isabella, and soon was to return to America on his third voyage.

Meanwhile in Portugal, when Manuel followed John in the kingdom, he also followed him in the interest of India. John II died on October 25, 1495. Manuel was going through John's chest of papers when he discovered an interesting letter about trade from a Venetian merchant who was a good friend and had negotiated and executed the dead monarch's commissions. The merchant wrote of India with its great riches and trade coming by seas and lands unknown. Rich merchandise and aromatic spices came to Alexandria when the Turks gained great profits. Should Portugal gain a searoute to India, it was clear, she and not the Turks would benefit. Merchants, he wrote, brought these products of the faraway to Venice.

Correa was to write that the merchant friend said that "this was the greatest trade which there was in Venice, because it went there to all ports, so that sometimes the galleys in Venice came to Spain, and went to sell at Lisbon, as he had seen, but in what port India lay, he was unable to tell him. This, however, was an affair for a great prince to undertake and endeavor to discover and conquer it, and adventure in this his whole kingdom and power; for if it pleased our lord to show it to him and make lord of it, he would be exalted in riches and grandeur over all the Christian princes, and he would be of glorious memory for the exhalation of our holy faith." The discovery of this letter moderated King Manuel and he commanded shipwrights to finish those ships partially prepared by John. He used the sailors who had gone to Janifant to supply these ships and chose a gentleman of the household, Vasco da Gama, to command the expedition of ships. Vasco gained the pardon for his eldest brother to go with him. Paulo da Gama had wounded a judge of Setubal.

In England, Henry VII of that nation granted to John Cabot in the wake of the Columbian discoveries patent letters to discover new lands. Cabot sailed from Bristol in the spring of 1497 and seven hundred leagues or about two thousand miles later he discovered land he first thought to be Cathay or China. He covered most of the Atlantic coast and saw no human beings, but found snares, a needle, and felled trees, which showed the land to be inhabited, but found no populated and wealthy land of Cathay. He received vast honors for his journey and the king promised him ten ships in the following spring. Sebastian Cabot, his son, recognized that this was a new land, and therefore when he undertook the voyage of 1498, he was looking for a northwest-passage.

Henry VII took a great interest in the Sebastian Cabot voyage and paid out of his regal purse, part of the expenses for a part of the gain. Sebastian went by way of Ireland, and not able to find the passage, he sought, he coasted like his father down to 38 degrees north. Sebastian later went on a voyage in 1516 or 1517, and discovered Davis's Strait and Hudson's Strait before they were seen and named after the two explorers. Meanwhile, the Portuguese were sending frequent fishing fleets to the shores of Newfoundland, followed by the French fishing villagers on the coast of Brittany and Normandy. The Spaniard, Esteven Gomez also coasted the mid-North American coast, and future maps, used the knowledge gained by Gomez from Maryland to Rhode Island, including the map of the Hudson River. Verazzano covered much of the territory a number of months later.

The next voyage to the New World is the trip undertaken by Americus Vespucci. There is no other record of this expedition other than the account of Vespucci himself. Further, there is information that on the date of this supposed voyage, he was equipping the third fleet of Columbus. According to the man who left his first name on the two continents, he set sail from Cadiz on May 10, 1497, with four caravels as navigator. This fleet passed throughout the Bahamas, along the coast of Yucatan, and passed the southern coast of North America, around Florida, and up the shoreline to anchor in Chesapeake Bay.

Back home in Cadiz on October 15, 1498, they sold their cargo of Indians into slavery. If such a voyage took place, it was a most notable one. Florida and the eastern coast is shown in the famous Cantino map of 1502, and this information could have come from Vespucci, or been used by him, for the latter described his voyage as navigator in a letter of September 4, 1504. One cannot be sure about the voyage, but it should be remembered in a history of the times just in case that the error was the case of wrong dates or someone else's doings. It does show the advances being made at this time.

Vasco da Gama had written to his brother to see the judge he had hurt and obtain his pardon. Having gotten the pardon of the king, he must come next and kiss the king's hand as was fitting. Paulo gained the friendship of the judge and presented himself before the king. Afterwards, the two brothers persuaded Nicolas Coelho, a friend of theirs and asked if the king would make him the captain of the other ship. The king gave his approval and commanded Vasco to make ready.

In the following days the explorer prepared for the voyage. He needed men adept with the compass and sounding plummets, since once past the known coast, there would be no navigation by latitude or known charts. Working hard and with great skill, Vasco da Gama equipped the ship and trained the waiting sailors in carpentry, rope-making, caulking, blacksmithing, and plankmaking. Drawing from the king's long purse, he paid the men more for their new skills. Because they knew the training would mean more pay, the men were eager for the education. Vasco da Gama kept in contact with the king, who gave him full support in his endeavor.

Once the ships were ready, the eagerness in the Portuguese monarchy and people launched them upon their voyage. King Manuel and Queen Maria went to hear Mass at the Cathedral of Lisbon, conducted by Bishop Calcadilha. The bishop praised the voyage and the holy design of his monarch to search for India, and he called upon the prayers of the people to pray to the Lord that this would exalt the holy faith and would increase the good and honor of their kingdom. While the bishop was speaking, near the royal curtain with the lords and gentlemen of the court, the three leaders of the expedition stood in rich clothes. After the Mass, Manuel came out from under the curtain and spoke to his men, who expressed their realization of the great honor paid them in their selection with rich words.

The royal pair left for the palace where the explorers paid court once again. This done, they left for the ships and set sail to anchor at Belen for three days until a favorable wind came up. While waiting, the sailors gave the names of parents and wives for use in payments upon their return. The married men received a hundred cruzados to give to their wives while they were on a voyage to India. Single men got forty cruzados. Vasco got two thousand cruzados, and his brother the same. Coelho received a thousand. With the right wind, they set forth down the river.

Vasco directed the three ships well out to sea towards Cape Verde and soon had met with storms. The crews suffered much hardship. There was some concern over strange lands, and Vasco da Gama encouraged them and told them the cape was near, beyond which they could find more seas they wished for. Correa wrote in his book that the explorer did not sleep or take repose. Vasco da Gama took part with his men in their hardships that were many, given the storms they met. Sick with fear and unable to prepare their food, the sailors "clamored or putting back to Portugal, and that they did not choose to die like people who sought death with their own hands, thus, they made clamor and lamentation, of which there was much more in the other ships." The Captains answered them that they could do nothing except what Vasco da Gama ordered.

At times angry, but always recognizing their hardships, fears, and the dangers which they all found themselves in, Vasco da Gama would not change his decisions nor his determination to continue. They were well to the south for the days in the winter of the Southern Hemisphere were very short and the fearful nights were long. The ships were letting in much water, requiring the hard work of the men. Next, cold rain fell and the sailors "cried out to God for mercy upon their souls, for now, they no long took heed of their lives."

Vasco was set upon sailing until he could round the expected cape. The seamen took heart when they saw land and the calmer seas near the African coast. They sailed on at night with lanterns so they would not part company. Then suddenly, there was no more land to be found eastward, and they were certain that they had rounded the cape. By this time it was late October or early November.

Sailing on toward the east, they saw some mountain peaks that gave the sailors great joy. Skirting the coast that was now to the north, then left. At dawn, on the following day, in the words of Correa, "they again set all the sails and ran to the land, so that at mid-day, they saw a beach which was rocky and running along it, they saw deep creeks, and such large bays, that they could not see the land at the end of them, they also found the mouths of great rivers, from which water came forth to the sea with a powerful current; her also, near the land they found may fish which they killed with fish spears." The sailors who ate the fish came down sick with fever.

They found the mouth of a large river and entered it. Vasco da Gama sent Coelho five leagues (about fifteen miles) up river, but Nicolas found no villages. The country was uninhabited. On the following day and sent up river, Coelho sent twenty leagues without discovering any people. After fruitless searches and explorations, Vasco da Gama directed the voyage east-ward, and once again, they ran into storms in the Indian Ocean, and suffered more hardship, but their leader would not turn back. He told the crews that once again, God would have mercy upon them, and upon their return, would receive honor and recompense for their duty. This steadiness did not hold, and they plotted an overthrow of their captains. Vasco da Gama discovered this and put some seamen in irons, once he learned of the plots.

The seas let up in time for the ships to put into a river with it's bay for repairs and water in January of 1498. Vasco da Gama's sailors fished for fresh good, which lifted their spirits, and the sick were fed, whose health improved. Many men died on the voyage. The survivors needed time on land. A change of work helped. Entreated by Paulo, Vasco released the prisoners. Because Coelho's ship had many of the ship ribs and knees broken, they broke it up instead of making a difficult repair. Nicolas Coelho found some aborigines that he took to the ships for a visit. After setting up a memorial of a marble pillar set in a stone, the Portuguese set out once again on his trip of explorations for the grand India.

Following the eastern coast of Africa, the explorers saw a sail. The Portuguese gave great thanks to the Lord. They were entering civilization once again. Vasco da Gama sailed his two ships after the sail, which fled seaward. It disappeared into the night. They found six cafres or blacks and one Moor in a canoe. The others fled and the Moor was captured to be entertained on Vasco's ship. The Moor understood a few words of Arabic spoken by an African slave, and indicated that there were people further on who understood their language. He went with the Portuguese along the shoreline to the shoals and land of Sofala. Later, they overhauled a ship with blacks from Mozambique at the end of March 1498.

After some troubles, the Portuguese set out northward up the coast until they reached Melinde with it's walled city and flags. It was the end of April. The king of Melinde made them welcomed. Because of their fine welcome and good treatment, they were there until the new moon of July of 1498. Sailing on to Canavor and Calcutta, they found in India the latter principal city. The Portuguese had reached India. All was not easy dealing with the Indians and after a time, they sailed for the home they had been so far away from. The return voyage was also long, but they reached Lisbon to an honorable reception.

In 1500, an ambitious and adventurous Gaspar Corte-Real proposed to the Portuguese king that he discover the lands to the north. He felt that the southern lands had already been found and he set out to find lands as yet hidden to the Europeans. After equipping one ship, Gaspar set sail in the spring. After crossing the Atlantic, the Portuguese captain saw a land that was cool and the site of great trees. The explorers found a very barbarous and wild people in the land that was probably Newfoundland or the area of Maine. Corte-Reale found a people of middle stature, who were active and great bowmen. Instead of spears, they used shafts burned in the fire. The land had provided them with skins of animals to wear. Finding a people who lived in rocky caves and thatched huts, he observed no religion in his terms, but a people much moved by signs. They were strict in their marriages. Corte-Real was the first Europeans since the Norwegians to see Newfoundland.

The explorer was to return in 1501 to coast Labrador, Newfoundland, and Nova Scotia. At this time, he brought back fifty Indian slaves to Lisbon with a black and some Venetian silver ear rings left by John Cabot. Corte-Real disappeared on the voyage back with his ship, but the two other ships in this trio of vessels setting out returned safely. His elder brother Miguel Corte-Real went to these lands in 1502 and remained to live among the Indians as chief of the Wampanoag Indians. The Portuguese made use of their discovery by fishing in these waters from 1506 for the next quarter of a century.

In 1504, small vessels from Biscay, Bretange, and Normandy crossed the North Atlantic to fish. Two years later, Jean Reneys drew his map of the Gulf of St. Lawrence. Fishermen found great profit in the fisheries and in 1517, there were fifty Spanish, Portuguese, and French ships in the area. Having helped the Cabots on their first voyage to equip their vessels, R. Thorne of Bristol capped his interest in the New World with a trip to search for a northwest-passage. He and his ship disappeared at sea. The year was 1527.

Chapter V

MORE ADVENTURES

There appeared at this time, a vigorous and able man by the name of Vasco Nunez de Balboa who had been born about 1475 in the province of Badajoz, bordering on Portugal. Young Vasco became a page in the service of Don Pedro Puerto Carrero, the deaf lord of Moguer, and in time was the fencing master. In the enthusiasm of the time, this Balboa joined the expedition of Bastidas to seek his fortune in that great maker of fortunes, America. He was present during the following events. Rodrigo de Bastidas was a wealthy notary who was eager to risk his life and savings to trade along the pearl coast of the Mainland or Tierra Firme, northern South America.

Coming from Triana, which was the maritime suburb of Seville, Bastidas secured from Ferdinand and Isabella a license to discover new lands in the Indies. This license was very inclusive. The monarchs authorized him to acquire gold, silver, copper, lead, tin, quicksilver including other metals, pearls, precious stones, jewels, slaves, monsters, serpents, fishes, birds, spices, drugs, and other things. The income from the journey would first be used to cover costs, and then to divide one quarter to the crown and three quarters to Bastidas. Fortunately, Bastidas secured the services of Juan de La Cosa to be chief pilot for those two ships have sailed with Columbus and Juan Ojeda was a logical choice to guide the expedition.

In October of 1500, they set sail. Steering for the Canaries, they soon reached this stepping stone to the New World and brought on water, meat, cheeses, wood, and other fresh provisions at Gomera Island. Off once again, they reached a green island in the Indies and collected fresh water in their casks. When they reached the north coast of Venezuela, the chief pilot guided them westward, going past the Cabo de la Vela, Ojedas' furthermost point of exploration in 1499. On their exploration of the coast, the Spaniards found Indians with gold and pearls and exchanged European trinkets for the valuables found so numerous in the region. Pass Rio Hacha, he found crowned natives at Santa Marta.

In March 1501, along the coast, Bastidas and his sailors saw the mouth of a large river. He named it Magdalena and entered the bay where the Spanish were to found and settle Cartagena. Passing the island of Baru and those of Arenas and San Bernardo, they reached another named Fuerte, where the Indians made such fine salt, that the Spanish had a great desire for it. Moving west and south, they saw more lands, islands, and turning at Punta Caribana, Bastidas thought he had found the strait which would lead past the land mass on the way to China. It did not prove to be the case. He found the water to be fresh and potable, and named the place Golfo Dulce (Fresh Water Gulf). Later it was the Gulf of Uraba or Darien.

Next, Bastidas directed his two ships along the Caribbean shore until sea worms had bored the wooden ships, and they began to leak. They turned around for home. The point of return was Nombre de Dios where Columbus was to land in 1502, the next year.

Setting an eastward course, John de la Cosas piloted Bastidas' ship to Jamaica for Jamaican wood and fresh water. Once again, underway, they found more trouble from leaks and put in for repairs off the coast of Haiti, but on the way once again, they immediately ran into a gale. Finding refuge, they were troubled by leaks and sailed into the port of Jaraqua, Haiti, only to sink. Chained Indians on the way to slavery were drowned, but the Spaniards made land and headed on these routes to better subsist, to the new town of Santo Domingo. There, Bobadilla imprisoned Bastidas for trading with the Indians without a license. Stripped of his property, the explorer was sent to Spain for trial.

Balboa gained valuable experience on this voyage of Bastidas and settled in Hispaniola. He learned that many of the discovered Indians used poison on their weapons. Seeing an Indian village in the middle of green and fertile fields, Balboa and the rest of the sailors had to contact, probably doing some training and learning that the natives of Darien did not use poisoned implements of war. Having a good experience with the Indians, Balboa was able to get an apportionment of Indians for laborers from Governor Ovando and became a plantation owner. There, he learned more about management of men, which doubtless brought him his later success, but his management the plantation for the next seven years was financially unsuccessful and he amassed such great debts that he was to be forced to default.

Cardinal Francisco Ximenez de Cisneros had risen to great power under Isabella with his missionary objective with the Moors and Amerindians in Spain and America. Cisneros was born of good, but poor family in Castilian Torrelaguna in Madrid in approximately 1436, and graduated in civil and canon law at Salaonea in 1456. Soon after becoming a priest, he practiced in the courts of the papal consistory in Rome from 1459 to 1465. Pope Sixtus IV promised him the next benefice in Spain, but the Archbishop of Toledo refused to place Cisneros in the place. The priest held out for several years, when in 1480, Archbishop Carillo restored him to his benefice. There were better things for a man of his talent, and Cisneros exchanged it for a chaplaincy at Siguena and then shortly became Cardinal Mendoza's vicar-general.

No sooner had he won approval from his fellow churchmen, and also fine opinions from laymen, Ximenez de Cisneros abruptly decided to adopt the austere life that was to be his hallmark for the rest of his life. He became a monk at the Franciscan monastery of Don Juan de los Reyes, which was recently established by Ferdinand and Isabella at Toledo. The usual hard life of the order was amplified by Francisco. He slept on the bare ground, wore a hair shirt, undertook more fasts than were ordinary, and scourged himself with vigor. When crowds came to see this holy man with their confessions, he retired further to a lonely monastery, and then lived as an anchorite in a rude hut in the neighboring woods. Later, he became guardian of another monastery.

Mendoza remembered Cisneros and now that Mendoza was archbishop of Toledo, he suggested to Isabella that she make Cisneros her confessor. The queen sent a message in 1492 and called Cisneros to her. She liked him and forced him to give up his monastery life. Since the queen carried to him her affairs of state as well as her personal life, Cisneros had influence upon such national matters as the New World. In addition to this, he used his growing powers to reform the church in Spain. His reforms went with the Spaniards across the ocean in his day and later. Cisneros worked to purify the clergy with a strengthened austerity and preaching missions.

A vibrant royal interest in conversion of the newly conquered Moors was brought forth by Cisneros in Granada and spilled over into Indian affairs across the ocean. Isabella spawned a religious fervor in Granada which was to become a systematic persecution for the Moslems in Spain. Since the Amerindians had a weaker and underdeveloped religion, the Spanish religion met with great success, requiring no persecution, which they considered so necessary in Granada. In contrast to this hardening of Spanish character, the peoples they met in America were generally docile and this gave the invaders, the conquistadors a decided advantage in government and religion. Not all the Amerindians were a quiet people, but once humbled, they were easily brought into the Christian fold by the mendicant orders, to whom the Crown entrusted the American mission.

Now that Bartholomew Diaz had rounded the Cape of Good Hope and that Vasco da Gama had reached Calcutta, the way was open to the Portuguese to reap some of the wealth of India and the East Indies. Da Gama had reached Kenya or Marindios as it was then called where he had hired an expert Arab sailor, Ibn Madjid, to guide the way to Calcutta. There he was faced with the opposition of Moslem Araas and Persians who turned a local Hindu rajah against him. With these troubles, he had to sell his cargo at a loss and could buy only a few spices. This had been the first direct European seaborne contact with the Indians. Vasco da Gama reached home again to the excitement of the Portuguese court and people. This began what was to become a successful trade between Portugal and India and control of the Indian Ocean by the Portuguese with their superior guns.

Despite some caution on the part of some Portuguese, King Manuel was eager for the sending of a new fleet in March of 1500. The king wanted to act promptly to prevent the Arabs from arming in time to prevent Portuguese trade and from inciting the Hindus against them. There was prepared a force of twelve hundred men and an ample cargo to trade for the imposing fleet. In order to impress the rumers of India, many of the ships were commanded by nobles. In order to begin the conversion of the subcontinent of India, Manuel sent Franciscan friars and clergymen, some of whom were to stay behind in India. This was a factor abroad, and the chief command was entrusted to the noble Pedro Alvares Cabral. Bartolomew Diaz was there to help navigate the ships. The ships set forth on the ninth of March of 1500 from the mouth of the Tagus.

To take advantage of the best winds, the ships sailed upon a course to land them in Brazil. Taking the steady northeast trade wind and the ocean currents, they soon passed within sight of the Canary Islands first and the Cape Verde Islands secondly. One ship was lost on the way and was searched for for two days. The northeast trade winds continued. Steerage and currents carried them further west and they coasted Brazil south of the equator just out of landsight. On the 21st of April, signs of land were encountered in a great quantify of lone weeds, and they saw Mount Pascoal on the coast of Brazil at the vesper hours on the twenty-second. The Portuguese had discovered their Brazil, and a land was made at the mouth of a river. The Amerindians there had painted, tattooed, dark, naked bodies with brilliant feathers. No Portuguese had seen the likes of this display before.

The natives came forth with their bows and arrows, and laid them down when motioned to. Nicolas Coelno gave them a red cap, a cape of linen, and a black hat. In return, they gave the Portuguese a hat of long bird feathers. They sought anchorage to the north, where they met more natives, who by sign language, told them there was gold and silver inland. They found fresh water to fill their kegs. Later, there was some more trading and the Portuguese took on more wood. A native was sent back about the discovery of the land. Sometimes, in the afternoons, the fleet was overtaken by a storm in the South Atlantic that sunk four ships, and left the remaining seven battered. The ships set sail for the Indian Ocean, and made it up for Mozambique for ten days of repair, and then sailed on to India.

The king and queen of Spain appointed the military knight of Alcantaro, Nicolas de Ovando, royal governor of the Indies, and on September 16, 1501, gave instructions for the duties to be fulfilled in the New World. They decreed that he must first of all work with diligence in the service of God. It was his responsibility to see that divine worship be performed with great edification, good order and reverence. The royal pair wished that a conversion and salvation of the natives be uppermost. This they believed was the greatest good that the Indians could receive. Pressure was not to be used, but Ovando was to furnish such favor and assistance that would lead to the success of conversion. Subjects of the Spanish Crown in the west must accept all regulations and decisions of the monarchs and their governor. The natives were to be well treated, neither hurt or robbed. Word that the Indians had been robbed in Hispaniola and elsewhere led to an order that their women, cattels, and goods should be returned, and any Spaniard wishing to marry an Indian was to be allowed to do so. Tribute owned to the Crown should be paid based upon the productivity of the land. Ovando and his officials should collect tithes as first fruits for the church.

There were also a number of minor detailed orders given by Shiels. Spaniards should pay Indians a just salary when hired. Bobadilla should have an office and debts to Columbus should be listed. Also, the monarchs instructed that settlements should be made on good and well-watered land. Three fortifications and other strong points for defense were to be established for protection. Payrolls padded by Bobadilla should be stopped, waste in cutting brazilwood should be ended; the lawless element was to be shipped to Spain; fraud prevented in gold mining; strangers kept out; and Bobadilla should be sued for the cattle he attached. Finally, Ovando was to rule with a firm and strong hand.

The archdeacon of Seville, Juan Rodriquez de Fonseca, was a valued councilor of the Catholic monarchs. They gave him charge of the affairs of the Indies from Spain. While directing these undertakings, Fonseca had occasion to advise them on who they should appoint to be the new governor in the West Indies. Ovando was highly respected, so the choice was fortunate. While Columbus had had trouble getting men and provisions, Ovando was highly favored. His fleet was made up of thirty-two ships and 2,500 men. This large force of sailors, soldiers, and colonists was well equipped. No other early expedition in the early history of the West Indies had such numbers. None had the wealth spent on them that Ovando had upon his expedition. Further, the Spaniards put numbers of domestic animals and useful plants aboard. Among the colonists were well-experienced farmers. The planners wanted the colony to be self-sufficient.

On April 15, 1502, Comerdador Nicolas de Ovando had arrived at Santo Domingo to replace Bobadilla, the governor of Espanola. Ovando had a large retinue, a man's importance being recognized by the largeness of his collection of couriers, officials, and servants. The new governor was filled with so much show of self-importance that he refused the great Columbus shelter for his ships from an impending storm when he sailed off the Espanola coast on his fourth voyage in late June of 1502. Columbus warned of an upcoming hurricane but Ovando refused to listen to him. What resulted from this refusal, was the loss of more than twenty vessels in a West India hurricane to the surprise of Columbus' pilots, but not to a sadder Christopher, the greatest explorer of all alive and an expert on expeditions to the New World. Five hundred persons lost their lives including Bobadilla and many of Columbus' bitterest enemies except for Ovando. Not only this, but 200,000 castellanos of gold were lost in the sinkings.

At this time, Ovando embarked upon a policy of successful development of the island. He managed people so well that he turned a turmoil of 300 Spaniards into an attractive colony of 12,000 colonizers in the four years after he arrived. The flood of immigrants continued so rapidly that the governor felt compelled to ask the Crown to limit the sailings of immigrants to a point at which they could be well absorbed. Restrictions against Jews, Moors, and converts were relaxed, opening up opportunities for them. They began arriving with the skills and capital, noted for their cultures, which proved to greatly benefit the economy of the Indies.

The governor successfully organized gold production from the rivers and mines and provided for the establishment of farms. He used a Spanish frontier land system that allotted large estates to suitable Spaniards, and gave responsible colonists powers to force the Indians to slave for them on the lands. This was the best way to develop vacant lands in view, and indeed, Spaniards were eager for these repartimientos. This was the way to get rich quick, second only to gold discoveries.

On the westernmost mainland, unknown to the Spaniards, there was a change of rulers. When the uncle and ruler of Mexico's Montezuma II died, he was selected as the new monarch. He was elected in 1502 to the emperorship of Mexico over his brothers because of his superior skills as a soldier and a priest. His skills as a soldier were expressed in the days of his youth and his skill as a priest took up the better part of his time by the time of his selection. There was much ceremony to be attended in the Aztec worship. Upon election the bearers of the good tidings found Montezuma sweeping the stairs of the great temple dedicated to the national war god. He accepted the honor with humility, a humility that marched his character. He spoke little but with prudence and lived his life with a grave and reserved demeanor.

Montezuma turned to war often in his early days as emperor. Frequently, he led armies in person. His first expedition as emperor was against a rebel prince. It was successful as he did back many captives for bloody sacrifices at his imperial coronation. There were games and religious celebrations for several days. The next expeditions included those on the coastal gulf and into Nicaragua and Honduras. Mostly, they were successful and the limits of the empire were expanded as never before. He favored and promoted a strict justice and tested the integrity of the judges and came into contact with the abuses of his city. He built many public works that included a new channel to bring more water into the capital. In the city of Coihuanan, he established a hospital or retreat for invalid soldiers.

His humanity of the steps gave way to an intolerable arrogance. He would have only persons of high rank serve him and poor soldiers of merit were precluded from imperial menial offices because they were unworthy of such august a person. Montezuma, by his own choice was seen less and less by the people of his empire. Increasing taxes to pay for a lavish court, he earned the disaffection of the people caused by the imposition of grievous taxes. Because there was no mixture of the peoples in his empire, his rule lacked cohesion. Each people were separate and subject to trouble and rebellion.

Queen Isabella established in Seville, the Casa de Contratacion on February 14, 1503, to regulate the trade with the New World. Before this, there were certain rules dealing with commerce, but this was the formal institution of trade. The Casa was also a customhouse. During the first voyage, the first fruits were to go to the Crown, except for one-tenth of the net proceeds for the discoverer. Columbus was allowed to contribute one eight of the coat of the cargo in return for one eighth of the returns, but it was awhile before that would pay off. Private individuals were prevented from carrying forth trade merchandise on the fleet.

Isabella had a customhouse for the receipt of the royal merchandise. Sailors, officers, and others had to present themselves for inspection, going and coming. Shortly, the subjects of the queen were allowed to engage in trade since so many Spaniards wished to go to the countries beyond the sea. Since moneys belonged to the Crown, it was only by royal grace that one third of their produce was awarded to the miner. After that, regulations were beginning to increase, and the Casa de Contratacion was the chief manager of those regal provisions, that guided the management of the trade in the western lands.

Spanish taxes were small at first. In the spring of 1497, royal decrees exempted all goods imported from the West from the manifold duties of Spain. Also, goods exported to the West Indies were exempt. However, in 1543, custom duties were levied on American trade. However, there were port duties in Hispaniola to the amount of 7 and a half percent.

Seville was chosen for the residence of the Casa because it was the wealthiest and most populace city of Castile. A single port was easier to regulate and although other cities made claims for part of the action, they were unsuccessful in getting anything done about their wishes. The colonies protested and Charles V took efforts to change the situation, but nothing was done. Lacking influence, the mariners could complain all they wished, but no one listened. They said that the city was sixty miles from the sea and that the channel was narrow and tortuous. Further, they said that the bar at San Lucar was dangerous to cross. Larger vessels that became more numerous over the year, made it difficult for trade, especially when the river began to accumulate silt.

Over the years, there were to be delays with the increased traffic of ships that made it more difficult. Some relief was granted for shipments at Cadiz down river, but those that were homeward bound still had to stop at Seville. In 1509, an inspector was appointed for the Cadiz port, but Charles V allowed the Seville bound Casa to appoint the inspector for the benefit of Seville. On some occasions, there were landings at other ports in cases where wind and weather prevented a landing at Seville or to avoid hostile squadrons, but these were exceptions.

When the Spaniards needed labor to replace dying Indians, they turned to black slaves from Africa. The first record of blacks in Hispaniola was a mention of slaves in 1503, and soon, there was a flow of Africans in slave ships to the Americas. These ships had been carrying blacks from West Africa to Spain for about one half of a century. They were used on large estates in southern Spain. Also, a this time, the cruel Spaniards captured large numbers of Bahaman Indians for Hispaniola. The islands were depopulated and the poor natives died quickly in the fields and mines, dying broken and despairing from hard work, which they were not used to in their earlier days.

At the time of Columbus' second voyage to Hispaniola, this island was divided into five native kingdoms with their kings. In addition there were other Indians who recognized none of their kings. These people of Hispaniola were faced with great pain after Queen Isabella died. One of these kingdoms was called Aqua that meant plain and an attractive plain it was. The length was eighty miles and it's width was between five and ten miles, surrounded by high mountains and well watered, gold dust was brought down form the mountains in the streams.

It was soon known that the Spaniards lusted for gold and King Guarionca's Indians presented them with gold as they had. He was a peaceful king who expressed his devotion to the Spanish monarch. A governor wanted the Spanish to fill the rich lands of Hispaniola. In return for this kindness, one of the Spanish captains violated his wife and the ruler left the kingdom, but the Spaniards made war upon him and destroyed the kingdom until they were later to capture the man and bound him back to Spain as a slave. This ship was wrecked along the way and at a great loss to the Spaniards. The slaves lost their lives.

The king of Marien called Guacanagarí had gold mines and treated the Spaniards well from the first. He befriended the sea captain and gave great assistance to him. In return, the Spaniards began their murders and robberies there. The Indians fled and their king died poor in the mountains and the nobles of Marien were enslaved. Next, was the kingdom of Maqoara, known for its sugar production and ruled by Canaboa. As he have seen he was enslaved too. Along the way, the ship which carried him, and five other ships were sunk. Las Casas later saw in this God's wrath. Canaboa's brother rebelled against the Spaniards. The Spanish depopulated a great part of the country in Indian wars.

The fifth kingdom went the same way as the other. Xaraqua had a brother and sister as rulers. The king died and the sister was left to be the sole ruler. Anacaona was sold as were her countrymen, but the Spanish governor got the three hundred peers and lands of the natives together, and many more were burned alive in a straw cottage. The rest of the people were murdered by the sword and the Spanish governor caused Anacaona to hang herself. Those that escaped were reduced to servitude. The fifth kingdom, that of Hiquey, governed by Queen Hiquanama, met with a similar fate. The aged queen was crucified, and others were tortured, burned alive, or partly torn to pieces. Those on Hispaniola who survived were enslaved.

When the wars were at an end on Hispaniola, the Spanish conquerors divided the Indians among themselves. The men were sent to the gold mines, at intolerable labor under the whip, and the women were also sent to hard labor manuring and tilling the ground. Eager to get the maximum for the least, the women were fed nothing but roots and herbs, drying up the milk of those with child so that the infants died. With men and women separated, there were soon no more children. Both sexes died of the hard labor they were unaccomstomed to, not to mention the heavy burdens for which the got blows of whips, cudgels, and fists.

Las Casas wrote about the beautiful islands of St. John and Jamaica, fruitful gardens when the Spaniards came. However, when freed from restraint, after Queen Isabella died, they killed and burned, and threw to the dogs these oppressed peoples, almost exterminating the natives. Las Casas witnessed or heard about much of it and wrote about it and campaigned against such behavior.

Chapter VI

MORE EXPLORATIONS

In 1504, only four years after the Portuguese discovered Brazil, a French ship from Honfleur reached that coast. French traders seemed to take to that country and overlooked Portuguese traders. Portuguese authorities did not wish to spend their flowing wealth upon armaments, but they were forced to take measures by the increased frequency of French merchants off Brazilian coasts. In 1523, John III gave orders to his subjects to sink any French interlopers they found. French mariners were strong enough to protect themselves, and in 1530, they attacked and plundered Pernambuco, recently settled. They also took an interest, increasingly, across the ocean in West Africa and connected the two territories in French trade, the Atlantic possessions in Brazil needing black slaves since they could not make the Indians in the west work, whereas the natives of Africa were used to hard and hostile conditions. Because the currents flowed northwestward to the West Indies, there was a natural move of the French pirates into the West Indies before sailing out of the Florida channel to Europe.

It has been suggested, but never verified that British merchants had discovered the island of Newfoundland between 1480 and 1494, but it is a sure thing that the west countrymen were experienced fishermen in home waters, off the Irish and Scottish coasts, and off Icelandic waters. Then the Danes established restrictions on Icelandic fisheries. The English still had the Hanse competition as before in the fish trade. These German critics had a formidable trade organization. The fishing merchants heard of new and rich fishing grounds of a newly found island to the west, which was named Newfoundland. When Cabot got back, from his voyage, the Anglo-Portuguese fishing expeditions followed him to the New World fisheries, which we have seen. Fishermen from the ports located from the Severn to Southampton sailed to the banks also and shipped fish to ready markets in France and Spain which they had earlier supplied with fish from closer waters. It was a bonanza for the people of southern England, the grounds being so rich that they were thought inexhaustible.

Fishing ships left England between January and April with prevailing easterlies. When they got near the coasts, they would take advantage of the Arctic current to sail southward to the banks off Newfoundland. They tried to be there in May since in that month, the codfish usually arrive offshore. Once there, the men went ashore for the construction of stages, flakes, cook rooms, and shacks to harvest the crops as they were brought in. Once prepared, they were stored in the hold completely water-proofed, not to be opened until their destination for sale, as dried codfish. Lack of salt required a long process for preservation. The ships began to leave in August for a four-week average voyage to England. Other nationalities had cheap salt and did not require their troublesome procedure.

Ojedas' ship entered the bay of Calmar. Juan de las Cosa, being familiar with the land and people advised Ojeda not to disembark. By not listening to the navigator, Ojeda was responsible before God for the deaths that followed. The expedition leader landed a force and took the Indian village of Clamar, enslaving the Indians and plundering them of their gold. Several leagues inland Ojeda found another Indian town. Because the town, Turbaco, was deserted, the Spaniards scattered throughout the town to loot.

Suddenly, the people of the town returned and began killing the surprised invaders. Casa lost his life as did many others. They fled for the ships, but only Ojeda and one other man reached safety. Chastened, the Spaniards set sail westward. At the limit of his grant, the Gulf of Uraba, Ojeda built a wooden blockhouse and some small houses within a stockade. This was the second Spanish settlement on the mainland.

Because he needed protection from the poisoned weapons, he named it in honor of, and supplication to the arrow-martyred San Sebastian. The Spaniards left in parties, searching for good and gold. The Indians ambushed the Europeans. Many died from arrows, other wounds, disease, and hunger. Ojeda himself was wounded. His belief that the Virgin protected him proved to be a mistake. Upon his orders, his surgeon cauterized the wound with redhot irons to save his life. Enciso had not reached him with the expected supplies, and indeed had yet to look up and sail, so he decided to go to Hispaniola.

In May of 1510, Ojeda left Francisco Pizarro in charge, and after some trouble, reached Santo Domingo, but he could not get aid from Diego Columbus or the king. Losing his "bray and bluster," Ojeda gave up his worldly ambitions and became a friar in the St. Francis Order. He was to die a few years later. After the expected fifty hungry days had passed, Pizarro following orders, took his men and sailed eastward. One ship was overturned by a squall and all drowned. In the other ships, Pizarro and thirty-five men made it to Calmar, where they met Enciso. Life was dangerous.

When the tardy Martin Fernandez de Enciso obeyed his instructions to follow the expedition with more men and supplies and set sail, he had a castaway abroad. This was a planter, Vasco Nunez de Balboa. He sought adventure and relief from his debt ridden life in Hispaniola. Since local laws forbade debtors from leaving the island unless they settled their accounts with their creditors, Balboa was unable to leave. Because he could not leave openly, he arranged to be secretly taken abroad the ship. Friends took his valued sword and his dog, Lioncico to the vessel. Bartolome Hurtado took a large cask with Balboa inside across the gangway and set it on deck. Safely hidden, Balboa got out and hid himself in an extra sail until they left on September 1, 1510, and he could reveal himself to Enciso. Fearful that Balboa was escaping, Enciso ranted, and threatened to leave him on some desert island. However, Balboa's friend interceded for the stowaway, and convinced Enciso that Balboa would be a good asset to the company of 150 armed men abroad the ship and brigantine.

After the westward sail and meeting with Pizarro, lawyer Enciso gave the orders to go to San Sebastian. Unfortunately, the ship under the command of Enciso was wrecked on a shoal, and the men on it had to walk to San Sebastian. The other two vessels followed along. At the settlement, Enciso found himself and his men terrorized by the deadly Indians. Although, they could not return to Hispaniola, everyone was for flight, as the only alternative, but Balboa suggested going to the fertile town he had seen in Panama. Balboa led them as a proclaimed Moses to safer territory.

They found the site, named Darien in what is now Panama and immediately prepared for conquest. Most of the expedition put into shore, found higher ground, and reconnoitered Darien. Chief Cemaco watched and when it was clear there would be a fight, he sent the village women and children away to safety. The five hundred warriors supplicated their gods and the Spaniards their promises, and immediately prepared for conquest. Because Balboa assured the men that these Indians did not use poisoned arrows and because it was a case of win or die in battle or face starvation, the Spaniards attacked just before dawn. Both sides were brave. However, the gunfire with its death dealing sureness stuck terror in the Indians and they fled. The invaders took the village with its food, cotton cloth, and stores of golden loot. They remained at Nuestra Senora de la Antigua del Darien and Enciso became the mayor.

On November 22, 1509, after Ojeda had deported Diego de Nicuesa, Nicuesa gave his orders to set sail for the far coast. Because little was known about the location of the coast of Veragua, his pilots steered to the Calmar-Uraba coast and then turned the expedition's ships for Columbus' Veragua River. They found it, but not listening, the leader of the ships directed them past its mouth, until they hit the islands of the Chiriqui Lagoon. The ships sank, off the island nearby. Nicuesa left the wrecked ships, and they went by land.

The pilot, Ribero stole away, found Lope de Olano, the leader's lieutenant at the site of Bartholomew Columbus' 1503 settlement, and brought Diego and his men to safety there. An angry Nicuesa put Olano in chains. When the Indians deserted the site (Belen) and left the Spaniards without food, which the Indians had supplied. Also, there was no loose gold, it had to be mined, and although they would suffer to hunt for it, they did not want steady jobs at hard labor.

Gregonio of Genoa who had been with Columbus guided his chief, Nicuesa to the harbor of Puerto Bello where there was a spring of cool water, but the Indians killed about twenty of the invaders when the Europeans tried to seize food. Nicuesa went eastward and stopped at Nombre de Dios, which he founded. On November 9, 1510, while his men were dropping like flies from disease and the conditions found in the tropics, he sent a message to beg for immediate aid. Then Colmenares founded them. Blaming Columbus for the "false report" that Veragua was a rich land, he saw it as a forbidding and poor land. We know now that his land was not the Veragua of the great explorer and that Nombre de Dios was on the Spanish trade route from Peru. Drake was to call it a treasurehouse. When the envoys from Antigua gave their view of the situation, and the town, Nicuesa gave a banquet and told them in his arrogant way that he would dispose of the officials there, seize all of the gold, and punish those who had taken the gold from his "subjects."

At this time, the Dominican Order in America was founded upon instruction by Pedro de Cordoba, who arrived in Santo Domingo in September of 1510. Cordoba took his religion seriously. He preached vigorously and fervently on behalf of the natives. Spanish planters and rulers, eager to exploit and feather that nest they had come across the ocean to gain, were angered and Pedro had to return to the New World to become an inquisitor under the authority of the Inquisitor General on January 7. 1519.

Although they were settled in a comfortable town and had grown crops in the fields surrounding them, the Spaniards were not at peace with each other. Their alcalde was a happy being by reason of the gold objects that he now owned, a rich man for his times, many times over his expenditures for his part in the Ojeda expedition. However, when Enciso made laws to regulate the conduct of the colonists and issued an edict to prohibit private trade for gold, he engendered opposition. Since they were so interested in gold and this was to be forbidden them under the pain of death, they could not contain themselves, and were determined to remove him. Enciso's authority from Ojeda was lost in the shipwreck, so he could not prevent it to the adventurers upon demand. They believed that Enciso wanted all the gain for himself and did not have authority over them. Indeed, as Balboa said they were in the territory of Diego de Nicuesa in Panama. They were now, naked, leaderless, and under Spanish law and custom, and could elect a town council for a government. This they did and Balboa and Martin de Zamudio were elected joint mayors of Darien, the coast of Panama.

Not long after this, in mid-November of 1510, the new citizens of Darien heard the faint reports of artillery and saw smoke in the east. They eagerly responded with smoke signals of their own and some hours later saw two ships approach the shore. They were the vessels of Enriquez de Colmenares, loaded with supplies and men to reinforce Nicuesa. The tactful lieutenants of Nicuesa gave supplies and received the respect of the colonists. Balboa and his partisans decided to invite Nicuesa to come there and govern. Enciso and his friends opposed this, but they could do nothing and Colmenares set sail with two delegates, both of them enemies of Balboa.

Chapter VII

LAS CASAS

One of the early colonial decisions to be made was that of the status, character, and capacity of the Indians. At first, it was decided by practical men on the spur of the moment. The early explorers treated the Indians as sources of information and the early traders moved any gold they had from native to Spanish hands. A few were enslaved and taken back to Spain. The Portuguese showed the way for this, and as we have seen, many of these captives were lost in shipwrecks. Later, the Indians would be eradicated or put to work in any of the gold mines, as suppliers of provisions, and next, to be enslaved to work on plantations. In a few words, they were to be exploited. After this, the theorists took over. The official chronicler of the Indies, Oviedo, declared them to be generally lazy and vicious, lying and shiftless, and a most cowardly people. Many Dominican friars moved toward the other view and exaggerated the capacity and lovable nature of the Indians. Las Casas went to the extreme of this in his obsessive praise of the Indians. Others were more realistic, distinguishing between various groups from the cannibals of the Lesser Antilles to the city dwellers of the Yucatan peninsula, who proved brave and long resistant.

So far, the Spanish had treated the native rough and in a mercenary spirit, and without any protest. But on this Sunday proceeding Christmas in 1511, Antonio de Montesinos spoke against this bad treatment of the Indians by the Spaniards. This brave man was a Dominican friar and he spoke out for human liberty in a straw-thatched church on Hispaniola. He spoke for Christ, and sought to make Spanish sins against the Indians public. Bartolome de las Casas wrote that the lowly friar preached, that the voice he was to proclaim everyone who treated the Indians with cruelty and tyranny were in a state of mortal sin. He asked what right they had to keep the Indians in such a cruel servitude. He asked them by what authority they waged a cruel war against the natives of the New World. The Indians were oppressed and ill-treated when sick and were not fed enough. The desire for gold on the part of the oppressors led the Spanish to virtually "kill" their slaves by their oppressive Spanish drive. They had not taken care in giving religious instruction to the Indians, who had rational souls. He asked his audience if they were not required to love the Indians as they loved themselves?

Finished with his sermon, Montesinos left the church. The colonists had not come to hear a message that would denounce them, and they were astonished, and muttered against their preacher. The sermon had not moved their heart and souls. With growing anger, they went to Diego Columbus' house. There, they gathered and uttered their protest against the sermon. Vicar Pedro de Cordoba was not perturbed by this threat. He would not swerve, and did not honor the delegations threat. The colonists wanted him to expel Montesinos. Cordoba said only that the friar had spoken for the Dominicans and promised that the religious would speak again on the matter. The delegation left, but they were so sure of themselves that they thought, they had carried the day. had they not been so arrogant, they would have realized that the vicar had said that the friar had spoken for the Dominicans.

Everyone in that part of Hispaniola thought that they would have a great victory against those who questioned their right and their morality. They were sure that Montesinos would back down. Montesinos surprised them royally. He advocated his subject and belabored the colonists greatly. With more passion, the friar warned the assembled and newly unholy colonists that the friars would not receive them for confession and absolution. In a further blow, he compared them to highway robbers. Knowing what they would do, Montesinos said that his hearer could write home to anyone they pleased, and say anything they wished.

And the colonists took their complaints to King Ferdinand II, who listened and immediately was angered. On March 20, 1512, the Spanish ruler ordered Diego Columbus to reason with Montesinos, and if the friar persisted, to send him home for punishment. The king wrote that the Dominican error on the island had been condemned ten years before. Canonists and theologians had held a conference on the matter of the Indians and made the decision. Ferdinand felt, if they preached further for Indian rights, they would do great harm. So pressure was put on Montesinos. Authorities reproached him and the matter passed into history where Montesinos was to be considered a shining beacon to historians centuries later.

In 1511, the Spaniard came in great numbers to Cuba, where they again expressed their cruelty and rage against the poor Indians. A refugee from Hispaniola, in Las Casas' account, the Lord Hathuey warned the people of Cuba of the Spaniards and their God. He told the native Cubans, that they could not be merciful in Cuba, but that they should dance to the Spanish deity who should command the Spaniards to let the Indians of Cuba alone. This deity of the Spanish was from the nature of the Spaniards. They believed that gold was the God of the invaders and in hopes of appeasing his rage, they adored a box of gold. They hoped this box would tell the Spaniard to leave the natives alone. The Hispaniolan then cast into the river to prevent it from being taken by the Spaniards.

The Hispaniolan Hathuey saw the Spanish come to Cuba and escaped them and fought to retain his freedom. He made a desperate resistance. Finally, the Spaniards caught Hathuey. Governor Velasquez decided to burn him at the stake. A Franciscan came to him before the burning to talk about God and about the articles of Christian faith. There was a time for him to find salvation before being burned alive. He could go to Heaven. He asked the friar if the door to heaven was open to the Spaniards. Yes, it was to the good Spaniard! the Indian replied, "let me go to Hell that I may not go there where they are."

Later, the people of one city came to submit to the Spanish and do them honor. Then they returned home. The Spanish governor and his men crept among them that night, and catching them asleep, and burned their houses. They murdered some of the escaping Indians and tormented captives to get from them, where they had hidden the gold. Later, the Spaniards murdered more of them. Another Indian gave a present of nine thousand crowns. They tortured him for more. Getting all that he had, they continued to torture him for what he did not have. The beasts from Spain continued this elsewhere, not sparing helpless women and children.

The crown had appointed Velasquez governor of Cuba after the conquest and the new governor concerned himself with the prosperity of the Spanish on the island. He directed the building of a number of settlements. His seat of government was St. Jago on the southwestern corner of the island. Settlers were attracted by liberal grants of land and slaves. They were encouraged to cultivate the soil with Indian labor, especially the sugar cane that became a great export for Cuba.

Bartolome de las Casas was born in Seville in 1474. His father became rich and shipped out on Columbus' first voyage, while his son was graduating from Salamanca at age eighteen. He and his father went out on Columbus' 1498 expedition. Back in Cadiz in 1500f, Las Casas soon sought again the New World. In 1502, he went with Nicolas de Ovando, who was the new governor of the Indies. There, he was ordained a priest and soon went to Cuba to help in the pacification of the island's population and observed Spanish methods. In one case, he was unable to prevent the massacre of all of the Indians in the vicinity. The Spaniards excelled in killing defenseless Indians. When the island was considered settled, the governor gave to Sos Casas of Pedrodela the Renteria plantation with Indian workers as serfs.

An impolite blunderer among the explorers of the American natives, Nicuesa was soon to enter into more trouble than he could handle. The envoys had gotten a glimpse of what he would do in his bragging and they were to learn more. For when Corral and Albitez whom Nicuesa had promised positions in Darien or Panama, came across a chained Lupe de Olvo, grinding corn like a woman, they learned what might have actually happened to them and the people they had left. The two men returned to Antigua de Darien, the main city, with a feeble and sick band of colonists, and told of what they had seen and heard in Nombre de Dios. The people of Antigua determined not to receive Diego de Nicuesa. The governor was in great spirits and took his time sailing for the town which seemed destined to be his capital. Sending Jan de Quicedo ahead to announce his coming, Nicuesa stopped off among the islands to kidnap some Indians for slavery. Not knowing that Quicedo was his enemy, Nicuesa had no way of knowing what the herald was telling men at Antigua to convince them to reject him.

When Nicuesa sailed into the port, he was met by Balboa, and asked not to step foot upon the soil. He should, he said, go back to Nombre de Dios. Taking back because he expected a warmer greeting, Nicuesa asked to be allowed on shore, and suggested that they could talk matters over. Afterwards, they could do with him as they willed. An angry people refused. Nicuesa begged but without favorable result. On the next morning, the governor came ashore, but he had to flee a hostile crowd and be rescued by Alcalde Balboa, who sent him back aboard the brigantine. Balboa punished Francisco Benitez with one hundred lashes, because he kept urging the population not to allow Nicuesa, such a bad man, ashore. By this, Balboa gained a mortal enemy. Nicuesa persisted so the people sent him out on the "worst brigantine in the port" and he and his ships disappeared, never to be seen by the Spaniards again. Next, the colonists exiled Enciso for tyranny and usurpation of authority.

Diego Columbus listened to information from Antiguan agents about what had happened there and about the needs of the colony. Favorably impressed, Diego decided to support the strong and able Balboa in his Spanish outpost on the mainland and exercise his own authority in that part of the new Spanish domains. On September 10, 1511, Christopher's son wrote Ferdinand about Antigua del Darien and that he had named Balboa to be his lieutenant on the mainland. The Spanish ruler approved of this and issued an appointment to Vasco Nunez de Balboa to be acting governor of Darien, followed by a royal commission in January of 1512. Meanwhile, Diego sent supplies to the colony of Darien in Panama.

Meanwhile in Panama, Balboa had sent food to Nombre de Dios on three occasions and then about July of 1511, brought the people to La Antigua del Darien, to prevent them from dying out from the climate and the elements of disease. The Spaniard in Nombre de Dios had seen five or six men dying daily. They were given town lots and lands for raising corn, cassava, and other crops. Colmenares had brought them back and on the return found two Spaniards dressed and painted as Indians on the coat of Cueva or Coilba province. They had been sailors who had deserted the expedition of Nicuesa the year before and had fallen in with the Indians in that province led by Careta. Well treated by Careta, they lived with the natives and one of them, Juan Alonso was appointed as a war chief. The two men told Colmenares that Careta had a lot of gold and provisions and they advised Colmenares to attack and loot the village. Because the chief had two thousand warriors, it was decided to avoid raiding them, but that one of the sailors should inform Balboa about the tribe, while Juan Alonso would stay to betray Careta.

An informed Balboa listened and decided upon action to gain the gold and provisions because the growing population of Antigua needed more food to survive. The governor led 130 men to the port where Careta lived and welcomed Balboa. When he was asked for food, Careta told Balboa that he was out of supplies because the war with his neighbor Ponca had kept them so busy, they had not been able to plant their fields. He denied having any gold. Alonso, having greeted his fellow countryman, spoke in Spanish which Careta could not understand, and advised Balboa to pretend to believe the chief, and leave and return by night to attack. This Vasco did and surprised the Indians, killing them and capturing them. He had the Indians load up their provisions and carried the natives back to Antigua.

In Antigua, Careta asked Balboa to release him and his tribesmen to cultivate the fields to provide the Spaniards with food. It would, it was clear, be better to have the Indians as allies producing provisions and not having to be guarded. Independently, they could be allies in case of war. He turned them free, baptized the chief as Ferando, and aided the Indians on their raid on Ponca. The best part for Balboa would be having Careta's daughter as a common-law wife. She gave him good counsel in his life and provided him with valuable information.

One hundred and twenty miles to the west were the lords of Chief Comogre and his people. They formed a large tribe of over ten thousand men, women, and children and could field three thousand warriors. The had learned of the white men, their coming, and of their great lust for gold. At that time a relative of Careta's known as a wise man among these peoples, advised Comogre to make peace with the Spaniards. Comogre sent a message to Balboa inviting him to visit the domain of his tribe, and when the Spaniards came, he greeted them and him at the borders with great ceremony. The Indian chief had with him his seven sons by as many wives, and many of his principal warriors and people. These tribesmen conducted the white men to their chieftain's house.

Balboa and his men were surprised at the great size and able construction of the palace, which was, they reported, one hundred and fifty steps in length and eighty in width, with great pillars and a stone wall. It had an attic of beautiful fabricated wood. There were many storage compartments and a spacious hall with desiccated cadavers of former chiefs that was the center of a great veneration, leading to a kind of ancestor worship. These remains were covered with cotton mantles, golden jewelry, pearls, and precious stones suspended from the ceiling, with cotton ropes.

Eager to gain favor with the whites, Comogre laid before what he considered a gift of superior gold pieces and seven Indian slaves. When they saw the jewelry, the Spaniards weighed it. After setting aside the king's fifth, they distributed the spoils among the soldiers. The Spaniards divided it, disputing and wrangling. Comagre's eldest son, Panquiaco, looked on in scorn. He had thought them superior, but now he expressed his disdain for such behavior by hitting the balance and scattering the gold pieces all over the ground. He told the astonished Spaniards that they should not quarrel over such trifles when to the south there was a province of great wealth. In order to do this, it would be necessary for the to have great numbers of soldiers, for these people were ruled by great kings who could be counted on to defend their lands with great courage and rigor. There they could see another sea with ships and great stores of gold in kingdoms in the seaside.

The Spaniards listened intently to the translation. This momentous statement provided history-changing information to the Spaniards. It was the first that they had heard of the great civilization in America which was to be called Peru with the great wealth which had motivated them to explore and plunder for the last two decades. Their greed and eagerness encouraged a nation to search for the Inca Empire of Peru. Resulting in many efforts, it led to Balboa's decision to go search for Peru and the parsimonious Ferdinand's decision to spend much treasure to prepare an armada for Castilla del Oro. It led also, to much exploration and conquest in narrow Panama and on the Pacific coasts of America to the south.

Balboa and his men heard this good news with unrestrained joy and some weeped for pleasure. During the next several days, the Spaniards remained there and learned about the routes to the near sea and the tribes on the way. Panquiaco offered to guide them, but they would need one thousand soldiers and all of his father's warriors to defeat the fierce Tubanamo. In return for the hospitality, gifts, and information, Balboa had the priest baptize the tribal family, and gave Panquiaco the baptismal name of Carlos after the grandson of Ferdinand and Isabella, who would soon reign as Charles V, and become a famous emperor.

Next, Balboa went back to Antigua to write to Diego Columbus and the king of what he learned and to tell the colonists in Panama about the great wealth of Peru. Back home, he learned of the arrival of provisions under Juan de Valdivia and his commission from Diego, which greatly strengthened the position of Vasco Nunez de Balboa.

Because Valdivia had done so well after six months negotiations, Balboa sent him once again to go to Hispaniola with reports of Peru and see if Viceroy Diego Columbus, Christopher's son, would ask the king to furnish the one thousand men needed for the conquest. Valdivia took the king's fifth for his majesty and many colonist share for their families in Spain. Seeking the necessary support in Spain, Balboa sent in secret, some choice pieces of Indian jewelry to the royal treasurer for his personal benefit. This man, Miguel de Pasamonte, so powerful in the homeland, had to be bought because of his influence, whether good or bad. Valdivia set sail to be wrecked and all but two to die by drowning, various suffering, and by violence in Yucatan.

Back in Antigua del Darien, Vasco Nunez de Balboa was having his troubles, with problems of subsistence, jealousy, ambition, and greed, but he was popular, able in command, and courageous and stayed upon top of things. His colony was still in danger and there were rightful fears about the friendly Indians coming to trade maize, cassava, and fruit for trinkets which the Spanish very cheaply bought or manufactured. But to the natives, these were valuable. These visitors could also talk to Indian slaves in the town and learn much about Spanish strengths and weaknesses. By this means, the small numbers of Indians who came, could report much to the chiefs and peoples. Balboa would also lead forays to get food and gold from the Indians without stirring up much hostility. The Spanish leader was a good diplomat as shown by the success of his ability. A rough commander would cause many casualties and hostilities in these forays, but Balboa was different from most of his fellows.

However, there was fighting to record because some of the Indians were not friendly and viewed with alarm the growing number of foreigners in their land.

Captain Francisco Pizarro was ordered to take six men for a reconnaissance toward Cueva. This small party was seen by Cemaco as a good chance to kill some Spaniards, but when Cemaco attacked, he learned differently. Pizamo's men warded off the hurled varas with their shields and killed some 150 Indians. The Indians pressed hard against the Spaniards and Pizarro left Francisco Hernan wounded on the battlefield. Wounded himself, Pizarro got the rest of his men out. Balboa was anger and commanded Pizarro to rescue the wounded Hernan. Balboa would not let any of his soldiers to be left alive on the battlefield. Pizarro rescued Hernan. The Indians had not harmed the wounded man. Balboa took action, heading to catch Cemaco with one hundred Spaniards. They were too many, so Cemaco sidestepped and used to jungle warfare could not be caught. The jungle was still the Indians when they were prepared.

Soon after the Pizarro incident, Balboa thought it was time for a project of importance. The Spaniards had been listening to words of a very rich lord reported to be descended from the powerful goddess Dabaiba, who was the mother of the creator of the sun and moon. The greedy Spanish, eager for gold, believed this story, and even after not finding it, thought it was surely true.

Balboa prepared to go to this land, and he set out with an expedition of 160 men in two brigantines and many canoes. On June 24, 1512, a couple of so days after they left, Balboa and his men discovered the mouth, or mouths of the Atrato River. Dividing his force, the governor of Darien of Panama took both units up two of the mouths, and found an abandoned village where the Indians had been warned by Cemaco. Some of his men were lost with much gold from the village in a tempest of the gulf where they had headed after looting the Indian town. He joined with the other unit that was under the command of Colmenares.

They were still exploring the river system when they came upon a town of five hundred houses. This town was defended by its inhabitants under the Chief Abenameche. They hurled long varas, and used wooden swords and clubs. It was no match; the Indians had to flee, Balboa and his men captured the chief and others. A Spanish solder who had been wounded by the chief, sought vengeance by cutting off one of Abenameche's arms, near to the shoulder with one stroke of the sword. The Spaniards sacked the town. He left half of his men to protect the rear. Again Colmenares was put in charge.

Upstream, the Spaniards found the interesting village of Chief Abideida, with its houses built on large and high trees above the lagoons and swamps and safe from the floods of various seasons. The houses were constructed of posts and wickerwork of canes with roofs of grass and large leaves. Balboa made a visit to the chief, but Abideida would nnot come down, and told them to go away, since he had done nothing to harm them. When the Europeans began to cut into the great tree, Abideida descended. Since the people of the land were fishermen and had no gold, Balboa grew insistent. The native chief said there was gold on nearby mountains, and in sight of Balboa and his men, and if allowed, he would bring the precious metal. He left hostage is wife and children and headed in that direction and disappeared. Other villages were found, but the were deserted.

While Balboa was gone, Colmenares sent out Raya to raid. Raya, with his nine men attacked the town of Chief Abraiba, but losing two men were free to return to Abenameche; they suffered an attack in the town by the revengeful chief who had lost an arm. The five hundred warriors would have cause great losses except that Balboa sent thirty men to reinforce Colmenares. Later Balboa and Colmenares returned home leaving Bartolome Hurtado of Abenameche to watch the natives. Hurtado raided until most of his men were sick. These sick men were sent downriver only to be ambushed. Only two escaped, and when Hurtado heard rumors of an attack by hostile Indians, he abandoned his post with his men and returned to report to Balboa.

There was a confederation of Indian in Darien. to the south, planning to utterly destroy all Christians in Antigua del Darien, but Balboa's concubine Fuluiz told him about it. He soon made preparations for a defense without telling his men the secret that they would not let it out and forewarn the Indians that their five thousand Indians were expected on this certain night. A brother of Fuluiz had been told by her brother so she could be safely away when the attack was made. For this reason, Fuluiz was told and because of her love for Balboa, he was told. Believing that the best defense was an offense, Balboa led his men against Cemaco, but the latter escaped the net being set for him.

Since he had heard nothing of Valdiva since January, Balboa could decide the had met with shipwreck, and so he sent forth Juan de Caicedo and Rodrigo Enriquez de Colmenares to Spain. They left in November of 1512. Caicedo died soon after reaching the homeland. Colmenares joined Enciso in uttering against Balboa, verbally abusing the governor and stirring up trouble for him in Spain. Both men were clearly jealous of Balboa and desirous of power and wealth.

Meanwhile, the dispute over Indian slavery in the West Indies was carried to Spain. When the colonists sent the Franciscan Alonso del Espinal to protect their peculiar institution, the Dominicans sent Montesinos to speak for Indian rights. Because Montesinos presented a list of Indian grievances, the hostile Ferdinand who was caught off balance, ordered a group of theologians and officials to consult, and decide upon laws to deal with the questions. Meeting for more than twenty times, the Spaniards discussed the reforms that were so obviously necessary.

Chapter VIII

BALBOA

Friar Bernado de Mesa was one of the king's royal preachers who spoke with power and a conservative establishment viewpoint. He presented his thesis with the use of logic and argument. According to Mesa and as free people, they suffered from idleness and it was the duty of the king to set them to work to remedy this. Absolute liberty was injurious to them. Further, Mesa felt that because the Indians were inconstant by nature, they required some kind of servitude in order to curb viciousness and compel them to devote their time to industry. The Licentiate Gregorio used quotations from Aristotle, Thomas Aquinos, Duns Scotus, and Augustine of Anchona to prove that slaves were in servitude because they were slaves by nature. To all this, Montesinos quoted the text, " answer a fool according to his folly, lest he be wise in his own conceit."

After this discussion, the officials and religious came to an agreement on seven propositions and then framed a code of Indian legislation known as the Laws of Burgos. Ferdinand had these laws promulgated or publicly announced and issued on December 27, 1512. In these laws, we see the royal view of the ideal relationship between the Indians and their masters. First, the Crown laid down manifold responsibilities for encomenderos or plantation owners. The slaveowners were to gather the Indians they were granted and house them in villages of new buildings. Then all native dwellings were to be burned, in order that the new slaves could not long to return to them. They should not use violence, but do all of this with much gentleness.

Chief in importance to these churchmen and officials both were the conversion and instruction of the Indians. The plantation or estate owners were to undertake, as an important matter, this education of these charges and to build churches with the proper equipment and supplies. Foremost, was native use of prayer, creed, and confession. These slave owners were to have the Indian children baptized and the young sons of chieftains educated by Franciscan friars for four years. After learning religion, reading, and writing from Franciscans friars, they were sent back to their villages, eventually expected to be a good example for the rest of the tribe.

Further, it was decreed that there get formed meticulous regulations to keep colonists from overworking and badly treating the Indians. They forbade the Spaniards from working any pregnant women. Also, they went into great detail what food, clothes, and beds were to be supplied the slaves. Native marriages were encouraged, and indeed, they were to be persuaded to marry. Getting drunk and dancing were expressly forbidden. The Indians were not to bleed and paint themselves. Two inspectors for each town were to enforce the law. The interest of these law writers included benevolence to the extent of providing provisions for native governments when the Indians showed an ability to manage their own affairs.

On the day of promulgation, Pedro de Cordoba arrived. The Dominican provencial of Hispaniola studied the laws and told the government that they were incomplete and insisted upon changes. The king agreed and they went back to conferring and discussion while amendments were delivered on July 28, 1513. These new rules were issued with provisions for more protection for women and children. Clothes were required to be worn and voluntary vocational training was provided.

Having received a letter from his friend Martin Zamudio in Spain, that the charges of Enciso were stirring up the anger of the king and Fonseca against him, Balboa would have great reason to be concerned. His future and even his life was at stake. With Enciso at the court, Balboa could lose his rightful commendation and reward for founding and supporting the mainland colony. Enciso claimed that Balboa was the one guilty for the death of Diego de Nicuesa, hiding his own support for the exile of Nicuesa. Zamudio informed Balboa that he was summoned to the court to answer charges made of his action at Panama. This did not worry Basco Nunez, and he would be replaced by a permanent governor appointed by Ferdinand, which did create anxiety for Balboa. Balboa himself wanted the honor and fame of discovering the South Sea, so he would not wait for reinforcements or replacements, but would go ahead with projects of exploration. Like most men of daring souls, he would not be crushed by real or threatened failure, misfortune, and defeat.

Although he did not have many men, five hundred at the most, Balboa selected some one hundred and ninety men with training and experience in arms, tropical conditions, and Indian warfare for an expedition to the great sea to the south. He told them of the unusual hazards of the venture. Failure might mean death for all, while success would mean wealth and glory for all. Any who wished might withdraw without prejudice. Not a single man did so! These were hardy adventurous men, ambitious for glory. Also, Balboa equipped his men and gathered necessary supplies for the journey.

On January 20, 1513, Balboa wrote the king about what he had done in Panama, and informed him that Ojeda and Nicuesa had done so poorly through their own fault, and by this means, caused their own destruction. They did not know how to use their own authority. The condition and state of the jungle was such that it required full attention and hard travel. Because of the many rivers, extensive marshes, and great mountains, the Spaniards found the land difficult to travel over and demanding of lives. There were bad nights and days in which it was necessary to face death a number of times.

He was careful to go with the advance at any time. He marched with the men through rivers, marshes, woods, and mountains. They all did so with high spirit even when it meant going naked through the swamps and water for several miles, with everything on their shields on their heads. It required a number of days to march in marshes. Any leader who does not go out with his men is depriving them of the best leadership. He needs to concern themselves and take a part in the work. Then Balboa showed his care in expressing the great need of the colonists for food and more men from Hispaniola. They needed to invade the interior and pass to the other sea.

The interior was a place for many rich gold mines. He told of the gold up the San Juan River and the news of rich rivers further on and of is trip to Dauaibe. Further on the way, there was news of great wealth and of cannibals who were lords of mines of great value.

There was also a report of most high mountains, and beyond it, a great plain. Tales he had heard of the lands Balboa relayed to the king, since he was anxious to gain royal support for their exploration and conquest. Next, he gave information on the lands he had seen, those of Careta.

He wrote that Spaniards in Antigua needed supplies to build boats for the rivers of the New World. Also, Balboa asked for masters in boat-building and master merchants to repair crossbows damaged by the frequent rains. In his defense of the charges leveled against him, Balboa noted that Ojeda and Nicuesa had together lost 800 men. For his part, Vasco had rescued Spaniards and arranged without aid their sustenance. He would send Sebastian de Ocampo to give the king more information about the situation in Panama. He told the king that he had reached the Pacific and returned.

Machiavelli, with a clear view from Italy, wrote "nothing gains estimation for a prince like great enterprises. Our own age had furnished a splendid example of this in Ferdinand of Aragon. Besides this, he always used religion as a cloak for undertaking great undertakings, and under pious guise practiced great cruelty." One of these great enterprises, his last great effort in his old age, Ferdinand wanted an armada for Darien of Castilla del Oro as it was soon to be called, an expedition to establish a Spanish official in Darien, protect the coast from Portugal, and search for the South Sea, which would lead to Japan. Fearing Balboa because of what Enciso, Colmenares, and Passamonte had lied about him, the king wanted a great force to subdue the Spanish followers of the explorer if necessary. These enemies of Balboa had lead Ferdinand to the belief that Balboa would use force to prevent the landing of a new governor.

On June 11, 1513, Ferdinand wrote the citizens of Darien that he wanted them to continue their labors and he would send a new governor, Pedro de Arbolancha carried the letter to Darien with the mission of gathering information, to spy out the land for a true account. The king wrote to Columbus and to Juan de Esquibel, governor of Jamaica, about the delegate. Over three weeks also, Ferdinand directed Miguel de Pasamonte to pay no attention to Diego's intermeddling in the affairs of the mainland. However, he informed Pedrarias that Veragua on the mainland did fall under the jurisdiction of Diego Columbus. Because he was jealous of the popularity of General Gonsalvo de Cordoba, Ferdinand had just called off his war in Italy. Balboa was daring and aggressive, and for this reason not to his liking. Also, he had heard that the explorer and governor was guilty of arbitrary and dictatorial acts.

The king appointed Pedro Arias de Avila, to be known in history as Pedrarias to be captain general of the armada and governor of Darien. His personality is revealed so in America by the name they often called him there. They called him "the Wrath of God." It seemed to run in the family because his brother, Juan Arias de Avida, became the first count of Punoenrostro, which translated means "Fist-in-the-Face." A colonel of infantry in Africa, Pedrarias served with such honor that Ferdinand chose him above all other applicants. He was the grandson of a converted Jew who took an aristocratic name out of thin air. The grandfather, Diego, was so able that he became chief auditor of the kingdom of Castile and set the stage for the success of his descendants. However, Pedrarias married an noble woman, Isabel de Bobadilla y de Penalosa, and by this fortuitous marriage, he was assured more advancement from the Crown than he could obtain otherwise. His wife insisted upon going with him to America, leaving their children under the care of a relative back in Spain.

On July 27, 1513, Pedrarias was formally commissioned with the usual ceremonies for the Triune God, but the object was to seize, protect, and enslave. There were detailed instructions for forcing the native to give up their lands, gold, pearls, and other valuables. Troops were sent for this purpose and to keep the Portuguese out of this territory. Pedrarias would also enslave the Indians to replace those who died off in the Caribbean islands under Spanish care. Ferdinand instructed the new governor to investigate Balboa in the time-honored method of Spanish administration for Spanish America where the new governor passed judgment on the old. If found guilty, Balboa was to be sent prisoner to the court of Spain. With this done, the Spaniards worked to prepare the fleet and collected two thousand men to go on the expedition. This took longer than the king had planned.

Juan Ponce de Leon was born into a noble family that had connections to Spanish royalty. The family traced its descent from Oserio of the twelfth century and became known as the Ponces. One of the family had married Dona Aldonza de Leon, who was the daughter of Alfonso IX of Leon and the sister of the St. Ferdinand who was the conqueror of Seville. Because of this tie, the Ponce family added "de Leon" to its name. Down through the centuries, other Ponces made their mark. Pedro Ponce de Leon was a count, and helped hold the Spanish frontier, while his grandson, Juan Ponce de Leon at one time held the city of Cadiz for his military services against the Moors.

His son Rodrigo Ponce de Leon led the conquest of the Alahama. A member of the younger branch, our Juan Ponce de Leon was trained in arms and fought in the last of the Moorish wars. He found his way over to Hispaniola on the second Columbian voyage, and once again proved his abilities by supporting the authorities during the island's state of discontent and trouble. Fighting in the province of Higuey on Hispaniola's eastern end, he was appointed Nicolas Ovando's lieutenant in the town of Salvaleon.

When the Indians told him there was gold on the island of Puerto Rico, Ponce de Leon was interested enough to get permission to hunt for gold there. Taking a small caravel, a type of small ship, he crossed the waters in 1508, and became friends with the chief there and discovered gold. He sent samples to Ovando and when Diego Columbus became governor in 1509, Ovando returned to Spain. There he told the king about Ponce de Leon's services and discoveries. Appointed governor of Puerto Rico, Ponce de Leon built a town and awarded its followers with recalcitrant Indians to be used as slaves on their estates. He had a great dog who would attack the Indians. They feared the dog, Bezerillo, more than soldiers. After Ponce de Leon had pacified the island, the king replaced Ponce de Leon as governor to meet the rights of Diego Columbus and his followers.

There was a rumor of an island called Bimini, our Forida, lying to the north of Hispaniola, which had a spring whose waters would restore people to youth and vigor. Ponce had heard the rumor. There were natives in the growing legend who had been actually restored by this fountain of youth or were witnesses to its wonders. Hispaniola's president of the island senate hesitated, but expressed a belief in this marvelous pool. Next, the Spaniards heard that not long before Columbus discovered America, certain Indians from the island of Cuba had entered a country supposedly to be Florida to search for a restorative river. The Spanish probably expected to find gold and slaves there also, so that there was great excitement that gave Juan the idea of discovery of this great fountain of youth.

At the court of the young Charles V, Ponce de Leon used all the influence he could bear and gained a patent to discover, people, and govern the island of Bimini. He would have to use his own money and credit to equip a fleet. Also, Charles provided the explorer and his adventurers to take Indians as slaves and peons. Ponce de Leon returned to Puerto Rico where he was so needed for the suppression of Puerto Rican natives with force that he had to defend the trip for one year. Finally, he was able to fit out three ships. There were soldiers aplenty, but no monks and priests were along.

On the 3rd of March of 1513, Ponce de Leon gave the orders and the sailors set the ships in motion from the port of San German in Puerto Rico. It was a Tuesday and Anton de Alaminos of Palos, the pilot of the expedition, gave the directions toward the Bahamas. Once there, they went toward the northwest. Off the coast of Florida, they saw the beautiful beaches, forests, and flowers of the Floridan spring. Ponce de Leon took possession in the first week of April. He named it Florida after the flowers of the Easter season. He had discovered it at Eastertide on the second and was probably near the mouth of the St. John River.

After setting up a stone cross with its inscription, Ponce de Leon sailed away and on the eighth of May doubled Cape Canaveral and within days, had reached the Florida Reefs to the south. He named this ridge of islands, The Martyrs because the high rocks of this island looked from a distance like suffering men, as Herreda related. Sailing on, he ran out of land, turned about, reached the southern end, and followed the western shore northward, its entire extension traveled around after seeing the coast turn to the west. Southward bound, the Spaniards discovered a group of small island and set in to take in wood and water, and careen one of the ships. Some Indians wanted them to land, but remembering two encounters when the natives rained darts and arrows upon them, they remained aboard. These inhabitants of the land also proved hostile, but when they discovered the white man's absolute greed for gold, they tried a different tactic.

Telling the Spaniards their chief would barter with them, gold for goods, they laid a trap for the intruders. The Indians used the carelessness of the Spaniards and attacked their ship under the guise of trade. They attempted to cut the anchors under cover of a frontal attack on the ship in canoes, but the commander noticed this, and sent a long boat against them. The Indians fled. Under guise of trade with the Spaniards, the Indians launched a futile sally, but were held back by the crossbow and great guns. Ponce de Leon returned to Puerto Rico, sure he had not found the island of the fountain of youth. The only positive result of the expedition was the discovery of the Bahama Channel, which became the usual passage for ships on their way from Havana to Spain.

Chapter IX

EXPEDITION

The prepared expedition for gold and discovery led by Vasco Nunez de Balboa with its 190 Spaniards had taken with it about 800 Indians. They left from Antigua on Thursday, September 1, 1513, and took the Indian trail that began at the port of Chief Careta. As we have seen from his report to the king of this expedition they were to have a hard passage. Balboa's Indians were vital for this trip, because they carried so much of the burden of supplies and equipment. They supplied the canoes and paddled them when going by, and carried the baggage, opened trails, built small bridges and rafts, constructed shelters, gathered and prepared food, and served as guides. As additional fighting men, the Indians added strength to the expedition and the protection often going with size. On top of these numbers were a pack of large killer dogs and Balboa's dogs, Leoncico. This dog drew a captain's pay when on forays such as this journey.

When he reached the village of Ponca, Balboa found once again that the people of this place had fled upon his approach. Not wanting to leave any unfriendly Indians in his rear, Balboa stopped there and sent out some of Careta's warriors to find Ponca and induce him to return. His messengers were successful. Ponca returned on the thirteenth and gave him some objects of gold, knowing that gold was the great god of the intruders from beyond the sea. In order to make friends and get Poncan warriors and carriers to take him into the territory of Ponca's enemy Quarequa, Balboa treated Ponca well, and gave him some shirts, hatchets, and glass beads. The Spanish governor was successful. Ponca provided him with what he needed, told of the land ahead, and verified the existence of the great sea to the south. In this place in Panama, the ocean was to the south. Releasing Careta's tribesmen with presents to go back home, Balboa set out on September 20, 1513, and traveled slowly over thirty miles of terrible trails and took rafts across rivers at great risk of life.

Seeing themselves in the territory of Chief Quarequa, the Spaniards found the men of this tribe lined up in the battle lines. The Indian leader asked Balboa who they were, why they came that way, and what they sought. He threatened to destroy them should they persist. When the Spaniards advanced, the Indians attacked with loud noises, brandishing their lances, bows and arrows, two handed swords, javelins, and clad in plates of gold for ornamentation and protection. The Indians were struck with terror when the Spaniards fired upon them with guns and crossbows. Spanish loud noises and smoke that killed so many seemed to be roaring forth from the mouths of the white men, and the Indians thought the invaders could control the thunder and lightening of the heavens. Swords also caused horror, cutting into the Indians and causing equal fear.

The Indians panicked before the Spanish superiority. They lost the battle and the Spanish gained supremacy over the Isthmus of Panama in this one battle. Promoting terror among the Indians was a key factor in the defeat of Quarequa. Six hundred warriors were killed, but no Spaniards lost their lives. Further Indian losses occurred when Balboa set his killing dogs upon Indian males wearing shirts. The Spaniards thought that because they were dressed this way, they were abnormal.

Setting out once again, Balboa and his men came into view of a mountain, which his Quarequa guides told him he could see the southern sea. The time was the morning of September 25, 1513, and it was the most exciting moment of Balboa's career. In addition, it was crucial. Success would mean preferment and fame. Failure would mean defeat and judgment. He began climbing the peak; it was strenuous and hard in his armor. Reaching the summit, Balboa looked toward the south. His anxiety vanished when he saw the sea with a gulf jutting inland toward the very mountain upon which he stood.

Balboa dropped to his knees, raised his arms heavenward, and gave thanks to Jesus Christ and all of the saints. When he called to his men to come join him, they rushed upward. Their cries of joy could be heard far and wide, demonstrating their happiness and eagerness to see this great sea so close to China and further wealth, and to Peru and rich rewards. The men reached the top and shouted, "the sea! the sea!" Embracing their commander, they renewed oaths to follow and obey him.

With a quieter joy, Balboa pointed with his right hand to their discovery and addressed his men, that the words of the Indians that the sea was there were true, so would be the words of a rich civilization to the south be true. They had seen already the object of desires and labor and would see more. Francisco Pizarro was one of the sixty-seven Europeans present. So was Andres de Vera, the priest. He led a worship service at this point and the notary Andres de Valderrano drew up a document celebrating the event and making official attestation of the discovery.

This done, and with the easing of excitement, Balboa led his men down from the divide, down the southern slope to the village of Chief Chiapes, where he defeated those Indians in a battle much as that which had taken place earlier. Treating the prisoners kindly, Balboa in his way made friendships with the chief and people of Chiapes. Next, they reached the gulf and the Spanish commander took possession. Alonso Martin was the first Spaniard to step into the salt water of the Pacific Ocean (as it later became known as). Pizarro was again present.

Once back in the village, Balboa talked to the Indians to learn what they knew about the region. They told him about their neighbor, Cuquera, who was their enemy. Cuquera, they said, had many pearls and much gold. Eager to harm his enemy, Chiapes offered to furnish canoes and paddlers to take the white men to subdue Cuquera. Balboa took him up on the offer and led fifty men in eight large canoes upriver on the seventh of October. The invaders landed in the night and marched over hard trails to the village nine miles away. When the Indians of Cuquera saw them come near, they fled in flight from the bold intruders.

At daybreak, the Indians came to attack, but seeing the bearded Spaniards in strange clothes and arms, were fearful, and fled again. Balboa sent after him and made peace to learn that the pearls he, Cuquera, gave Balboa came from an island out in the gulf. Since gold was becoming common and heavy with each accumulation, pearls were becoming more sought after by the Spaniards. In the greedy end of going there, and sure God and the saints would protect them, the Spanish headed toward that place of pearls, but when forced by a storm and almost killed, they were eager to seek the mainland which they reached in the dark.

Balboa and his men marched in the dark for the village of Chief Tumaco. At midnight, they reached that goal and defeated the Indians. Since they did not poison their weapons, the Indians were faced with a brave charge that the Spaniards knew would break Tumaco's line of warriors. Tumaco fled, but came back, after his envoy son was treated kindly and given a shirt and some trifles. The chief gave Balboa gold and pearls of great wealth. Balboa named the province after St. Luke, because it was on Luke's day that it was taken.

When the Indians roasted the oysters for their meal destined only for their chiefs, their pearls were dulled by the heat, so the Spanish showed them how to extract the pearls a better way. Would be they had taught Christianity with such diligence. Tumaco told, under questioning, of land and sea far to the south and people with gold and draft animals. He drew the picture of the llama. Pizarro was present and was to prove the truth of Tumaco's assertions. Not everyone believed what the Indians chief told of the animal, different from what they had known before.

Balboa then took possession of the gulf and land in a ceremony on the 29th of October of 1513, and on the third of November, began his return by a different route to subdue new tribes and take more loot. Going up a large river, the Rio Sanano probably, Balboa came upon more Indians. Soon, by a surprise attack, Balboa had captured the tribe of Chief Teoca, who surrender his wealth and was relieved to speed the Spaniards along their way, when they were ready to go. Teoca's son guided him forward. Their usual action netted them the next chief, Pacra. Told he had gold mines, the Spaniards tortured Pacra to get their location, but he insisted he had none. His enemies, the surrounding chiefs, begged Balboa to kill him. Balboa had Pacra and his three principle officials murdered by throwing them to the dogs and eaten. When they heard of this criminal action, other alarmed chiefs came to give gold and slaves to Balboa. The Spanish left the land of Pacra on the first of December.

During December, the Spanish explorers toiled through mountains, swamps, and suffered because of a scarcity of food and dried springs. There were no Indian villages on this part of the route, so there was no help outside for the expedition. Some captives died of thirst before Balboa's Indians found a water supply. This lack of water was the most critical time they saw on the journey. On the fifth, they found a suddenly deserted village of Buquebuca. Next, a chief gave homage to get Balboa to help him attack an enemy, but anxious to get on, Balboa deferred aiding this Chionso. The chief did receive three iron hatchets, beads, and other trinkets.

The way was improved, because on the eighth, he found the mountain village of Pocorosa with its stock of food. Balboa wrote later that this place was thirty-six miles from the Caribbean Sea. Pocrosa returned five days later to give pieces of fabricated gold to the Spanish. Other chiefs sent presents or delivered then, but Balboa had to defeat Chief Tubanamo, the great chief Balboa had heard of years before as being so important. Neighboring chiefs wanted Tubanamo's death, but the chief begging for his survival and his people brought to him, all of the gold they had. He denied having any mines. Back in Pocorosa, Balboa set out for home.

At Comoare, they learned that Comogre was dead and his son, Panciaco was ruling. He had told the Spaniards of Peru. Leaving Comogre on January 14, 1514, they arrived at Ponca where they learned of the arrival of reinforcements at Antigua from Hispaniola. Balboa hurried on ahead, with twenty soldiers, gold and slaves to be back at Puerto de Caveda three days after Comogre and at Antigua on the nineteenth for a day of great rejoicing and procession. The city council petitioned Ferdinand to continue Balboa as governor.

Growing in impatience because he had expected the armada to set sail five months earlier, Ferdinand wrote on January 19, 1514, to Pedrarias that he was hourly expecting to receive news that the fleet had sailed from Seville down the river, fifty-four miles from the sea. The weeks passed and spring brought milder weather and the fleet sailed after Pedrarias held a grand review in Seville. A storm off the mouth of the river struck the fleet and there were losses before the ships made the safety of the river.

Back in Seville, the sailors and soldiers disembarked. Soon, there was good weather and on April 11, 1514, they were again underway. They reached the Canary Island and took on supplies of meat, fish, cheese, wood, and fresh water while making repairs. The flagship had lost her rudder and this was replaced. They stopped off at Dominica where they took on water and Pedrarias. Far from royal restraint and a law within himself, he had hung a old servant of his named San Martin. The true character of the man was now showing up.

Then at the port of Santa Marta, in view of the Snowy Mountains, Pedrarias landed a force of Spaniards, who killed and took prisoner for slaves some of the Indians. One man was wounded and died of a poisoned arrow, all for the greed of the Spanish and their notable cruelty. They sailed on, Indians escaping them at Isla Fuenete, but they found baskets of salt finer than that produced in Spain. Then they anchored off the coast near Antigua del Darien on June 29, 1514.

Balboa welcomed them and promised his loyalty to the king and his acceptance of the new governor. Still, the original inhabitants, including Balboa, could look with resentment upon those new settlers who would crowd them out. There were now more to feed and supply, to take part of the gold and jewels of the land, but most of the newcomers would die of disease and starvation. Pedrarias drained Balboa of all of the information he could and then in jealousy and hatred for Balboa prosecuted him and seized all of his property, but on the advice of Bishop Quevedo, freed him, where Quevedo could use him to counter-balance Pedrarias.

Meanwhile, in Rome on September 24, 1513, Leo X had issued a bull naming Juan de Quevedo to be bishop of Darien. Ferdinand of Spain had asked him to provide a bishopric for Panama, as Darien was later known, the first bishop on the mainland. It was also the fourth in the New World. The popes had in 1511 established sees in Hispaniola, namely those of Santo Domingo and Concepcion de la Bega, and in Puerto Rico, that of San Juan. Meanwhile, Balboa continued on his famous expedition. Quevedo was to prepare for his trip and arrived with Pedrarias in July of 1514 with other churchmen to carry forth the church's work. He was to be critical of the governor because of his cruelty to the Indians, and was to return to Spain in 1519 on orders of Pedrarias. There is a disputation before Charles V, where he and Bartolome de las Casas disagreed on conquest such as the treatment of the Indians. On December 24, 1519, Quevedo died in Spain.

Bartolome de las Casas had had an interest in the America from the time he was a boy. When Christopher Columbus came back from his first voyage, Bartolome was there in Seville and saw the parade. According to the one account, his father gave Las Casas some Indian slaves while the boy was a student at the University of Salamanca, sometime after the second voyage. While in America, the young man obtained Indian slaves for his mines and estates, for his part in the conquest of Cuba. He did not mistreat them. Interested in getting rich, Las

Casas did not concern himself with the idea of the rights of his workers, and although he had taken holy orders, he opposed Montesinos' plea for decent treatment for the slaves.

He found time for the religious duties of his calling and when preparing a sermon to deliver on Whitsunday of 1514, he read these words in Chapter thirty-four of Ecclesiastics: "He that sacrficeth of a thing wrongfully gotten, his offering is ridiculous, and the gifts of unjust men are not accepted." In the next several days, he thought upon this verse, and upon the ideas of Montesinos whose words had passed him by. Then, conversion came in a rush. It was his fortieth year and set his course for over fifty years to come. Immediately, Las Casas gave up this Indians and preached his sermon. The Spaniards were shocked at the preaching against Indian slavery. He embarked upon a reading of Latin and Spanish works, where he found reasons and authorities for a course of correcting the injustice and crimes against the Indians.

One of the many instances Las Casas would be concerned about was the desolation of Trinidad, where a tribe of friendly Indians, used to defending themselves against the Caribs, were met with massacre. A certain Juan Bono was employed by the self-seeking audiencia or public court to gain slaves from one of the islands of the Caribbean. He and his fifty or sixty men landed on Trinidad. These Indians on the island met the Spaniards and asked them who they were, and what they wanted. Juan said that they were good and peaceful people, and had come to live with them. The Indians built them a large bell shaped house, large enough for one hundred people to live in as requested by Bono.

This was done, and Juan Bono gathered the Indians together in the house. There they were entrapped by the sword drawn Spaniards. Bono came and said that they must be still or be killed. He set fire to the house and the Indians rushed the door and were massacred or captured according to their luck. Others were burned within the house. Juan Bono and his men took them to Hispaniola, and acknowledged before Las Casas that they had never met with such kindness as on the island of Trinidad. Bono was following the instructions on the audiencia to take them in peace, if he could not take them in war.

On October 8, 1515, Juan Diaz de Solis sailed forth from Lepe, a southern port in Spain in two or three caravels. His goal was to search out the coast of South America to find a passage to take their merchant vessels to the Spice Islands. The way had been traveled by the route of the able navigators from Palos, the brothers Pinzon. The first South American land they saw was at Cape San Augustin on the easternmost extension of Brazil. Solis was highly regarded in his time as a pilot who was Spain's chief pilot for two years before the voyage.

They sailed south from the cape along the coast, sailing through yellow waves. Curving around the southern coastline of Brazil, they saw on their right, the hill which became the capital of Uruguay, Montevideo. There were the rolling prairies with their purple blossoms with woods. Staying close to shore, Solis sailed his ship to the island of Martin Garcia. The various tribes on land seen from the ships friendly, so Solis went forth to kidnap an Indian to return with to Spain. With him were armed followers. No sooner was he landed, than Charruas warriors came out from the bushes, and with a rush murdered them all, while their horrified crew and soldiers watched from the flag ship. With this, the ship headed back, naming what was to be called River del la Plata or at the time, El Rio de Solis.

At this time, the Tezcucan, kin to the emperor of Mexico, and a wise adviser, died in 1516, still advising Montezuma. In the battle for the succession of Tezcuca, Montezuma supported the elder Cacama, but the younger Ixthilxochiti appealed to the patriotism of the people in his subject kingdom. There was a civil war that ended in a compromise. Cacama retained the southern half of the kingdom with its capital and Ixthilxochiti gained the northern portion and became a mortal enemy of Montezuma. Also, against Montezuma was arranged the republic of Tlascala, midway between Mexico and the Gulf of Mexico. They had retained their independence for more than two centuries.

Cortez was in Cuba at this time, but the events and conditions in Mexico would soon influence and determine his life. The people of Mexico were disgusted with their emperor's arrogance and with his extracting, and enemies within his empire, as well as out of it, were eager for Montezuma's downfall. However, the emperor was powerful and his very name stuck terror in the minds of his subjects. His armies were still valorous and disciplined. They were well-drilled in Indian tactics. In the last years of his reign, Montezuma led his armies less and less, devoting himself to priestly functions, allowing his generals to manage the army.

Even more foreboding for the existence of the Mexican empire was the belief in the legend of Quetzalcoatal, a deity with a fair complexion and flowing beard, who had according to legend had fulfilled a mission of benevolence among the Aztecs, sailed into the east, and promised to come back to Mexico. This day was looked forward to with hope, or with apprehension. There would soon be a return, it was said, and the people of Montezuma's empire expected its arrival to be soon. Comets and other phenomena made it seem immediately at hand.

In his reign, rumors of a white man, bearing in their hands the thunder and the lightening found their way and word of the landing of Grijalva found its way and to stern Montezuma was filled with dismay. He was attuned to their arrival again and sentinels were posted to tell of their return. Montezuma showed a moderate program, neither welcoming them as gods, nor meeting them with the fire and sword.

Bernal Diaz Del Castillo had come to Panama with Pedrarias and after the governor executed Balboa, Bernal and others sought different adventures. They gained permission from the governor to go to Cuba. When they arrived there, the governor of Cuba promised them the first land that fell vacant. When they received none, one hundred and ten of the Spaniards without prospects in the island elected Francisco Hernandez de Cordova to lead them upon a voyage of discovery. The group purchased two vessels and obtained a bark that Governor Velasquez was willing to give on credit. His condition for the use of the bark was that the party make a descent upon the los Guanages, and seized for slaves a number of the natives in exchange for the cost of the bark. The indignant soldiers refused this condition because, it was so just to make slaves of free men. Neither God nor king permitted this. Valasquez saw the justice of that and asserted so.

Preparing their ships with provisions, the adventurers brought hogs that were then sold at three crowns each, and cassava bread. There were no oxen or sheep in Cuba at the time, which limited what they could store in the skip. They engaged three pilots for the voyage. From the port of Agaruco, they got on board the ship with a proper officer in case gold should be found, and the king's rights should be attended to.

On February 8, 1517, they set sail from Agaruco after religious ceremonies in which they recommended themselves to God and the blessed Virgin. Having passed through a storm, they reached land where they saw on the coast exceeding in size any town in Spanish Cuba. Five canoes came to visit them, carved out of large trees. Many such canoes could carry fifty men. More canoes came up and the Spanish adventurers under Cordova were invited to land. They did and were ambushed. Fifteen of the soldiers were wounded with arrows. The Indian warriors with thick coats of cotton, bows and arrows, lances, shields and slings advanced against Spanish crossbows and musketry. The Spanish won and the chaplain, Gonzales, seized the chests of idols early, and with two prisoners, the Spanish returned to the ships and sailed up the coast.

They passed a large town and went ashore to fill their casks with water. Fifty well-dressed Indians came up and invited them to town. Cautious now, the Spaniards noticed the natives collecting in large numbers. They watched native hostility grow and they prudently retired to their ships and coasted for six days. After this experience, they were again cautious and did not go past the beach. They spent the night and on the morrow were attacked by large numbers of Indians who surrounded them. It was hand to hand fighting and many Spaniards fell. Two of the Spaniards were captured. After heavy losses, the adventurers had to cut their way out form the swarms of native warriors.

They reached their boat, but in retreat, it accidentally sunk, and the men had to half-wade and half-swim to their ships. They lost fifty-seven men in action, losing over half in an hour. Unfortunately, they left their casks of water behind and they were to suffer for long hours for lack of water. They stopped and sunk wells before another Indian attack endangered them. The Indians tried to drag away the Spanish boat. Yucatan was discovered on this voyage. They were finally driven ashore by a violent gale of wind, and some had to make their way by land to the Spanish town Yaguarrama where Bartolome de las Casas was then parish priest.

Chapter X

CORTEZ

Meanwhile, Florida was visited again. The pilot Diego Miruelo sailed from Cuba in 1516 to barter with the Indians, his toy of iron and glass for gold. Strange for a pilot, he failed to note the latitudes, so no one now knows what parts of Florida he visited. Soon afterwards, in February of 1517, Francisco Hernandez de Cordova undertook an important voyage of exploration with some noblemen just arrived in Cuba from Spain a few months earlier. He left Havana in three ships with 110 men. There was a priest for mass and sacraments. They were to raid the Lucayan Islands for slaves for Governor Diego Velasquez in payment for his sale of one of their ships for the expedition. Some of the Spaniards in the expedition who were in a minority of their countrymen, felt that such slave hunting was not right. The soldiers told Cordova that neither God nor the King had directed them to make slaves out of freemen. They prevailed, and Cordova decided upon a search for new lands.

A westward storm at sea blew them into the Gulf, but they reached Yucatan where they lost half of their men in a battle with Indians. Sadly returning home, they ran into another storm and sought refuge in Florida. There, Alaminos was wounded in the throat. Back in Havana, the Spaniards reported to Velasquez, and Cordova died of wounds he had received on the trip.

Black slaves were early introduced into the West Indies, having been in Spain at an earlier time. When Fernando III conquered Seville in 1248, black slaves of the Moors were taken by the Spanish. More black slaves were introduced by the Portuguese into Spain. Slaves of men traveling to America were among the first to see the New World. In 1501, the Crown was concerned about the type of people who might go into the new country and was fearful that the might contaminate the faith of the Indian neophytes. Royalty forbade slaves, Jews, Moors, and new Christians from going from Spain to the West Indies. Again in 1526, Spanish speaking slaves were forbidden to be shipped into Spanish America. These orders did not prevent these people from moving to the Americas.

In 1505, seventeen slaves were listed among passengers going to America. The House of Trade of Seville needed slaves for mining since the Indians were not proving suitable. They appealed to Ferdinand, who in 1511, allowed them to import fifty blacks to work in the mines of Santo Domingo. Alvaro de Castro, dean of the Church of the Concepcion of Santo Domingo needed slaves to work on his lands, and Ferdinand allowed him to import two hundred slaves.

There was an early movement in the Indies to replace Indian slaves with black slaves. In 1510, the first religious order in the new country, the Order of Predicator, wanted to replace Indian slave labor with blacks. It was argued that one African slave was worth any four Indian slaves. A more influential proponent of this idea was to come. Blacks were imported to America even before Las Casas suggested it as an alternative to enslaving Indians.

When he heard of the adventures of Cordova and what they saw, Velasquez became all the more interested in exploration and conquest on the coast. Various items of what they saw interested the governor and none more than specimens of curiously wrought gold. Velasquez arranged for a small fleet of four ships for his exploration of Yucatan and chose as it's commander, his nephew Juan de Grijalva. The fleet left St. Jago of Cuba on May 1, 1518. It followed the course pursued by Cordova, but the wind drove it on a southern course and they saw the island of Cozumel. Sailing along the coast, he was struck at the architecture and large stone crosses. It was evident to him that this was more than an average Indian civilization.

They stopped at points that Cordova had reached. The Indians were sure of themselves having driven the Spanish off when the Cordoba expedition had come to its shore. This time Grijalva disembarked half of his force, of these men, one half were wounded before land was reached, but the results were different. Grijalva used reinforcements to drive the Indians of Champoton into the marshes with only three men killed of the Spanish force. The village was deserted. Four days later, they re-embarked to coast westward. At the next town, they were met with friendship and an exchange of gifts. The Indians gave of what gold they had and told of more in Mexico. They headed along the shore until they reached settlement under the domain of the Aztec, Montezuma.

Officers representing that emperor traded gold for glass beads, objects of which interested many Indian tribes and nations. Along the coast, they saw their first Aztec sacrificial pyramid and arrived at Vera Cruz. The Aztecs were noted for their sacrifice of people, cutting out hearts and severing limbs while the victim was still alive. Grijalva sent Pedro de Alvarado to Cuba for reinforcements. However, an Indian attack changed their minds about going into the interior and they returned to Cuba despite their commander's wish to establish a settlement. With the Aztecs so powerful, a single settlement would have been a mistake. The realm of the next conquest was found and Velasquez asked permission of the Spanish court to order the seizure of Mexico and prepared to undertake it or send a lieutenant for the task.

Hernando Cortez was born at Medelin in the Spanish province of Estremodura in 1485 to an ancient family, whose descent has been traced to a Lombard king. This genealogy is doubtful, but it must be said that Hernando's father, Martin Cortez de Monroy, and his mother, Catlina Pizarro Altamiraro were noted for their honorable and excellent qualities. The young Hernando was a weak child, but he grew stronger in the years ahead. His father had greet hopes for him and when the boy of fourteen, sent him to Salamanca for a law education, but Hernando did not care for books, and wasted most of his time while at school. Two years later, he returned home with the ability to write prose and verses, but short of great skill.

Buoyant spirits drove the young man at home and in the community. He was set to go out under Nicholas de Ouando, when an accident led to time in bed. He had scaled a wall on the way to the apartment of a ladylove, when the stones gave way. Falling hard to the ground with a panoply of stones over him, Hernando was confined to bed until after the ship was left.

Delayed at home for another two years, he finally shipped out in 1504, at age nineteen, for the New World in a ship under Alonso Quintero. The fleet Quintero was with stopped at the Canaries and took in more supplies. Cortez' captain thought he would beat the rest of the fleet to America, and he stole out by night. The captain paid for his mistake, because he ran into a storm which demasted his ship. Returning to the islands for repairs, he had to face the other captains whom he tried to beat. The convoy waited. They all sailed out, but Quintero repeated his tricks and ran into a storm once again. He made his way to Hispaniola and found his fellow captains were there with all of their cargoes sold.

In the port of Hispaniola, Cortez went to see Governor Ovando, but he was absent at the time. The secretary assured him he could receive a liberal grant of land to settle on. Cortez replied, "but I came to get gold, not to till the soil, like a peasant." Ovando returned and Cortez has to settle for a plantation tilled by Indians, and the position of notary of Aqua. In Hispaniola as in Spain, he was engaged in affairs of honor usually resulting from amorous involvement and was scared in various swordplays. Whenever the Indians would revolt, Cortez joined Ovando's lieutenant, Diego Velasquez, in his expeditions to suppress the insurrections. He learned the tactics of Indian warfare in the field. Illness prevented him from suffering the fate of Nicuesa's expeditions.

In 1511, he served under Velasquez in the conquest of Cuba and did so well that the governor of Cuba, Velasquez, made Cortea one of his secretaries. Cortez friendship did not remain constant nor could it survive a rebuke over a lady when Cortez was courting, and then friendship cooled. When opportunity presented itself, he joined a disaffected party in Cuba. This group gained an open boat and convinced Cortez to undertake a voyage across to Hispaniola to complain about Velasquez in Cuba. The governor learned of the conspiracy and seized Cortez before he could leave.

He was loaded with fetters and placed in strict confinement. He might have been hanged except for the imposition of his friends. Cortez escaped from jail, loosening one fetter, and using it to open a window on the second floor where he was, and fled to a nearby church for sanctuary. Careless of his sanctuary, the escapee was outside the church portals taking his leisure when seized. Shipped to Hispaniola for trial, Cortez was on board, when he escaped once again to sanctuary, swimming from boat to shore. At this point, a forgiving Velasquez and a chastised Cortez became friends again, and the future conqueror tended to his lands and offices once again.

His recovery of friendship wit Velasquez opened the way to Mexico for Cortez because Velasquez soon selected him to be captain-general of his expedition to fabulous Mexico. Rumors of its richness, being doubled and redoubled in Cuba, interested the Spanish to distraction. This friendship was not steady and it behooved Cortez to proceed as quickly the supplying and preparing of the fleet that was to take him to Mexico. Also, he worked on gaining the friendship of those who had the ear of Velasquez. Cortez was good at this, which might have left the door opened for him, and according to Bernal Diaz del Castillo, the governor soon wished to deprive Cortez of his command. However, Cortez quickly skipped out of the harbor at night from Havana, to other waters to complete his preparations. Velasquez raced to the harbor, and to his dismay, saw Cortez underway.

In the Mexico to which he was bound, there was a long-lived civilization. In this ancient past civilization in Mesoamerica there had developed a high state of the art with priests as the key to society in elaborate religious buildings, but there as a collapse. More warlike peoples came through central Mexico. First, there were the Toltecs with their peace-loving deity, Quatzalcoatl, but they disappeared, leaving behind their legendary god. Secondly, there were the Chichimcas, a people who included the Aztecs who were the latest invaders from the north. These Aztecs were oftimes deported and settled on a number of islands in the corner of the lake region that was the valley of Mexico. The glories of these people were ahead because from this event, about 1325, the Aztecs began to expand and become allied with the people of Texcoco and Tiacopan (Tacuba). Moving forth in the east, south, and west, they had an empire in the years ahead.

The Aztecs were agriculturists and warriors. They had two chief gods. Tlaloc was the rain and vegetation god. Huitzilopochtli was the sun war god. The superior classes were that of priests and warriors, blurred and often the same. Many classes provided a manifold gradation. Because traveling merchants, metalsmiths, lapidaries, and feather artists were so useful in preparing for war and achieving the fruits of victory, they were ranked high in society. There was opportunity for moving up in the upper classes for those excelling in success in war, distant trade, and craftsmanships. The priesthood of course needed talented men also.

Their religion required war to keep the Aztec system going, because they believed sacrificial victims nourished the sun and gods, and therefore kept the universe working. Only destruction would come with peace. Men depended upon war to grease the wheels of their success in society and there was a general human greed for expansion and power. Man had created the state and it had a life of its own, but suited to the desires of its people in the raw. Men gained glory by bringing back captives and joined the sun in heaven, if they died in war or under the knife of sacrifice. Women gained glory when they died in childbirth or were sacrificed. They were feted before the act as heroes.

Later, the Aztecs were to recall omens beginning ten years before the Conquest with a sight of a great tongue of fire piercing the heavens before the sun arose to destroy it. According to the old men this cycle continued for a full year, that of the Twelve House. There was a fire that destroyed the wooden Uitzilopochtli's temple of its own accord. There were other signs with a lightening hitting the temple of the old fire god, a comet which burst into three heads, a boiling lake, weeping in the dark of the night, a vision, and vanishing two headed people. It is to be doubted that there was any basis in this. It is possible that there were fires and there were comets enough to be seen.

The old men were to tell that at first there was only one vessel. Juan de Grijalva had arrived off the island of the Sacrifices, after sailing off the coast. Alert Indians saw the strange ships and reported the sightings to the authorities. Pinotl, the high steward of Cuetlaxtlan, learned of the arrival and set out with two stewards and two guides to see for himself and to spy out the strangers. Thinking that it might be Quetzalcoatal returning, Pinotl took with him a gift of precious capes reserved for their emperor, Montezuma. Men of the sea coast paddled them out to the ship and made obeisance. When the Spaniard asked who they were, they said, Mexicans from Mexico ruled by Montezuma. They gave their capes with the sign of the sun and fantastic decorations. In return, the Spaniards gave them necklaces of blue and yellow. Grijalva said for them to go. They were going back to Spain, but would not return.

When the steward and his group saw the ship disappear beyond the horizon eastward, they hastened as rapidly as they could to report to their emperor, Montezuma. At an audience with the ruler, who sought after their comfort, Montezuma instructed them to keep the arrival and departure of Quetzalcoatal secret. They were to keep the coastline watched wherever the strangers might return to land. Once the stewards were gone, Montezuma informed his deputy, two big warriors, and the high judge of what had happened. He said they must safe guard well the turquoises beads in safe keeping, for the return of the whites. Should the keepers lose even one piece, he would take from them, their houses, children, and wives. So time passed.

On February 10, 1519, Cortez sailed the entire fleet for the island of Cozumel, with one ship ahead of the others, when they discovered that the natives had fled. They found there some fowls, idols, toys, and ornaments of debased gold, in the local temple. Cortez sailed up and punished them for taking things from the natives. He ordered the items returned and paid for the fowls, since they had already been eaten. Seeing this good treatment, the Indians returned. During the three days they were there, Cortez had a review of the troops that numbered five hundred and eight soldiers and one hundred and nine marines, with eleven ships. Their cavalry numbered sixteen and there were thirteen musketeers, ten brass field pieces, four falconets, and thirty-two crossbows. Francisco de Orozs with military experience in Italy was captain of artillery.

The Indians of Cotoche repeatedly used the word "Castillan" and Cortez thought it referred to Spaniards held captive on the coast. Eager to please, the Indians of Cozumel said that there were captives on the mainland. Indian merchants on the island told the Spanish chief that they had spoken to the prisoners a few days before. Anxious to obtain their release, the Spaniards sent letters to them by two light vessels for their ransoming of the captives. The merchants of Cozumel were entrusted with the communication of the ransom to the captors, but the captives remained confined. Meanwhile, Cortez replaced the Indian idols on Cozumel with the image of Mary and a crucifix. Mass was then said and soon the expedition shipped out. Next, one captive was rescued. He, Jeronimo de Agiular, had been wrecked eight years ago. He was a cleric and refused to marry despite pressures while he was among the Indians.

On the fourth of March, Cortez and his fleet set sail for Yucatan. A wind separated the ships, but all were soon joined again. While the ships were detained, several of the Spaniards went ashore and found four temples with idols. Aguilar was able to tell them about the country for he had lived here. Grijalva had already been at the point because the two greyhound dogs they left behind greeted Cortez and his men joyfully. They reached the river of Tabasco or Grijalva on the thirteenth.

At Tabasco, they found the mangrove banks of this river contained an array of canoes and twelve thousand Tabascan warriors at the town. Cortez directed Aguilar to talk to the chiefs to ask the reason for their hostility when the Spaniards came as friends and brothers. However, should they attack, they would live to regret it. Because of this, they were more violent. The Indians threatened them with instant death should they approach their fortified town with its parapets and palisades. The Indians would not let them procure wood and water, or to interview their chieftains. Shortly, the natives withdrew to their town. Cortez did not urge the matter any further that evening, but disembarked on a neighboring island.

At dawn on the following day, when the Spaniards next saw the natives and found them more numerous than ever on the opposite banks. Cortez prepared for his attack and landed one hundred men, commanded by Alonso de Avila, downstream to proceed on a road to the town, while he advanced in front of the Indian army. Once he was in front of the Indian defenses, he asked for passage, but the natives showed defiance and unloosened their arrows at once.

Cortez led his forces in boats alongside the Indian canoes and the two peoples grappled until they fell into the water to continue the struggle that benefited the superior strength of the Europeans. The Indians retreated to land, followed by the Spanish who at length gained its bank. When some order prevailed, the Spanish opened up with a brisk fire from arquebuses and crossbows. The roar and flash of these weapons stunned the Indians. They retreated to the barriers and were force back to the town and its palisades. At this point, Anida came to their side and the Tabascans fled the empty town. Cortez took possession of the town and its territory. There was no sign of the natives on the next morning, but reconnoitering parties found them and Cortez forced them to retire. The few prisoners they found told them that the entire countryside was in alarm and eager for the fray. Fourteen Spanish soldiers were wounded and eighteen Indians were killed.

After a sleepless night of checking the sentinels, Cortez gathered the troops on the morrow and declared his purpose was to march against the evening on the level ground where they were. The infantry and artillery would attack them on the front and Cortez would lead his horsemen against the evening on the level ground where they were. After mass, they proceeded along their way. It was the twenty-fifth of March of 1519. Marching was difficult because of the canals, patches of maize, and plantations of Cacao.

The Tobascans used their volleys of arrows, stones, and other missiles to their advantage, until the Spanish could apply their artillery and musketry on the massed natives. In reply, the Indians used their superiority in numbers to blanket the Spaniards. At length, Cortez and his horsemen swept into view. Applied against a fearful Indian force, the man and horse combatants put the Indians into a fleeing disorder. They had never seen horses before and thought the man-horse combination. a new and fierce animal. The Spanish infantry led a charge against the back of the Indians, and the Spanish won the battle. Only two Spaniards had lost their lives versus the many on the part of the Indians. The Spanish were well protected by their armor.

The Tabascans had had their fill of battle with the white foreigners and their chiefs came to make peace and bury their dead soon after this battle of Santa Maria de la Victoria. The Indians gave twenty female slaves and supplies, including a few gold ornaments, which had come from central Mexico, to the Spaniards. On the following day, the celebration of Palm Sunday, with its color ad pageantry impressed curious and astonished Indians. They began with these displays, the conversion of the Indians and brought forth to interest them in Christianity by Catholic images in place of the pagan ones, and the Cross, which was to the Indian a sign of the rain god. Peace was established and the Spanish reembarked and sailed up the coast for Mexico. They now had on board an interpreter and lady of high rank, Donna Maria, as one of their slaves. She had been captured from her people by other Indians and knew various languages.

On Holy Thursday of 1519, Cortez' fleet came to Vera Cruz, and on the following day, disembarked cavalry, infantry, and artillery on the sand hills of the coast, where they were well treated by the Indians. There, he met a noble vassal of Montezuma's expanding empire. They exchanged presents. Cortez received a great plate of gold, the size of a wheel and one even larger! There were golden animals and plumes of feathers.

While the waited, the Spanish band was suffering from pestilence, malaria, and from the stings of mosquitoes. Thirty of their number died, a loss the army could no longer endure. There was a search for a better port and a more healthful climate, but after days had passed, the Mexican envoys had returned with the same formality. When the Spaniards sought to change the faith of these Aztecs, the natives disappeared in the night. Cortez then found a better place to camp and anchor the ship. Before they moved, they were met by a different peoples who congratulated them upon arrival, and said they would be proud to serve under the Spaniards. Cortez was glad to learn that Montezuma had enemies within his own empire.

The Spaniard told them that he would visit them, the Lopelucios, in their own land. This would shorten their need to stay in such a pestilent climate as Vera Cruz.

There was a difference of opinion between the parties favoring Velasquez and those favoring Cortez. The former wanted to return to Cuba to report and Cortez was not ready to abandon this expedition., He had naught to profit him in Cuba, when Mexico beckoned so happily in the west.

To forestall those who wished to go back, Cortez gathered his partisans in the night, and the next morning they elected Cortez their general. Alvarado was sent into the interior at the head of one hundred soldiers, principally made up of the party of Velasquez. He soon returned with two prisoners, and had seen sacrificial altars where humans had died.

Cortez soon embarked into the west and met the chieftain of Cempoal. The Spaniards found a fine town of whitewashed and plastered buildings. They remained there in their quarter that night to avoid any drunken skirmishes that would alienate the people of Cempoal. The fat chieftain of that town and province complained of Montezuma's extractions and his own enthralldom to the emperor of Mexico. Cortez promised that he would free him of this tyranny. Next, they set forth through this province with their baggage carried by the natives, used to this service for the Aztecs, when they traveled through. The Indians to the west also supplied the Spaniards upon request. At this point, he gained the alliance of this chieftain and went westward closer to Mexico City seizure in the friendship of the Aztecs, and gaining friendship along the way from Aztec enemies, who had been subjected to the Aztecs in previous wars.

Next, the conquistador set forth with four hundred soldiers and one thousand of them Cempoal allies and reached the town of Cingapacinga which the Cempoalianc had proceeded to loot. Cortez ordered a return of that which was stolen. This owed him the favor of the people there. He effected reconciliation between the two peoples. The cacique or chieftain of the countryside provided ladies for a marriage alliance between the Spanish and their own people. Despite the agitation of the natives, Cortez ordered the destruction of the Indian idols. The pagan temples were turned into Christian temples after a purification and cleansing.

Chapter XI

MONTEZUMA

When Montezuma received news of the Spaniard's arrival, he believed that indeed, Quetzalcoatal had landed, returning as he had promised so long before. Since he was a god, he was due a god's array and the emperor sent four complete sets of dress most elaborate, rich and decorative. Two in this collection were made for Quetzalcoatal. First there was a smoke mask in turquoise mosaic, for masks denoted high worship in the Aztec religion. Only the first outfit had a mask, which was noteworthy of its superiority, but other gods were also coming and they must have their own finery. The other two sets of dress were for the god, Tezcatipoca and for the god Tlaloc. With the clothes, Montezuma sent five priestly and important warriors to represent him and say that he, Quetzalcoatal had come to occupy Montezuma's "poor home" in Mexico. As the god's deputy governor, he was sending the most suitable gifts.

Now, the first array of Quetzalcoatal also had, in addition to the mask, a fan shaped head ornament made of quetzal feathers. Around the neck was to be placed some neckbands. One plaited jodeite neckband centered by a disc of gold. The others were made of jodeite and golden shells which were to entice Cortez. The shield the gods were to carry had bands of gold or of gold and seashells that were crisscrossed with quetzal feathers and a quetzal flag from the lower edge. The mirror was equally decorated and had a turquoise back. There was a turquoise spear thrower with a snakehead-ornament and black obsidian sandals.

The second costume for the fair god consisted with a peaked jaguar skin cap with pleasant plumes with a large jodeite stove tip. Next, were earplugs of turquoise mosaic with pedant golden seashells. This set had a neckband like the other with its gold disc. The caps for the god to wear were red-bordered. For the ankles, the thoughtful Aztecs provided golden shell ornaments. This shield was similar to the first. The wind god's curved hooked staff, with its spread of white jodeite stars, would be presented. White sandals finished this set of ceremonial garments.

The array suitable for Tezcatlipoca began with a gold starred feather headdress. His earplugs were formed with gold to resemble shells. Regular seashells were used for the necklace breast ornament. A sleeveless jerkin had a design, eyeleted borders and feathered edging. There was a mirror of mosaic for the small of the back, and golden shells to ornament the calves of the legs. White scandals finished the outfit.

A characteristic Tlaloc heron featherhead dress was made entirely of quetzal feather, under a band of shells crossing another of gold. The jodeite earplugs had snakehead carvings.

There were a sleeveless jerkin, a neck ornament, a mirror, rattles, anklets of golden shells. The cape had an edging of red rings. Finally, a turquoise mosaic staff was designed like a snake.

When the imperial emissaries reached the coastline, they went by boat to the Spanish ships. The Spaniards sighted them and had their interpreters ask who they were and where they came from. The emissaries assured them that they were not fugitives as the invaders first thought. Allowed aboard, they arrayed Cortez in the costumes. In return, in European fashion, the Spanish under orders fettered their necks with iron, shot off the great lombard gun, and had to revive the emissaries who panicked with sudden fear. Released, the Indians returned to Montezuma who was unable to rest, to sleep, or to eat.

First, Emperor Montezuma had two Indians killed, tearing out their hearts and sprinkling the emissaries with blood. Later, these emissaries told the emperor of the gods they had seen and had spoken to. He was informed of their wargear, and their animals that looked like deer and were as high as the rooftops. Montezuma was shocked, terrified, and felt faint at the tale of the whites with beards and yellow or black hair and the fierce gods they had brought with them.

It was necessary for Montezuma to send more emissaries. However, this time he sent doers of evil to deal with the white and the black gods. The Mexican assumed the slaves to be gods too. They set out the magicians, wizards, and soothsayers and the elders and warriors to requisition food for the gods and to care well for them. Also, there were captives to provide blood that the Aztecs supposed the gods drank.

The Spaniards, nauseated by the sacrifice they saw, and repelled by the blood soaked food, would not eat, and the Mexican had to change their minds about what gods ate. Cortez and his men ate the food of the Mexicans and their horses enjoyed the fodder of deer. Then came the twist. The magicians and other evildoers tried their skill upon the Spaniard with spells, enchantments, and incantations, but they could not sicken, kill, or turn back the gods. Powerless, they reported back to Montezuma that they were nothing compared to them.

The Aztecs were alarmed about the power of the gods who had arrived in their time. Montezuma wept over the distress he felt for Mexico City. His people also wept over their fate. Some were dejected and hung their heads. Their emperor was even more alarmed when he learned of Marina's service as a guide to lead the Spaniards to his capital. The emissaries of Montezuma began turning their backs upon the Spaniards. When the emperor learned that the Spaniards had begun to inquire about him, the mature slender Montezuma was afflicted with great apprehension and thought to flee as the soothsayers were encouraging him to do, but he knew that he must wait.

At this point in time, the Spaniards returned to their newly constructed city in Vera Cruz and found a vessel from Cuba in the harbor. It was commanded by Francisco Saudedo and contained the able officer Luis Marin and ten soldiers with two horses. Saucedo told them that Velasquez had received the imperial authority of Charles V to colonize in Mexico. Cortez sent a deputation to Charles with gold and articles of value to Spain and a statement of what had been done in Mexico up to this time. After Mass on July 26, 1519, the agents left for Spain and bypassed the island of Cuba, leaving an angry and disturbed Velasquez to find out by other means what had happened.

When he learned of the events in Mexico, Velasquez prepared for himself a fleet and expedition under the command of Pamphilo de Narvaez. In Spain, the agents of Cortez found an angry bishop of Burgos, then president of the royal council on the Indies, taking the part of

Velasquez. The bishop wrote the emperor Charles, but so did the agents and Charles was appreciative of what Cortez had done, and for many days, the Court talked of nothing else but of the services and adventures of the conqueror of Mexico.

Meanwhile in Mexico, Cortez learned of a plot against him and hung two of the conspirators and severed the feet of a third. To prevent any of the partisans of Velasquez from escaping, he dismantled and sunk much of the fleet he had off Vera Cruz. Soon after this, Cortez led his army into the interior bound for Mexico City. In the month of August, he took with him one thousand and five hundred of Cempoal's principal warriors, plus, one thousand to draw the Spanish guns and carry the baggage. He learned much of the typography of Mexico City and of the great wealth of Montezuma from native allies. His allies advised them to pass through Tlascala. Recognizing good advice when he saw it, Cortez followed the suggestion.

Summer rains made the roads nearly impassable, but the ascent into bland, salubrious air revived their spirit. However, the steepness of the ascent was only one of his troubles. The expedition reached a rocky eminence where they put up a cross. They did not fear the dangerous terrain because they were still among friends, which helped because of the opportunities for native armies were so great. There were also cold winds from the mountains. The poor Indians suffered the most being used to the warm lands of the coast and some perished along the way.

Reaching the plateau, they advanced and were confronted with a thick stone wall, nine feet in height. There was a passageway of ten paces, which was exposed by the inner wall. It extended more than six miles rising at each end in a natural buttress. Unfortunately for Tlascala, they did not guard this entrance originally meant for the Aztecs. The Spaniards and their Indian allies made their way through and were on the soil of the republic.

In the land of the Tlascalano, the advance guard sighted thirty of the enemy watching them. Cortez sent out a cavalry detachment to take some prisoners, but the Tlascalans fought so heard with swordplay, that they had to kill five Indians and prepare for an attack by three thousand hidden warriors. The Spanish and their allies would have been overwhelmed if it was not for the killing effect of the Spanish artillery and musketry that forced a retreat by the Indians. Once again it was the superior weaponry of the Spanish that carried the day. During the Indian retreat there was some more fighting, but evening came upon them and the Spanish broke off the fight.

On the following day, the Spanish advanced and met two units of a total of 6,000 men using missile weapons. Cortez ordered a halt, and dispatched three Indian prisoners on the first day to relay a peaceful suggestion, but the Tlascalans fought all the harder at this "weak" sign. The hostile Indians suffered heavy losses on this day, the second of September of 1519. The Indian allies of Cortez killed multitudes of the native soldiers.

There was another battle on the fifth where four hundred men plus allies sustained the attack of hordes, completely surrounded. The Indians used arrows, stones, and two headed darts that would pierce armor. There was an onslaught of close hand to hand fighting, but less than in previous battles. The cavalry carried the day. Without the horsemen, the battle would have been lost. The fierceness of the battle forced the Tlascalans to retreat. Counting casualties, the Europeans found their losses to be one man killed and over seventy wounded. The losses of the allies were probably much greater. All of the horses were wounded also. When the priests of the Indians said they could be conquered at night, an Indian night attack was carried out, but the Spanish were not caught by surprise, and the enemy force was forced to retreat. Only one Indian of the Spanish forces was killed in that battle.

Cortez consulted with his chief advisors, who stressed the Heavenly favors which had come their way. They advised the conquistador to release their captives to make a second offer of amity with the Spanish determination to destroy them if they did not immediately negotiate with the Spanish leader. The Spanish proposed an alliance with the Tlascalans against the Aztecs. This would have worked if it were not for the Tlascalan chief in the field who wanted to attempt another night attack. His Indian allied advisers proposed going to Zumpacingo which Cortez did and make peace there. At Zumpacingo, Cortez had the help of the chiefs in gaining peace with the Tlascans. The discontents in his army wanted to turn back, but Cortez noted the valor of the army and the relief that they would continue to be blessed by God. It was better to continue onward, than to turn back with its perils. Cortez quieted the dissentents with these words.

Shortly after this, Cortez was granted the false peace with the Tlascalans, who still planned another night attack, according to the confessions obtained from four Indians whom Cortez seized. Next, Xicotenga, chief general of the Tlascalans who had delayed peace came to Cortez and made peace at last. The Tlascalans brought provisions to Cortez and his army. They went on to the chief city of these Indians, where they were greeted with flowers by the garlands. Cortez tried unsuccessfully to end their sacrifices, freeing victims, but once he was underway to Mexico City, they re-instituted their pagan practices. Montezuma did not wish a Tlascalan-Spanish alliance and asked him to come to Mexico City. However, Cortez did take two thousand of the best Tlascalan warriors with his army.

The Aztecs were still hostile, but were divided as to what they should do. This divisiveness provided Cortez his opportunities, and they were soon safely at Cholula on the way to Mexico City. However, the general learned of a plan to destroy the Spaniards in that city. He confronted the plotters after he discovered their plan. They told of the entire plot for the sacrifices and destruction of the Spaniards in that city, planned by Montezuma. Cholula was pacified with a bloody massacre, one unnecessary, because of the advantages the Spanish already had. The Aztec troops for the ambush left and returned to Mexico City. Once again, Montezuma sent the gold and fine mantles, when he learned that seven soldiers had been killed by Aztecs near Vera Cruz.

Once again, the Spanish conquistadors were on the road to Mexico City. Soon out of Cholula, they felt the cold weather and watched a snowfall. Along the way, they received, and were welcomed by the nephew of Montezuma borne on a litter by eight Indian lords. Soon, they viewed Mexico City with its lake site. Cortez dismantled from his horse and greeted Montezuma.

Distrusting the changes of the superior mind, Cortez affected the seizure of the emperor and burned four of is chief officers to death. Montezuma was taken to the quarters of the white conquerors and great attempts were made to convert the emperor to the Christian religion, but he did not swear allegiance to Spain. In 1520, a large tribute of gold was levied by the Spaniards, and divided among them, after the royal fifth was set aside for Charles V.

Meanwhile, in far different surroundings, in January of 1510, Alfonso d'Albuquerque dispatched a fleet from Cochin to Portugal in which sailed the severely wounded Ferdinand Magellan of the king's household. The two ships convoying this fleet struck on the shoals of Padua opposite the Maldive Islands in the Indian Ocean. Neither broke up, but remained aground and upright. The captains, pilots, and as many as could board the ship then returning to Cochin in Asia. Ferdinand was left to oversee the salvaging of the two ships. He played policeman and prevented the chests from being opened and robbed.

Soon, a caraval arrived to load, to the gills, the most important of the goods which could re rescued. They set fire to the two wrecks that had taken on much water. Although he was a key man in the rescue, Magellan was unable to save his own property and returned home poor despite his services against the Turks at Calcutta and in the fleets generally. When the king of Portugal would not or could increase his stipend, he turned to Spain where he was welcomed and where he was to make his major contribution to exploration.

Magellan denaturalized himself and arrived at Seville on October 20, 1517, and negotiated with the ministers of Charles V for a new exploration voyage to find a westward route to the East. There was a delay partly because of the intrigues of Portuguese agents. Finally, however, Magellan sailed his small fleet of ships from Seville on August 10, 1519, while Cortez was in Mexico. Magellan stopped at the bar for forty-two days before being able to steer southwestward for Tenerife. There were 237 men in the five ships he set sail with, and they took additional provisions for them there. He stopped at Monterose to supply the fleet with pitch. Passing Cape Verde in varied winds, they sailed into the water of the South Atlantic.

Sailing down the eastcoast of South America called Patagonia, they continued until they found a strait that was a hundred and ten leagues long. It emptied into a peaceable bay surrounded by large and high mountains covered with snow. There was no bottom to anchor, but moorings were found at twenty-five or thirty fathoms length on shore. Magellan sought an outlet, but the fleet suffered a great storm. The ten found a hidden strait and proceeded to find more bays and straits. After two days they found the two ships which had sought a passageway, but Magellan sent them out again. By this means, a way to the cape was found. There on November 28, 1520, the Spanish expedition passed from the straits into the Pacific Ocean.

Magellan set out across the ocean reaching Samar Island in the Philippine group on March 16, 1521. The journey had been long, but landfall was appreciated all the more. They were joyously welcomed by the people and traded red caps, looking glasses, combs, bells, ivory, and other things for fish and palm wine and victuals. The Spanish and the Portuguese commander met the king, who knew languages other than his own. On Good Friday, Magellan emphasized the military superiority of the Europeans, to the king. There was feasting on Sunday and a grand mass attended by Magellan and fifty Spaniards dressed with swords in their best. The ruler and his fellow king, a brother, promised to display a cross on the highest mountain in each of their domains.

Next, Magellan promised to fight the kings' enemies for them, but the king did not think the time was ripe. The people were naked and were painted, and therefore seemed defenseless to Spanish arms and armor. After seven days here, Magellan took his leave and sailed through the islands of the Philippines. He talked to the people there, informing them that their ruler was greater than the Portuguese king. The Spaniard now taught Christianity to the people they found there, but they could not avoid a fight indefinitely, and sixty Spaniards set out with arms and armor. There was a fight in which the furious natives wounded Captain Magellan on his leg with a poisoned arrow. This killed him. The Spaniards retreated, and soon set sail further upon their journey with Duarte Barbosa, a Portuguese, and Juan Serrano, a Spaniard, who was captured and probably killed before they moved out.

The Spanish voyagers went from island to island in the Philippines, and communicated with the various native kings they met. They reached Borneo, where there were elephants. The Spaniards got a chance to ride elephants for the first time in their lives. The Spaniards told the native king, that the King of Spain was his friend. Meanwhile, there was a skirmish with junks. These natives in Borneo were Islamic. They were soon underway again, reaching a very beautiful island named Sanghir and then their objectives, the Malucco Islands, where they were welcomed. The king of Tidore had learned that the ships were coming, and he, Raja Sultan Manzo, was highly honored on board the European ships.

After a long visit in the Moluccos, and the loading of slaves on their ships, the Spanish were still faced with a long voyage to Spain. They set sail westward among various islands. Many were Moslem isles, of naked inhabitants and adept in the growing of pepper plants. They heard tales of Amazons of Java and other islands. Passing the seas to Timor, they began to take precautions to prevent encounters with the Portuguese, who were more numerous than they in this part of the world. They crossed the Indian Ocean and passed to the south of the Cape of Good Hope. Extreme necessity brought them to a stop at the Cape Verde Islands, where they lied to the Portuguese to get provisions! They reached Seville on Monday, the eighth of September of 1522 to visit shrines and give thanks for the safe voyage of those who were not lost along the way. Of the 237 men who undertook the journey, only thirty-one remained to see Spanish soil. Once home, they learned of the wealth of Mexico..

When the news of Magellan's findings reached those with knowledge of the geography of the New World, it scattered the theory that North America was a cluster of outposts on the way to Asia. However, there was a long awaited strait to the south, and should be, they thought, a similar one to the north. The northern strait was later called Anian, connecting the Gulf of St. Lawrence with a short way, by sea, to the North Pacific Ocean. This would be an easier one than that to the south. Some thought there was a closer strait than that, one leading from Florida, an idea which should have been discarded by now, but which still existed.

Chapter XII

VERA CRUZ

In 1519, the Spanish official Francisco de Garay sought the great wealth he had heard was to be found in Yucatan. He had been with Columbus on the second voyage and had been governor of Jamaica under Diego Columbus. Now he wanted to conquer the province and capture the gold of the Indies. When he obtained permission from the prior Order of St. Jerome to lead an expedition there, Garay fitted out four caravels with plenty of provisions and men, and sent them first to the Florida coast under Alonzo Alvarez de Pineda to search for a strait or passage. This commander took the ships northward until he reached land. Turning eastward, he found the coast of western Florida and prepared information for the use of other Spaniards and his own claims.

Next, Pineda sailed westward to the Mexican coast near Tampico. There, in Mexico, he met Cortez. He next turned northward and eastward until he discovered a great river with a large town and forty Indian villages on both banks. He remained upon what was probably the Mississippi to observe, and also to careen his ships. He found a healthily rich country, and according to him, golden ornaments, giants, and pygmies. No one knows how he got that idea except from fiction. For eight or nine months, he searched for a strait to the Pacific between Florida and Georgia. Florida, he decided, was a part of the mainland. Later, Garay got a grant for the land that his agent Pineda coasted. A map was drawn up for Charles V.

The emperor gave Garay a grant that dealt with church-state intention to promote the interest of the Indian and the moral well being of the conquerors. He wanted to end the atrocities of the recent past. River transportation was suggested in order to avoid the necessity for using native and Spanish backs to carry baggage and provisions. Because dice and cards led to trouble and injuries and set an evil example to the Indians, these were to be prohibited.

The Spanish should not take women and children away from the native men, nor live with Indian women. This last was, Charles believed, the chief cause of evil in Hispaniola. Charles directed that his subjects should not attack the Indians. The invaders of America had enslaved Indians in the course of war. A state of war had been used for this purpose. They should treat the Indians kindly, and not assign them to labor on Spanish estates. Kindliness would result in many conversions to Christianity. For the young emperor, voluntary conversions in America in the hundreds would attain more of the Kingdom of God than a hundred thousand forced conversions.

Before he had word of the imperial grant, Garay sent Diego de Carmego on an expedition, but it failed. On June 26, 1523, Garay and the discoverer of Yucatan Grijalva set out from Jamaica to colonize Panuco in northeastern Mexico. Hardships along the coast led to deaths and desertions, and Cortez, eager to have Mexico all to himself, captured Garay, who was shortly to die in Mexico City.

The bishop of Burgos, Juan Rodriquez de Fonseca, still favored Velasquez in the absence of the emperor and sent orders to the governor of Cuba to seize Cortez, his army and take them prisoners. As soon as he received this command of the president of the Council of the Indies, the powerful Velasquez fitted forth a fleet of nineteen ships and sent to Mexico one thousand and four hundred soldiers under the command of Pamphilo de Narvaez.

When the court of the royal audiencia of St. Domingo, and the brethren of the Order of Jeronymites learned of this, they sent Lucas Valesquez de Aillon to Cuba with orders to stop the Velasquez fleet, but he had already spent all of his money upon this expedition, and refused to listen to the orders of the religious body. Narvaez lost only one small vessel on the way to Vera Cruz. There, they met the discontent of some of the dissentents, unhappy with their rightful share of gold, gathered by the Spaniards. Montezuma plotted with Narvaez who told him that they were to free the Indian emperor and kill Cortez and his men.

Narvaez sent three men to demand the surrender of Vera Cruz from it's governor Gonzalo de Sandoval. The governor prepared for the trouble that appeared ahead. Narvaez's envoy Guevara and two other envoys met with Sandoval and demanded Sandoval's surrender to Narvaez. Sandoval resented being called a traitor and told Guevara to settle his business with Cortez himself in Mexico City. He seized the three men, threw trammels over them and bundled then up on the backs of natives for the Aztec capital. Carried day and night, they were deposited before Cortez who shrewdly condemned the bad treatment the three had received and treated them with the greatest hospitality, giving them gold. Sending them back as lambs, compared to the lions they had been before Sandoval; Cortez won a domestic diplomatic victory.

Cortez wrote Narvaez "not to give cause by his conduct for the Mexicans to rise and destroy them all, assuring him that they were ready of do anything to liberate Montezuma, whose disposition had also greatly altered since the time that Narvaez had begun to correspond with him." The conquistador sent letters with presents to the interpreter. Narvaez felt that this was a sign of weakness. He ridiculed the first letter, calling Cortez and his army traitors and promising death for them all. The interlopers did not reply, however he got a shock when Guevara and his two associated returned with praise for Cortez, being in honor of a junction of their forces in the continuation of the conquest. In a rage, Narvaez put them out of his sight, but Guevara and his men told of the wonders of Mexico and of Cortez to their comrades. A priest from Cortez also came and told how anxious the conqueror was to put himself under the Narvaez command. When this did no good, he passed out rich presents from Cortez, and to Narvaez's avarice, dividing his troops.

Marching his troops inland to Cempoal, he seized all the gold, mantles, and women previously given to Cortez and his officers. Friends in the Narvaez army and Sandoval kept Cortez informed of what happened. Cortez then marched a force from Mexico City to meet the numerically superior army of the interloper's. The conqueror subverted the army of Narvaez and then he attacked at night and carried that force. Cortez had won over an army, but Narvaez had brought with him a Negro with smallpox that spread among the Indians and caused a great death among them, as the Indians died by the thousands.

Cortez marched his army, including the conquered troops for Mexico City arriving there in June of 1520. More trouble was ahead. Unfortunately, Alvarado, with his command, gathered six hundred of the leading Aztecs in their dance, song, and religious chants, and while they were performing without arms as requested, Alvarado and his men rushed upon them, and massacred the Indians. They then plundered the bodies of the dead. When the news reached the people of the capital, there was an immediate uprising of the Aztecs, and a great body assaulted the Spaniards. This was to be major setback in the campaign of Cortez for the conquest of Mexico.

As ordered by Cortez, Captain de Ordoz took four hundred men to check out the account of the insurrection one soldier had informed him about. He wished him to pacify the minds of the people if necessary. The commander left the building half a street away, large numbers of Aztecs attacked and killed eight soldiers on the spot and wounded large numbers. They attacked from all sides and from the roof of the buildings, forcing the Spanish to take refuge in their quarters and prepare for the ensuing fight.

At dawn, they sallied forth with their whole force against the Aztecs, who with their desperate force excelled that what Cortez' men had seen in their European experiences. They fought against the Mexicans in which, after a day's battle, they lost ten or twelve soldiers from the native onslaught. Next, they built four military machines of strong timber with towers for twenty-five men under cover with porthole for Spanish artillery, musketeers, and crossbow men. These required a full day to construct since they also had to repair breaches in the walls of their quarters in the city. The drawbridges of the city were up, which proved difficult for the Spaniards to travel in the city. They did arrive at the great temple and were rushed upon there by four thousand Aztecs. It was a bloody affair with artillery and swords, but the Spaniards had a hard time of it also. They had the aid of their Alascalan allies, who also lost many lives.

Returning to their quarters, the Spaniards found that the Aztecs had almost gained control of the buildings. Montezuma was persuaded at length to appear before the people. Cortez and his Spaniards thought that he could persuade the people to give up their attack upon the Spaniards in return for which the Spanish would leave Mexico. He did his part, and the Aztec attacked him after listening to his speech, and Montezuma was wounded. He refused help and shortly died of his wounds.

Cortez made a new sally for the section of the city that had firm ground, but he lost twenty soldiers killed. They tried, but could not get control of a single bridge. Their troubles thus increased. The Spanish astrologer cast the horoscope of them and came to the conclusion that they must leave Mexico City that any night or none of them would get out alive. Cortez would undergo a lost fortune and would return to greater fortune than before.

The great conqueror decided to move out that very night, and gave orders to make a portable bridge to replace those torn down by the Aztecs. The bridge detachments consisted of 150 Spanish soldiers and 400 of the allies. Cortez next gave orders for an advanced guard and a rear guard. The prisoners were to be protected and write the Marina and Luiso. Next, Cortez brought forth all of the gold, and left it there, for each to take what he wished rather than to leave it to its previous owners, the Mexicans.

Shortly before midnight, they set out in a dark and rainy night. They made some progress, when the alarm was given by the Aztecs. Soon the enemy was upon them by land, and in the lake, and in the canals by boat. Heavy rainfall then startled the horses, they fell into the water with their baggage and men. At this point, the Aztec broke the bridge and the water was soon filled wit dead and dying men. Many were lost by drowning and others fell to the Indians alive, to be sacrificed later in the sight of the Spaniards at a distance.

Those on horseback, including Cortez and his captains, but their spurs to the horses and galloped off to safety. Other were saved only by defending themselves with their swords. They reached firm ground. When the count was made, it was learned that 150 or more Spaniards were dead at their point in their flight. Most of those following Narvaez were killed and large numbers of Tlascalans were killed because they loaded themselves down with gold. The gold weighted them down in battle when they fell into the water. Now they had to fight along the way to the land of the Tlascalans for safety. On July 8, 1520, the Aztecs met them at the Battle of Otempan. Finally at that battle, they killed the Mexican general, and its people retreated, and were pursued by the Spanish for awhile, at great loss to their lives. There were 870 Spanish lives lost at that point. Over 1,200 Tlascalans were killed and lost in the uprising and in the flight. There is no record of Aztec losses, at that time, but they must have been exceedingly large.

The defeated army of Cortez and their Tlascalan fellow soldiers were hospitably greeted by the people of Tlascala. Cortez wrote to his garrison at Vera Cruz and asked for reinforcements that were granted them in the number of seven invalids. The younger Xicotenga, however, maintained his hostility and made designs upon the Spanish force now that they were defeated. He had enemies however, and his plot was exposed and the Tlascalans expressed their friendship by kicking him down stairs from the building where the inquiry w as held. The soldiers of Narvaez were less total and memorialized Cortez to return to Cuba, but they were not listened to, and had to go along with the Spanish leader.

Mexico had another emperor. The Aztec sent large numbers of troops to those provinces nearest the Spanish presence, but these men proved disorderly, robbed, and outraged these people. The suppressed natives sent four chiefs from among themselves to negotiate secretly with Cortez. They told Cortez they would submit to the Spanish if they would expel the Aztecs from their land. He answered their plea and sent his cavalry and crossbow men aided by the Tlascalans. Captains who had come with Narvaez had command in this detachment. These soldiers did not care for the tough fights and mutinied, but Cortez angrily ordered them to proceed.

Native chiefs told Christoval Oli how to proceed and he marched against the Aztecs and sharply defeated them. The Aztecs fled and the allies killed many of them. When the Aztecs paused for action, they were defeated for the second time in a matter of hours. Aztec control of these provinces was ended and gave alarm to the successor of Montezuma, and notice that the Spanish were not shorn of their power.

Cortez determined upon the siege of Mexico City with Spanish vessels made for action on the lake of Mexico. The excellent shipwright, Martin Lopez, was charged with making these ships. They marched for three days after Christmas for Mexico City. For ninety-three days before Mexico City, the Spanish held their siege, fighting continuously, encounter after encounter. On one dismal day, they heard the captured Spaniards being sacrificed on the temple mount. Soon, however, the Spanish fought their way into the city. On August 13, 1521, the emperor surrendered and this part of the Spanish conquest was completed.

About this time, an intelligent Lucas Vasquez de Ayllon of Toledo who had had no military experience in Spain or in Hispaniola took an interest in exploration and conquest. He had come over with Ovando and had become an important official on the island. In lieu of salaries, he received a repartimento of four hundred Indians, as was the custom of the time. In 1520, Ayllon sent forth a caravel commanded by Francisco Gordillo to the northern continent, but it was joined on the sea by Pedro de Quexos and the two men sent their sailors and soldiers on a slave hunting expedition. In June of 1521, claims were made to the country, then found. The fleet was not very successful.

While Gordillo was capturing Indians for slavery, Juan Ponce de Leon made his fatal attempt to colonize Florida. The great searcher for the fountain of youth had become richer over the years, but he was restless and sought greater independence. Despite discoveries already made, Ponce de Leon believed Florida to be an island. Perhaps he based his opinion on the Da Vinci map.

In 1521, he embarked in two ships for Florida. He had with him two hundred men and fifty horses, domestic animals, agricultural implements, powder, crossbows, monks, and priests, and other arms. Soon he was across the water and building a village for his settlers. The Indians attacked, and when Ponce de Leon led his men forth, he was badly wounded by an arrow and many of his men lost their lives in the furious encounter. He re-embarked and returned to Cuba where he died of his wounds. On the return journey one of his ships lost its way and fell into the hands of the great Cortez.

Chapter XIII

PIZARRO

After the conquest of Mexico City, Cortez and his soldiers left the city for their camp. Following this exit, the Mexican people in the metropolis streamed out of the city for the countryside. The causeways were crowded for three days and nights with this exodus of men, women, and children. Once the passage of the three causeways was over, Cortez sent soldiers into the city to observe its condition. Arthur Helps wrote that the Spaniards found the houses to be full of dead people. Those that still survived could not crawl out. Others just stayed. The Mexicans had searched the ground for roots to eat during the siege and eaten the bark of the trees. There was not fresh water.

Cortez ordered that the Mexico City aqueduct be repaired and a thanksgiving to be held for the victory. The conqueror went to the neighboring city of Cuyozcan where he held a great banquet. His soldiers indulged in such great excesses after long abstinences that Cortez suggested to Father Olmedo that they should hold a solemn procession with a mass and sermon. The sermon should inform the troops that they should not rob, take Indian women, or quarrel among themselves, but act as good Christmas should. This was done. Next, he dismissed his Indian allies and ordered the Mexican to clean the streets of the new Spanish capital of New Spain or Mexico. They were ordered into one quarter divided from the Spanish quarter by a canal.

Because the whole spoil was worth only 380,000 pesos of gold, the Spanish soldiers were disappointed and murmured against Cortez, claiming he concealed some of the spoil for himself. Cortez was concerned and feared being placed in such a position. In order to raise the amount of booty for division, Cortez ordered Quauhtemotzin and his cousin, the king of Tlacuba tortured until they told where they hid their treasures. Suffering agonies from the torture, the king looked to his king lord paramount to allow him to tell, but the tortured young king was content. One of the kings did confess and the hiding place was then known.

Having made some havoc of Mexico City, Cortez sent his men into other parts of Mexico, killing some natives, and enslaving others. They laid waste of the people of Panuco and other large populated provinces when they did not yield to the Spaniards and pledge allegiance to Charles V. Cortez sent his minions for gold to the south into Guatemala and Honduras, and there, dealt death. According to Las Casas, there perished over two million Indians leaving a mere two thousand left to work in the fields under a harsh master. Las Casas has been rightfully of exaggeration in a usually accurate account.

In Guatemala, the chief ruler was carried on a litter to welcome the Spanish with great joy, gave them plenty of provisions and housing. Ever eager for gold, they awoke the next morning to demand gold that was not to be had by the natives. The Spanish proceeded to burn the natives alive, to get out of them the secrets that did not exist. The nobles fled, lest they be destroyed by this insatious demand for gold by the Spaniards. The people were willing to submit, but they too had to flee. The Spaniards wished for gold, but their efforts were for naught. The Indians rebelled and marched against the invaders only to be deported, to be taken into captivity, separating families, and forced to carry Spanish ships from sea to sea, from the Caribbean to the Pacific Ocean.

For all of the first hoard of gold from the Mexican capital, Central Mexico was rich in Indians and not that rich in gold. It has been estimated that in the extent of central and southern Mexico, there were at least twelve million people and perhaps twice that number. The lower feature was still a vast addition to the population ruled by Charles V. Before the Spaniards came, these Mexican peoples had neither the wheel nor drought animals. There was a marginal surplus that went to the upper class and the soldiers. For the Spanish, as well as the Aztecs, taxes were generally paid in personal service and large amounts of maize or corn, beans, and cloth from the Indians.

Cortez distributed large groups of Indians to work on plantations, called encomiendas. Some of his soldiers received as many as 20,000 Indians for their services in a feudal system. The soldiers could levy tributes in the form of services upon these natives. The land however, and the government jurisdiction over these people did not belong to the natives or to the Spaniards. At this time, the Indians continued to be governed by their nobles and chieftains. Theoretically, they ruled in a feudal system like that dying in Europe. In this system the land was held by the king. The Indians were owned by the owners of the plantations.

All of this was insufficient for the Spaniards who sought gold or a commercial product in order to become richer. Greed was a natural component for the Europeans. Some encomenderos imported livestock from Europe, and seized land to be sown in wheat. When Peru was opened up, Cortez began trade between Mexico and Peru; His Indians began gold placer mining to the south. Others of his Indians raised great herds of cattle, sheep, and hogs. He and other Spaniards called upon their Indian vassals to work for free. As the century passed, the Indians began dying off in large numbers, especially at first. By 1568, there were only two and a half million people alive in the area of New Spain. Two generations later, there were only a million Indians remaining.

Sixteenth century Spain and Spanish America saw a great religious fanaticism which was developing in the final reconquest and would have been strong even if Luther had never been born. As it was, the radical and reforming activities of Martin Luther presented a threat to orthodoxy beyond the minor infractions of a weak populace or the occasional heresy or cult. Churchmen of the Catholic faith felt the peril and determined or drastic measures throughout Europe. They wished to suppress heretics of all kinds, fearing those heretics who were spreading what the Catholic hierarchy believed was error. In the Spanish politicization of state and religion under the crown, crimes against the church were also crimes against the state and so the division between heresy and treason was vague.

There was another reason expressed by Greenleaf, that "since heretics robbed the community of its faith, sacraments and spiritual life, it was deemed just to execute them as traitors and formentors of social revolution." Even orthodox liberal and reforming Catholics were damned in this earth. They were called Lutherans and were suppressed. Also finding dishonor were Spanish mystics and those who were influenced by Erasmus. Spaniard believed that even minor moral deviations would allow major heresy to come and thrive. Indeed, trial and punishment was common in both worlds.

Early in New Spain or Mexico, in 1522, the Mexican Inquisition tried an Indian, Marcos of Acolhuacan, for the crime of concubinage. In 1523, the Inquisition directed an edict against heretics and Jews, and another edict against any action in word or deed that the Vatican called a sin. The Franciscan Martin de Valencia was the first friar who had specific inquisitional power in Mexico, but there were those who served as inquisitor in the case of Marcos and others.

The governor of the province of Nicaragua, subdued that country in all its glory of fertility and a plenitude of fruits. The people were subjected there to their tormentors being unwilling to leave their domain. He sent over fifty horses and men to extirpate people by the sword. They seized many of the Indians and made slaves from among them. The Spaniards then took the peasant lands for themselves and burdened the slaves they had made, even the children as much as they could bear. This murder and enslavement deprived the country of its people. Brutal Spanish captivity saw many lives lost. The change of climate brought by their transfer to different lands, and the policy of the Spaniards to work the sick as well as the healthy brought about large-scale deaths from among the captive Indian population.

Before the end of the year 1523, Cortez received Charles' royal commission as governor and captain general of New Spain. This was most beneficial because legally, he was still a rebel under Diego Velasquez. This enabled the conqueror of Mexico to expand to the south in competition with other Spaniards. Cortez sent Alvarado to the west to advance from Tehuantepoc and sent Olid by water to Honduras. Alvarado conquered the Amerindians of Guatemala and went into Salvador, while Olid was involved in a four-corner fight.

Olid rebelled and so the Conqueror of Mexico sent Francisco de las Casas to arrest Olid. Also, in the fight were two lieutenants of Pedrarias, Hernandez de Cordoba and Hernando de Soto, using the town of Leon nearby founded as a base for operations. Gil Gonzales Davila had discovered Lake Nicaragua in 1522 and was also in the field. Olid defeated Davila and Fernando de las Casas then took Davila prisoner, taking him to Mexico City. Cortez was called upon to establish peace and dominance in Central America, but after a very difficult jungle trip, he had to return to Mexico to take care of the disorder there.

Back in Mexico in 1524, Cortez had more troubles. Charles V had sent a corps of royal officials to New Spain or Mexico to check up on the conqueror. Luis Ponce de Leon was sent to conduct a judgment on Cortez' administration, but he died two weeks later. Marcos de Aguilar succeeded him and after he too died, the treasurer, Alonso de Estrada took over as judge. During the judgment, officials interfered with Hernando's Pacific Ocean ventures.

On January 17, 1524, John de Verazzano sailed his four ships for America under the orders of the French king. He passed a desolate rock near the island of Madeira. In the next twenty-five days he and his crew made eight hundred leagues. Suddenly, on the 24th of February, the ran into a violent hurricane but survived to make four hundred leagues in twenty four more days and reached the shores of North America. They knew it was inhabited because of the fires they saw from the waters at night. Verazzano then followed the coast southward, but seeing no port in the next leagues of about 150 miles, he reversed his ship and headed northward in search of new lands. Some of the natives fled, but the French, in most cases, traded for provisions with the near naked Indians along the coast.

In his letter to the king, Verazzano thought the Indians were much like the Ethiopians with thick black hair, tied back. They were of middle stature with broad chests and strong arms and well formed legs. However they had broad faces or sharp faces with large black eyes and a fixed expression. The natives were not strong, but they had acute minds and were swift on their feet. They were liked the people of the east, particularly of the Far East. Because of the short stay, they could not learn much more.

Verazzano's expedition sailed farther north, and reached the Hudson River at the great harbor that it opened into. There, they were visited by many natives without fear and who delighted in the Europeans and the bells and other trinkets unusual to the Indians. From here they headed eastward along Long Island Sound and discovered Narrananset Bay and the harbor of Newport, in future Rhode Island. Rounding New England, they sailed further north and noted the large trees such as firs of which the north abounded. Soon after reaching the north-country, Verazzano brought his fleet home.

Meanwhile, on May 15, 1524, there arrived in Mexico City Franciscan friar Martin de Valencia who was commissary of the Inquisition in New Spain for a while, in which office, he melted out capital punishment. He drew the power to act from the authority of papal bull Omnimoda, though an implied grant of inquisitorial power. Conflict with the civil authorities followed, because Valencia claimed that he had credentials for civil and criminal jurisdiction as well as ecclesiastical jurisdiction. He had arguments from March through July of 1525 with Cortez' deputy, Gonzalo de Salazar, and the Cabildo or city council of the capital. He had on the ninth of March presented these credentials and demanded obedience.

The Cabildo found with consultation of its lawyers that it could find no grant of authority for Valencia's Franciscans to exercise civil and criminal jurisdiction. They ordered the friars to refrain from this authority and forbid them from exercising it. In 1526, the next year, the Dominican Thomas Ortiz arrived to assume Valencia's office, to return almost immediately to Spain. Fray Domingo de Betanzos then replaced Ortiz and pursued nineteen blasphemy cases. Next, Fray Vicente de Santa Maria served in the process of which he had two people, a Jewish blacksmith and a Jewish trader, burned at the stake. Another Jew was reconciled to the Christian religion.

Like Mexico, Peru had its legends of a white person, in this case a god and goddess, white in complexion and bringing the arts of civilization to the Indians. The Incas claimed thirteen princes before the conquest, which amounts to about two and a half centuries of descent, not the four hundred years that they claimed. However, there was a civilization that preceded the Incas, according to Inca history, upon whom the Incas based their own knowledge of civilization. The greatest expansion came with Topa Inca Yupanqui, grandfather of Pizarro's monarch, who surmounted the barrier of the terrible desert of Alzacma and drove into Chile to the river Naule with his troops. This man's son Hoayna Capac marked northward to add the powerful kingdom of Quito to the Peruvian Empire. Cuzco was the capital with its narrow streets and ample buildings. Its peak was the great Temple of the Sun, the sun being the traditional father of the Inca rulers.

The man who brought down the Inca was not born in the high society like an Inca, but was an illegitimate Spanish boy, born about 1471. This was Francisco Pizarro, born to Colonel Gonzales Pizarro of the Castilian infantry, who had fought in Italy at Navarre, and his girl friend Francisca Gonzales in the town of Turxills, a woman of the lower class. The boy was poorly cared for and received no education and grew up as a swineherd, but he could dream and share in the popular enthusiasms of the time. In time, he was shipped over to

America, for we first find Pizarro in Hispaniola in 1510. He took part in the expedition to Uraba in Terra Firma under Alonzo de Ojeda. The Ojeda colony failed and as we have seen, Pizarro was later associated with Balboa and then with Pedrarias.

In 1515, he and 27 cavaliers were assigned a position on the Pacific shores of Panama to trade with the Indians for gold and pearls. Next, he fought against the tribes of Verzgua. In 1522, Pascaul de Andogoya returned with tales of the opulence and grandeur. The Spanish pulse could quicken as the individuals in the New World could dream of another great conquest like Cortez in Mexico, which they were hearing about. The country to the south was made of high mountains and little was known of the Incas, but the Spaniards could dream. No one knew of the distance and form and it was as much of a tremendous undertaking as could be imagined, but Cortez' conquest told of difficulties overcome, and the Spanish could dream still.

Pizarro was to be the man and he found two colonials to help him. Diego de Almagro was a soldier of fortune, somewhat older than Pizarro and like he, a foundling, perhaps from the town of Almagro in New Castile. He was a gallant soldier, frank and liberal, and sometimes hasty and ungovernable in his passions. Also, they had Hernando de Luque, vicar at Panama and one time school teacher in the Cathedral of Darien. He had influence and controlled funds. The three men got together and formulated their plans. Pizarro was to head the expedition and Almagro was to be the quartermaster.

They obtained a ship and refitted it and Almagro signed up two hundred men for the expedition. It was an untimely departure in November of 1524 in the midst of the rainy season, but they survived contrary winds and reached the river Biru and up the stream they went until they found a good anchorage. They were in the midst of a swamp and had great difficulties marching on slipper mud and tangled undergrowth. The hill country they found inland was so rocky that their feet were cut, and they sank down on the earth amid the oppressive heat. But Pizarro was as optimistic as Cortez and kept up his courage. While Cortez had sought a better place in Mexico, so did Pizarro in South America. Pizarro and his men re-embarked and sailed down the coast. They were harassed and almost foundered from a heavy sea. Once calmed, the sea was traversed for a watering place and a place to gain provision. The forests and the landslides were funeral and full of nothing but insects.

At this point, Pizarro tried to lift the spirits of his men, but he sent half of them back with his ship for provisioning under a man named Montenegro. He tried to discover an Indian village, but none could be found in the virginal forests. They ate shellfish, the bitter buds of palm trees, and berries and herbs, some of which were poisonous and tormented those that ate them with pain. Pizarro sufficed to be cheerful and provide sustenance and empathy to keep his men going except for those who were starved to death. Twenty died of various causes, and the men felt abandoned by Montenegro and the rest of the adventurers.

Finally, they found a native village. Its occupants were frightened and departed to leave their food to the frightened Spaniards. There were supplies of maize and coconuts. The Indians returned with their golden necklaces and told of a powerful nation, the Inca nation. At this time, the ship commanded by Montenegro reached Pizarro and had plenty of provisions aboard. The men naturally enjoyed this change of fortune.

They all proceeded by ship and sailed southward along the coast. They reached the territory of a cannibal tribe and hostility set out along the coast by boat before the Indians returned to their village, they had just fled. The weather was tempestuous. Anchoring further to the south, they had a battle with the natives, a warlike race, which they barely won. This was enough: Pizarro turned around his ship and returned to Panama to talk of gold and adventure.

The first twelve Franciscans to arrive in New Spain 1524 included Toribio de Benavente, born in Benavente, Leon, Spain, who took the name of Motolinia, which in Nahuatl meant "poor." In keeping with his name and the vows he had taken, Motolivia lived in abject poverty while he evangelized throughout New Spain and Guatemala. In his years in the New World, he was guardian of convents, founder of missions, suggested the foundation of Spanish settlements in Puebla, took a political stand against the first Mexican audience, and won souls. He opposed Las Casas and criticized his confessional rules governing the granting of absolution to penitents, although both men wanted to defeat the Indians. In 1555 Motolivia wrote a letter to Charles about Las Casas, and in his time, he wrote two books about the Indians before and after the conquest. He died in 1569.

Once fully established in Mexico, Cortez sent Pedro Alvarado to conquer Guatemala. Alvarado used brute force and killed many of the natives in the process. With this accomplished, Cortez sent a party of the oldest and most battle scarred conquerors to the province of Coatza coalcos on the Gulf coast. They were to investigate the possibility of building a ship canal across the Tehuantepoc Isthmus to connect the Gulf and the Pacific. Cristobal de Olid explored the Honduran coast. Two fleets were sent along the coast of the Pacific. One went south and another went north.

News came back from Honduras that Olid had founded a colony in the province and had revolted. In order to subdue Olid, Governor Cortez immediately gathered an army to go overland so that he could explore the country along the way and add to his conquests. He appointed the men to govern Mexico during his absence and took with him Cuauhtemoc, ruler of the Aztecs, and a bunch of petty rulers and chiefs, all as hostages. He took with him three thousand warriors and many carriers and Dona Marina to serve as interpreter. In his private household, he had in state, a mayor domo or superintendent, two masters of the household, a brother, two chamberlains, a steward, a doctor and a surgeon, pages, grooms, falconers, five musicians, and entertainment provided by an acrobat and a magician and puppeteer. In the province of Coatzacoalcos, he stopped and ordered the settlers to join his expedition.

Cortez set out in the rainy season when the plain was overflowing with its rivers, swamps, and morasses so that he had to build many bridges, rafts and floats. Because so many people were on the expedition, it was hard to get enough food to feed them all. It was a struggle against the rivers, bogs, and starvation. Four of the five musicians died. There were many losses due to deaths by drownings and starvation. There were many desertions and many Indian carriers collapsed, so overweighed were they with burdens of iron tools and other necessities. At one great river, it took four days to build a great bridge until Bernal Diaz de Costillo, adept at such things, returned from foraging with one hundred and thirty loads of maize, eighty fowl, honey, beans, salt, eggs, and some fruit

With rumor of a plot reaching Cortez, the leader ordered Cuauhtemoc and his cousin, the Lord of Taculoa, to be hung and they were. Finally, past a range of hills, Cortez in Honduras found the first settlement of fellow Spaniards who were in a worse condition than his force and learned that Olid had been seized by his own men and beheaded. Cortez and Pizarro faced the jungle in their respective marches south. Both had similar difficulties.

Chapter XIV

AMERICA

Meanwhile, in Santo Domingo, there was a Spaniard who two decades and one half earlier discovered the coast of Columbia. Rodrigo de Bastidas was settled there and once again sought adventure. With approval from the Spanish government that conceded to him the right to construct a fort and build a settlement on the Colombian coast between Cabo de la Vela and the mouths of the Magdelena River, Bastidas set sail in July of 1525 with four ships. Anchoring off Santa Martha, he landed his fellow Spaniards and began the town. Humane as always, he treated the Indians well and made treaties of peace with nearby tribes. The Spaniards hated cutting the wood for their houses, and were unhappy that Bastidas did not enslave the Indians and force them to do the work. When Bastidas traded for gold so the precious metal could cover expedition expenses, the men grew angry because they expected that the gold be distributed among themselves.

Some Spaniards sought to murder Governor Bastidas and the lieutenant of the governor's named Juan de Villafuerte led a group into his bedroom to accomplish that aim. Confined to his bed with a fever, Rodrigo could not defend himself. They stabbed him repeatedly and left, sure that he was a dead man. Outside, Captain Rodrigo Palominio heard the cries of the wounded man and came to his assistance. The indignant majority were angry at the attackers and the latter fled into the forests, where most were captured and sent to Santo Domingo to be punished. Bastidas appointed Palominio to be his successor and returned to Cuba where he died of his wounds, a shining light among the explorers and conquistadors, and like Balboa, a martyr to his humanity.

Palomino was not the same man as Bastidas and he treated the neighboring Indians well in order to get needed supplies, but he raided beyond them and enslaved the natives as most Spaniards did. He oversaw the arrival of supplies and settlers and the planting to fields of corn and vegetables. Still there was not enough to sustain the people and the neighboring tribes could not make up the difference, so Palomino had to go forth to steal from distant tribes. Entering the rugged mountains inland, he undertook to raid, but he could not take his horses with him because of the wild terrain. The mountaineers defended their homes. Since they knew the country, the Indians could easily defeat the Spaniards at selected points. Fleeing back to the plains, the Spaniards were followed by native warriors.

More troubles faced Palomino. The Audiencia of Santo Domingo appointed Pedro Vadillo to succeed the former governor Bastidas, of whose death they were informed. The official governor and his lieutenant, Pedro de Heredia came with 200 men but Palomino would not allow him to land. He went up the coast to build his own fort and a priest was able to preserve the peace. The two governors would serve jointly, until a ruling came from the emperor. Both men attacked the natives and issued forth with a combined raid that was repulsed. While pillaging the most hospitable tribe they had found, Palomino fell into a river and was swept away and lost. With the cruelness of the majority of Spaniards, Vadillo devastated every tribe he could, but when at Santa Martha, he began to imprison, torture, and kill Palomino's followers, he was replaced. Then a judge imprisoned Vadillo and had him tortured. On the way to Spain for trial, the deposed governor's ship was wrecked and he was drowned.

One of the Spanish dreamers of these times was a judge in Santo Domingo, Lucas Vasquez de Ayllon, who decided upon a colonizing project of his own. With a royal patent authorizing him to settle the Carolina coast and noted Cape Hatteras, where there was a small broad mouth bay which no longer exists, he sailed his ships to land. Settlers were landed in 1526, but soon afterwards Ayllon died and his colonists dissented and left the colony.

Lucas Vasquez, seeking glory and wealth, returned to Spain to gain a grant from the emperor for his discoveries. His servant, Francisco Chicora, was a captured and converted Indian with a lively imagination. In order to stir up interest and return to his homeland with an expedition, Chicora in his excellent Spanish told great stories. Since Ayllon believed in the Indian and the people of that day easily believed in marvels, he and the rest of the sixteenth century Spaniards were intrigued and the stories were wide spread and reported by Peter Martyr. Chicora told of white Indians ruled by a king and queen who had been stretched as infants to reach a great size. They were a race of natives with long flexible tails. The Spaniards, he related, could find great treasures and rich land in the interior.

Charles V probably heard these tales, but what influence it had upon him is unknown. The emperor did however favor Ayllon and granted him power to discover great lands as Ayllon's personal cause. His greatest interest was that the explorer discovered a passage to the Spice Islands, that great hope of western mankind for two centuries. Details of requirements for Ayllon and rights of fisheries and land for the proposed explorer and mines for the ruler occupied officials of the emperor for awhile. Each ship had to have a captain and Ayllon was required to take with him a doctor, surgeon, and an apothecary. Charles wanted him to develop and agricultural colony and to use voluntary labor. He noted that countries had been depopulated where Indian slavery was introduced. Religious instruction for the Indians was stressed. This was to be paid for out of revenue derived in the new country.

An eager Ayllon returned to the West Indies, but suffered delays in setting out on the expedition he envisioned. In early 1525, he sent Pedro Quexos to explore the coast, much of which had been already seen before. Quexos explored the coast, much of which had been already seen before. Quexos found some gold and silver and a few pearls. Finally in the middle of July of 1526, Ayllon was able to sail forth himself. He had with him five hundred men and women, and eighty-nine horses. The explorer obviously sought to conquer and colonize the Atlantic coast of North America. They landed near Cape Fear. They tried but could not find a strait or Chicora's marvelous countries. Francisco Chicora deserted. A coasting party returned with news of a better country and Ayllon took his people to found the settlement of San Miguel de Guadape near a great river, probably the Pedee. It was an unfortunate colony. The people starved and were sick; Ayllon died on October 18, 1526; and anarchy began. Only 150 people were left by the time they set out for home from the Carolinas.

Pizarro, Almagro, and Luque (standing in for the Licentiate Gasper de Espinosa) formed a new agreement for profits for the second attempt at the treasures of Peru. This time they purchased two vessels, larger and better than the previous ore ship and stores were laid in on a large scale than before. Only three-fourths of the original two hundred men were left. They had a hard task to get enough men for the second voyage and they had to make do with 160 men against an empire. They knew now that transportation would be so hard so they must limit the amount of bulky goods and provisions. They set sail with an experienced pilot aboard by the name of Bartholomew Ruiz. Breezes were favorable this time and they set sail for the Rio de San Juan, the utmost limit reached by Almagro.

The banks of this river were lined with Indian habitations and Pizarro launched his great adventure by a successful surprise attack on a small village. For such a small place it had a considerable booty of gold. He also captured a number of natives. At this point, Almagro, as agreed, returned to Panama with the gold to gather needed reinforcements. Ruiz would scout ahead along the coast and Pizarro would go into the interior along the river to find comfortable quarters as suggested by Indian prisoners. Ruiz explored the coast and discovered the Bay of St. Matthew. Next, he headed for the deep sea and encountered an Indian balas boat sailed by Indians in time honored method. The Indians told of a port and wool, gold, and silver in great amounts in Peru. Then Ruiz returned to a troubled Pizarro.

Also exploring, Pizarro and his men were fearful and often under attack by the Indians suffering losses. He and his men had searched for the promised fairer lands and found only dense forests and ravines of frightful depth. Reptiles, boas, and alligators carried off some of the men, and the natives much of the rest. Famine and mosquitoes drove them to destruction, and soon, all but Pizarro and a few others wanted to return. Then Ruiz came with his reports of gold, silver, and wool and Almagro arrived with refreshers and volunteers, newly arrived from Spain, for the most part. This was a welcome relief.

They all embarked upon their vessels and sailed the southward pass the bay and were struck by appearances of cultivation. They reached the busy port of the recently conquered Inca territory of Quito, eager for a different conquest by themselves. This was the port of Tacamez and its ornaments of gold and precious stones. There they met a hostile force and were in danger had not one of the cavaliers not fallen from his horse to the astonishment of the Indians, who were unprepared to see an animal and its rider fall into halves. Chastened by the powers before them in the port, Almagro went back for more troops.

Bad word got out in Panama and Governor Pedro de los Rios was incensed enough to send two ships to recover the men from the bad situation Pizarro had gotten them into in Peru. The ships arrived but a small band stuck by Pizarro and stayed behind. The governor gave Pizarro another chance, and he having suffered some more, returned with his men. They visited along the coast and were soon in Panama. Pizarro went forward to Spain to tell his story and gain support for the taking of the Inca empire.

Meanwhile, in 1526, the governor of Yucatan set upon the people of that peninsula and proved a tyrant who with 300 men made war on the natives. Because they had no gold, he forced them into a slavery in exchange for wine, oil, vinegar, port, and horses. There the Spaniards hunted with the use of their dogs for the lost Indian. One woman could not escape and so hung herself. Her year old child she suspended around her waist. The dogs bit into this child, but he was rescued and baptized before he died.

Charles V entrusted Sebastian Cabot with a mission to pass through the Straits of Magellan to discover Tharsia, Opin, and Japan. On the way to the southwestern passage,

Cabot sailed up the Rio de la Plata in Argentina. He built a fort on the banks where the Tercero flowed from the mountains of Tucuman. The Portuguese were searching the area and Cabot sent this message to the emperor. After two years, he returned to Spain, leaving an officer, Lara in charge of the fort. Lara gained an ally in a nearby chieftain. When the ally fell in love with a Spanish lady at the fort, the Indian surprised and massacred the garrison, being killed by Lara in the battle. Indians carried off the body and her companions.

The English had traders in Spain to get benefits from the trade of the New World. These merchants lived mainly in Andalucia. Some resided in Seville, the chief center for all of America's official business. Larger ships had trouble in sailing up to Seville, and much of the loading and unloading took place at San Lucar and Cadiz, which were to grow in importance. The English merchants chiefly lived at the former where the Spanish monarch recognized the English company as a regulated company, and allowed them to worship in their own church, that of St. George. Londoners, Southampton men, merchants of Bristol, and the west country were present. Some were transient, while others were residents. These connections were real beneficial and included the Plymouth Hawkinses.

While the Anglo-Spanish alliance endured, this colony was important and well received. The English king, Henry VIII was married to a Spanish princess and Englishmen could take part in the American trade with their goods transshipped in the regular colonial convoys. About 1526, one could find Englishmen in the Indies. In that year, the Thornes of Bristol had a factor named Thomas Tyson in Hispaniola. Later on, Englishmen were in Mexico where they were merchants and served the Spanish government in official capacities. These were English Catholics who sailed under the flag of Charles V like subject Germans and Flemings.

The Portuguese were very interested in Spanish lands. Under great secrecy, the Portuguese king sent forth an expedition under Diego Garcia, the captain, and Rodrigo de Cerca, the pilot, to claim for themselves, the land that Solis had founded. With one large ship and two small ones, Garcia sailed from La Coruna on August 15, 1526. Sebastian Cabot, then in Spain as chief pilot, learned about the Garcia operation and decided upon an expedition of his own. He talked to several rich merchants seeking the way of Magellan's straits for the wealth of the Moluccos for Spain. They all came to an agreement and Charles V thought it was a good idea. the emperor granted a subsidy towards the equipping of the fleet. Cabot was detained by rivals, but in time, sailed forth with four vessels and six hundred men.

Because his provisions were short, Cabot was forced to drop in on the Guaranis and Tupis Indians for a supply of food, which they readily granted. He carried off four sons of the powerful chiefs and marooned three gentlemen of quality upon a desert island to die. Probably, because of lack of food, he gave up the idea of going through the straits and sailed instead into the River Plate and anchored upstream off the island of St. Gabriel, in Uruguay. There he recovered three sailors who were captured earlier and who were now half-Indian, and useful as interpreters. Cabot directed the construction of a small fort. Next, he sent Captain Juan Alvarez Ramon to explore the Uruguay River. When Ramon ran his ship ashore, he marched his men along the shore, pulling a boat with others of his crew. The Charruas Indians destroyed most of the men under him in an ambush. A few of the land party swam to the boat, making it back to the fort.

Cabot sent one Captain Cesar to find a road across the Andes to Peru with a detachment of three men. He was to join the conquerors of Peru at the end of a hard trip filled with dangers and one that took time. Meanwhile, a second fort, Santi Espiritu, had been built. Cabot explored the river system and reached the Guaranis in the interior. Once this was done, the Spaniards directed by Cabot, returned to Spain with a prize of silver obtained from the Guaranis.

Meanwhile, the Portuguese were busy in South America. They had sent Alejo Garcia with four companions to search for the mines. There was no gold or silver in Brazil and they entered Paraguay, and gained the company of two thousand Graranii to join him to find the mines in Peru. Upon reaching the Andes, the Portuguese found a large amount of silver, but along the way on returning, the Indians massacred all but a small boy. The Portuguese also sent some sixty men. Many were drowned because of their heavy armor when the Indians opened holes in their canoes in which the explorers were being ferried. The remainder were defeated in battle, and all except for a handful died.

Francisco Montejo was the first Spaniard to attempt to subdue all of Yucatan. He had had many experiences in the New World and had followed Pedrarias Davila in Darien, Grijalva in Yucatan, and Cortex in Mexico. He was in charge of gold shipments to the king and later the messages to Charles V from Cortex. Both times he was in Spain. During the second stay in his home country, he lingered and married a rich widow. When his old friend, Alonso de Auila came back to Spain to tell of his adventures and wealth, Montejo decided to return to America. His wife sold her jewels to finance his proposed expedition and Charles V made him governor of Yucatan with ten square leagues of land for him and his descendants in return for which he was to conquer and colonize Yucatan and the island of Cozumel.

In 1527, Montejo and his expedition and lieutenant Alonso de Avila set forth in three ships from Spain. He paid his sailors, but the soldiers were to share in the cost of the encounter with supposedly rich Mayan Indians. They were well received at the island of Cozumel and went over to Yucatan where they were also greeted and helped to build a camp. Because of insects breeding in the nearby swamp and in back of the settlement, the Spaniards were infected, and soon fever ravaged them, until they moved from this Salamanca town to a better locale. They got better there and Montejo put on a display of one of his best horses with a covering of bells. When he led it through the province, the natives were terrified. Some fled and some fainted, so frightened by the horse, and the noise of so many bells.

The expedition moved into the interior where they met more friendly natives. Further on was the city of Chuca with its storehouses and large numbers of merchants. The natives fled that night, but came back to fight the Spaniards. Montejo was mounted and frightened the Indians with his horse until his men could arm themselves and use their horses, guns, and great swords. Their guns looked like they controlled killing, thunder, and lightening. The Indians fled once again, but made peace soon afterwards. Other Indians were routed at a battle and then came forth to submit. Once again, the Spaniards reached the coast. By this time, mostly lost to fever, the Spaniards had lost so many that there were only seventy-two left of the 382 men who had landed, and so ships returned to Spanish territory. Montejo, with too few soldiers to conquer the land, returned to Columel Island, and left Yucatan behind uncolonized.

Reaching Seville early in the summer of 1528, Pizarro met Bachelor Enciso, who played a role in the colonization of Tierra Firme and had a claim against Francisco Pizarro, for which Pizarro was put in prison. The court learned of this and had him released to appear at court. The emperor was at Toledo briefly and listened and touched the gold and llama wool brought by Pizarro. He was commended to the Council of the Indies by the emperor. The empress helped Pizarro and there was made up the contract in Peru. Grants and titles were made and the expedition was financed, chiefly with promises, but Pizarro had an okay to conquer Peru and was ready to go back for the gold of that country.

Friar Juan de Zumarraga was appointed the first bishop of Mexico by the crown. He left Spain in August of 1528 and reached Mexico in early December, on the sixth. The son of a Vazayan landowner, Zumarraga received a higher education and joined the Franciscan order to enter a monastery at Abrojo. A guardian there, Juan was pegged to serve as provencial of a new province. When Charles V visited Abrojo during the holy week of 1527, the emperor met Zumarraga. Impressed, Charles commissioned him later to investigate witchcraft in Pamkpiona and then, to be bishop in Mexico.

This new bishop found a particular interest in his duties to protect the Indians from exploitation and of course came into conflict with the Spaniards in the New World, because they were there for the purpose of exploiting these natives, to get rich quick and return to prominence and glory in Spain. The soldiers in America thought of the gold of the new conquests and the labor of the Indians that would enable them to live well. Most officials in the New World looked to get rich serving the allied or bribe paying Spanish classes of rule and profit. Other officials were derelict what was thought of as their duty as seen by Ferdinand and then Charles in the theory. The kings were unable to deal with the parochial aspects of the problem. When their able officials ran into trouble with the exploiters, the monarchs had the claims of their corrupt and oppressive men to go through, but they met difficulties in finding the truth, even when that was their desire.

Because he believed that the Indian was a rational human being, capable of salvation and that he was empowered to inform himself of the social and economic conditions of the Indians and determine maltreatments, Zumarraga acted to protect these oppressed natives. He made known his jurisdiction and invited appeal to him. When the natives responded in large numbers, the officials of the audiencia of Mexico reacted strongly. They met and forbade him to interfere and let it be known that any Indians who appealed, risked confiscation and hanging. When faced by this stand, Zumarraga denounced the oidores or judges of the audencial or provencial court in a sermon from the pulpit.

Stung, the audiencia tried to destroy the bishop. They fabricated false charges and dragged a Franciscan father named Ortiz from his pulpit for preaching against them. Zumarraga reacted by excommunicating the judges. The president of the audiencia, Nuno de Guzman, censored what the bishop was writing to Spain, while the judges were denouncing him to the Council of the Indies. Trusted sailors carried the bishop's messages in secret to officials there. One person threatened Zumarraga's life, and another made a sword pass to kill or frighten the prelate. In a strong move, the bishop placed Mexico City under interdict. He granted absolution to the judges when they asked for it. The controversy wore him down, and so the relinquished his position as protector, because the conflict interfered with his spiritual government of souls.

Zumarraga did however continue to investigate and recommend what was good for the Indians. With of course an interest in the native's religious well-being, he was also interested in their education and economic affairs. He wanted to transport flax and stimulate a linen industry among the indigenous people of Mexico. He brought various seeds from Spain to experiment with in Mexican soil and climate. Silkworms, mulberry trees, and Moriscoes were imported to establish another industry in the colony. The bishop was to found some schools, edit and publish books for Indian religious instruction, work for a university, and found hospitals for the conquerors and conquered alike.

Cortez lost power in New Spain, since it was rumored that he wanted to seize power in Mexico, and went back to Spain to plead his own case. He was only partly successful. The emperor did not return him as governor, but reinstated him as captain-general. In addition, the crown named him Marques del Valle de Oaxaca with its 23,000 natives to work in his plantations. He was promised the governorship of any new islands or coasts not already known or granted specifically to others. This was a great incentive for Hernando Cortez and he resumed plans to explore along the Pacific coast when he arrived back in New Spain in 1530. Under his orders, Diego Hurtado de Mendoza in 1532 discovered the Tres Marias Islands off the coast of the Sinaoa River southward to the Rio Fuerte. A 1533 expedition under Juan de Grijalva and Fortun Jimenez discovered some more islands and the peninsula of Lower California, believed quite locally to be an island in 1533.

Chapter XV

PERU

In a small village five miles from Mexico City, there lived a lowly Indian named Juan Diego, taking care of an aged uncle in a hut with its thatched roof. Because they were members of the Aztec servant class, they were among the poorest people in their village. Their huts had little beyond the dirt floor. Juan Diego was a widower, but had no children. He, his wife, and his uncle were early converts to Christianity among the Aztecs. Two years after the event the wife had died. Now in 1531, he was fifty years old, well advanced in age for the times.

Leaving his village before daylight on the Saturday of the ninth of December in order to get to the village of Tlatilolco in time for Mass at the church of Santiago, Juan Diego passed around the base of Tepeyac. There had been a shrine to the Aztec mother goddess nearby and this was appropriate for the unfolding of the story where church and pagan ties intertwine in legend and fact as they had in past times also. The Indians often combined church and pagan. Christianity had grown more rapidly throughout history by establishing churches on heathen sites and this was again the case, but not the exact site as was usual in such events. A Mexican church was built here as a result of the events experienced by the old Indian and his vision.

Juan Diego later told that at the foot of Tepeyac, he heard birds sing and looked up to see a bright light on the summit. Then the bird song ceased and he heard a voice calling his name. In reply, he quickly climbed the hill to find a young woman in her teens standing in the middle of a golden mist. She asked where he, "the most humble" of her sons was going. To hear Mass, he said. She was the Holy Mary and wanted a temple set up there. Juan responded when Mary told him to tell the bishop in Mexico City by promptly going to the bishop's palace. He was to be kept waiting for house before he was able to see Juan de Zumarraga, who listened with sympathy, but no urgency as the interpreter translated what Juan Diego was saying in Nahuatl. The Indian was to come back sometime, Zumarraga said.

Realizing that he was not believed, Juan Diego went by way of the hill and again saw the vision. He preferred, he said, that someone more important be sent, but Mary commanded him to go once again. After additional difficulty, the Indian saw the bishop once again. Zumarraga questioned him more closely and was impressed with the detailed account, but he was fearful that if it was a hoax and the Spanish built the church, the revelation would lose ground already gained with the natives. The bishop would gladly build another church; that was no problem. Zumarraga asked for proof, and the proof was to be forthcoming.

Under the instructions of the vision, the Aztec found roses blooming in the December air and put them in his tilma, a loose cape made of two pieces of cactus cloth. She arranged them and told him that this was the proof the bishop needed. The Indian was to show them to the bishop only to gain his support to the erection of the temple. When the bishop's servants saw the out of season roses peak form the cloth, they told Zumarraga; the Indian was received. When he untied the tilma, the roses fell to the floor and an image of Mary appeared on the rough cloth. The bishop and all there fell to their knees and soon the Shrine of Our Lady of Guadalupe was built. The image has survived as bright as ever on cloth which should have disintegrated s long after the event provides proof of its authenticity to scholars and scientists in our modern age.

The first noted Hawkins at sea was William Hawkins of Plymouth, one of the principal sea captains in the west of England, who set out in 1530 on a voyage to Brazil. He sailed his ship of 250 tons burden, named the Pole of Plymouth on the first of three voyages. First, he touched at Rio Cestos on the Grain Coast of African Guinea, where he traded with the African blacks and took commodities with him. He and his men went westward to Brazil where he entered into a friendship with the natives.

Returning on his second voyage, he brought back one of the kings of the Brazilian coast to England, leaving behind Martin Cockeram of Plymouth as hostage. Hawkins gained recognition by presenting the Indian king to Henry VIII and his court. His strange appearance including holes in his face with extruding bones and gems caught the interest of Englishmen. After almost one year, Hawkins returned. The king had died on the way, but the natives, trusting in the Hawkins good treatment, believed him and allowed Martin to return to England in the English ship. Thus in trade and fame, the Hawkins voyages were a success.

There were more voyages to Brazil for Brazil-wood, some of them sent out by Hawkins, for Hawkins wrote about the continuation of trade with Guinea and Brazil. He expressed his hope of expanding his trade. English custom records record a regular export of that wood to the Mediterranean, where Italians used its dye to make superfine cloth in Florence and other cities of the Peninsula. One of the exporters was Nicholas Thorne of Bristol. His ship was partly owned by the minister in Henry's government, Thomas Cromwell. Southampton merchants followed William Hawkins' lead. John Pudey even built a fort on the Brazilian coast in 1542 near Bahia. Frenchmen operated out of Normandy's seaports to send ships to Brazil for its famed wood. The king of Florence briefly forbade the trade in 1538, but changed his mind despite pressure from Portuguese envoys.

In early January of 1531, Pizarro gathered his men together and sailed forth for Peru. When they reached the Bay of St. Matthew, the commander and Almagro disembarked their men and marched down the coastline. They crossed a swollen river and reached a village in the province of Coaque, whose villager fled in terror. There, Pizarro and his men discovered and plundered foodstuffs, gold, silver, and emeralds. After a fifth of the valuables was taken out for the crown, the rest was divided among the officers and pirates of the expedition. Gold and the rest of the plunder, when viewed by the gold hungry men of Panama, provided the reinforcements for the Pizarro expedition. Soon, Pizarro was joined by officials selected in Spain for the voyage and ore troops under an officer named Belalcazar, who was to distinguish himself in the land of the Incas.

Pizarro continued his march to the shores of the Gulf of Guayaquil and encamped on the island of Puna prior to the descent on the Indian city. There he was to wait until violent rains had finished. Learning of the plots of the chief of the island, he surrounded them with his soldiers. He sent these prisoners to the men of Tumbez, who immediately massacred them before Pizarro's eyes. The mistake enraged the people of Puna, and they grabbed up their arms upon the Spanish cantonment, where they were badly defeated. However, they did not accept defeat and Pizarro was rescued only by the reinforcement of a hundred volunteers under Hernando de Soto, who late rediscovered the Mississippi River.

At this time, the conqueror learned of a civil war among the Incas and crossed over to the mainland. There was a hostility between two brothers who were Incas, each of them ruled one half of the empire belonging to their father. Inca Atahualpa defeated his brother's army and laid waste to the rebellious district of Canaris with the same ferocity of the Spaniards, allowing no male capable of bearing arms to escape his wrath. His enemies were so fearful, that they opened up their cities to him. The opposing Inca Huascar met him in battle outside of Cuzco, on the plains of Quipaypan. Superior discipline and military practice won the battle for Atahualpa, who destroyed the enemy, captured Huascar, and took the capital of his part of the empire.

Pizarro crossed over near the port of Tumbez, mostly in European ships, but the Indians captured a number of balsa boats with baggage and the military stores. Three men were seized off the boats and killed in the woods. Another balsa boat was under Indian fire when Pizarro came to the rescue on horseback with other horsemen and scared off the Indians. When the Spanish entered Tumbez, they found it deserted, and almost entirely demolished. The eager Spanish were gloomy over the sad fate of two Spaniards Pizarro had left behind for treatment because of illness the last time he was in Tumbez.

Early in May of 1532, Pizarro set out for the conquest, maintaining a rigid discipline during the march. Most of the natives did not resist and those who did were pushed aside. Pizarro proclaimed that he came in the name of the pope in Rome and the sovereign of Spain, requiring the Indians to obey them. The conqueror founded a settlement in the fertile valley of Tangarola and ordered his men at Tumbez to come there immediately in their vessels. Using timber from the forest and stone from a nearby quarry, they built a church, a magazine or warehouse for public stores, a hall of justice, and a fortress. Pizarro organized a municipal government with regidors and alcaldes. Encomendos or plantations were established with serfs from the native population. He picked a very unhealthy site and the city had to be abandoned. It kept the name of San Miguel.

On September 24 1532, Pizarro and his men marched from San Miguel, leaving people to care for the Spanish rear, enjoining the settlers to treat the Indian vassals humanely and maintain a good relationship with the surrounding tribes. He headed in the direction of the camp of the Inca. Hernando de Soto followed orders and went to the camp, and after a week, returned with an envoy from the Inca himself. While the envoy was there, Pizarro entertained the Peruvian royally. The envoy was told that Pizarro would aid the Inca in his fight with his enemies.

The Spaniards moved into the sierras, often on narrow ledges, where it was possible, with one misstep, to fall hundreds or thousands of feet. After a march, they reached the crest of the Cordillera. When word reached them of the approach of the Inca, Pizarro sent messengers to the rear to hurry his men, so that they would not be short when the Inca arrived. Soon the Spaniards were in the city of Calamalca and Pizarro had his interview with Atahualpa. There was to be another since the Inca could not fear the small numbers of the Spaniards, minuscule in a large and prosperous empire with its large army and population.

When he came, he was greeted by Fra Vicente de Valverde, a Dominican friar, with his Catholic version of the Deity, the mysterious doctrine of the Trinity. He told of the creation, the fall of mankind, and their redemption by Jesus Christ. Speaking of the power of his monarch and that of the pope, who had commissioned the Spanish to bring under his sway, the Peruvian monarch, Atahualpa and his kingdom. The Peruvian emperor asked his authority to give away lands that were not his and he would not change his faith, nor would he give up the empire. The scandalized friar told Pizarro that the Inca could not be talked to. Now was the time. "Set on, advance; I absolve you."

When Pizarro gave the signal as planned, a gun was fired and the war cry roared forth from Spanish throats. The Spanish set upon the Peruvians and massacred the Indians with artillery, muskets, and charges by the cavalry. Trying to flee, the Inca people were crushed in terror. There was no way to escape in their fear, the exits being blocked, but Pizarro preserved the Inca from complete death, receiving a cut on his hand. He was the only Spanish injury in the encounter. The Inca was a captive of the Spanish now and his supply of gold and silver plate was Spanish. It was the emperor who suggested a ransom of gold filling a big room as far in height as the Inca could reach. Vast amounts of gold were brought in, but he was not released. The Inca ordered his brother Huascan to prevent him from being used by the Spaniards. Atahualpa was executed by the Spaniards soon afterwards.

In Columbia at this time, Governor Garcia de Lerma of Santa Martha was an active governor. He devoted his time to building, sending raids forth, and dispatching explorers. Houses were built, a church was constructed, and a masonry house was erected for his abode. His raiders went into the mountains seeking provisions and gold. The Magdalens was explored by the Portuguese Melo and others. Despite humane orders for the treatment of natives from Spain, the Spaniards in America committed outrages upon their enslaved Indians.

Meanwhile with a concession for settlement, Pedro de Heredia returned to the Colombian coast with a force and a large load of supplies. He had ample numbers of implements, tools, and arms and full amounts of ammunition, clothing, and provisions. On January 14, 1533, they landed and founded Cartagena, making peace with the inhabitants of the land and sending out parties to search for gold in the interior. Heredia found gold in large amounts, including a large golden figure found in a temple. The plunder was worth one and one half-mission ducats. One year after his arrival, Heredia and his brother, Alonso, set out on Pedro's second expedition and discovered a numerous and prosperous people in the Cauca Valley. Once back in Carthagena, his men accused the Heredia brothers of hiding gold form them, and they were thrown into prison. Once sent to Spain, they were exonerated, and returned to Cartagena to resume their services to the crown.

Pedro Sancho, secretary to Pizarro, wrote a report to the emperor in order to counter reports of the conqueror's enemies complaining of the actions which he took in Peru. First, Hernando Pizarro had sent the royal fifth to Charles V of one hundred thousand pesos of gold and five thousand marks of silver. A peso is about one ounce; most substantial for the time. Meanwhile more gold was coming in small pieces, and later, over five hundred plates of gold torn from house walls in Cuzco. One-foot stool of gold weighed eighteen thousand pesos. There was an entire fountain made of gold, worked with great skill. All of this came to one million, three hundred and twenty thousand pesos. the fifth to be sent to Charles amounted to two hundred and seventy thousand pesos, which was the total amount. Of silver there was one hundred and seventy thousand pesos and fifty-five thousand marks. Also, there was more to meet the expenses of the campaign against the Turks in Europe. The remaining rich haul was divided among the participants of the conquest; making many men very rich.

Pizarro was releasing tired soldiers to go back to Spain after their great service. He hoped that they would give good account of this wealthy conquest so that Spaniards would come to settle Peru and advance the Spanish cause in Peru. The land was large and the Spaniards were few who came with Pizarro and more people were needed for holding the land.

Once the golden treasure was melted down, Pizarro had the notary with him to draw up a document freeing and absolving Atahualpa from the promise to ransom himself. He made this decision known publicly. However, Pizarro would keep the ruler prisoner to prevent him leading an uprising against the Spaniards from among such great numbers of people who would follow his command. His general, Calicuchima, was also held in detention. Writing to the king, Sancho noted the kind treatment granted to the Inca and his poor faith, and wished to destroy the Spaniards. He claimed kindness that was a lie, which ignored the conquest by the Spanish. He put as much blame as possible upon the "proud tyrant," the Inca, who would kill the Spanish if he could. Of course the conquest was the cause of the trouble, but Sancho worked to put Pizarro in a good light, claiming that the despoiling of the Inca was for "just causes."

Atahualpa allegedly gave orders that Indian troops should come from Quito to attack the Spaniards at Caxamalca from five directions. The Indians found thirty or more Spaniards on the way from San Miguel where they loaded a ship with gold and decided to kill them before the Spaniards reached Casamalca. Meanwhile, some natives voluntarily confessed the plot to the Spanish. Pizarro acted by tying Atahualpa to a stake and had the churchmen teach him the Christian religion there in the city's plaza. They had told the Inca "that God wished him to die of the sins which he had committed in the world, and that he must repent of these and that God would pardon him, and he did so, and was baptized at once." Because he received the Spanish religion, he was strangled to death instead of being burnt at the stake. They interred his body in the church. In his place, Pizarro installed a puppet Inca or emperor.

Having executed Atahualpa, Pizarro installed one of the Inca's brothers and set out from Cassmarca to Cuzco with the design of becoming master of Peru's chief city. Almagro went with him. Hostile Indians along the way were routed. The depressed puppet, watching the failure of his people to stop the Spaniards, died two months later. Pizarro regretted this death as he had not the other, because he no longer had a figurehead to give some legitimacy to his rule of the domain of the Inca people. Another death followed. General Chilicuchima was suspected of communications with his people and was burned at the stake on the orders of Pizarro.

The Spaniards were in high spirits and Pizarro sent De Soto to restore bridges. The Inca defeated De Soto but reinforcements arrived and the surprised Inca fled. They had thought they had defeated De Soto and were free of the Spanish threat and here were more soldiers! Before the Cuzco, they might have been defeated because of the desire for resistance of the people there, but a brother of Huascar, named Manco Inca, in command there came out to meet Pizarro as his friend, and there was slight resistance. The Spaniards entered Cuzco on November 15, 1533, one year after they had entered Cassamarca.

There was enough treasure left in Cuzco to provided four thousand pesos for each soldier in Pizarro's army. They found ten or twelve golden statues of female figures, as large as life forms, and seemingly from a distance, to be alive. There was building to be done also. The conqueror had the idols pulled down, crosses erected on the highways and a church built. In the presence of a notary, and witnesses, Pizarro took possession of the land in proper form and in the name of Carlos the First, the invincible King of Castile and Leon. Charles was the first king of that name in Spain, but the fifth Roman Emperor of that name.

Meanwhile, Sousa, an experienced Portuguese sea captain who explored the coast of southern Brazin in 1531, founded the pioneering small settlement on the island of Sao Vicente in 1533. He had limited exposure to the New World. Martin Afonso de Sousa returned to Portugal in 1533 to receive Sao Vicente as a hereditary captaincy (1534), but he never returned. Instead, he went to Portuguese India to serve the Portuguese crown and when back to Lisbon. Sousa served on the Council of State. Overseers administered the captaincy very well and introduced sugar cane and a sugar mill financed by Erasmus Schetz, the Flemish capitalist by 1540. The Portuguese colonized Brazil in the decades ahead.

Words of the richness of Peru reached Pedro de Alvarado, who had fought under Cortez, and he gathered five hundred men at arms and descended upon the northern coast of Peru. In his turn, Pizarro learned of Alvarado and hastened to send Almagro to conquer, or win over, this new invader before he conquered what was left to take, or what Pizarro believed belonged to him. The danger lessened when Alvarado undertook to go to Quito to conquer from that coast. His force had hardships upon their pathway until they were so plagued by cold and hunger that they became so weak that they could not carry the gold and emeralds they had earlier been given by the Indians. Almagro reached Alvarado and while there was some desertions on both sides, the main field was one of words.

Negotiations were undertaken and terms were agreed upon. Almagro pledged to give Alvarado one hundred thousand pesos if he would turn over his armament and leave Peru. They all marched toward Cuzco when Pizarro paid the amount and the negotiations were put into effect. The men who had come under Alvarado took the other side of Almagro when dissension later plagued the Spaniards in Peru. Alvarado left Peru at this time. Pizarro then gave Almagro powers to rule at Cuzco and seek conquest to the south.

At this time in Spain, Fernando Pizarro reached Seville, and went to negotiate with the court. As a result of these talks, Francisco Pizarro was made the Marquisate of Aravillos, Fernando Pizarro obtained the habit of Santiago, Vicente de Valverde became the bishop of Cuzco and Almagro received a governorship in the south where Pizarro's ended, in return for this, he gave the emperor hope that a large donation was possible to enable Charles to commence his expedition against Barbary.

Almagro learned of his honors and was much affected by the news. He prepared to march into Chile in the area of his emperor granted land as governor. A popular man, he was joined by large numbers who in hope of great gain and gave up what they had already to follow him. The Inca then gave him the services of his brother, Paullo and of the high priest, Villaoma. While Pizarro was building his new town, Lima, Almagro was under way to Chile and Juan Pizarro was in command in Cuzco.

Chapter XVI

ST. LAWRENCE

Meanwhile, Jacques Cartier, a native of St. Malo, which was Brittany's principal port, had been on many fishing voyages and proposed in 1533 a voyage to the American coast to continue Verazano's work. Writing a letter to Philippe de Chabot, Sieur de Brion, France's high admiral, Cartier gained through him, the interest and support of the French king. The French king, Francis I provided the explorer with two vessels of sixty tons each. On April 20, 1534, Jacques set sail with 122 men equally divided. Encountering good weather along the way, they reached Banauista Cape of Newfoundland on the tenth of May. Because of the ice along the shore, they could not land but had to sail to Catalina, then called St. Katherine Haven, where they mended and dressed their boats.

Next, the French captain and his men explored the vicinity. Unaware of a southern entrance to the Gulf of St. Lawrence, Cartier directed the ships northward to Funk Island, where there were multitudes of birds. They killed enough birds to fill two small boats, probably the great auk, and supplied the entire expedition with fresh birds and salted away five or six barrels of the species. There were other birds in the profusion also. While there, the explorer's killed a polar bear that had swam to the island to eat birds. Continuing their searches, the French found straits, capes, islands, and rivers aplenty. They fished for salmon and discovered natives who fished and hunted seals in boats constructed of the bark of birch trees.

Down the northwestern shore of Newfoundland, they found and described a land of hills, dark mists, and fogs. There, they discovered schools of cod and soon reached St. John's island. There were other islands alive with birds, walruses, bears, wolves, and fields of berries, damask roses and parsley. In addition, there were forests of cedars, ewe trees, pines, white elms ashes, willows and trees of which they knew not the names. At one point, the French were chased by Indians in seven boats, but were frightened off by French weapons. This was repeated with other natives, but soon opportunities presented themselves for Cartier and his men to trade with them. After more exploration, they returned to St. Malo.

Cartier had been preceded to Canada by the Florentine, Giovanni Verazzano, who ten years before 1534 was sent by France's Francis I to explore the North American Atlantic coast. No record is left about the success of that voyage. In 1535, he arrived off the coast of Florida and sailed northward or twenty degrees. Verazzano took possession for the king.

Four years after Cabot returned to Spain from Paraguay, the rich Pedro de Mendoza fitted out an expedition with his own money for Rio de la Plata. Mendoza was a member of the royal household and a gentleman who had served the emperor in his Italian wars. Since he was financing the expedition and was associated with Charles V, Mendoza easily gained the support of Charles, who appointed him governor with the title of Adelantado. He was granted the right to rob the Indians of items of value, to retain and divide the wealth, after the king's fifth was deducted.

Mendoza was to take some missionaries with him. Unfortunately, Mendoza had no Christian forbearance himself. He had an able lieutenant by the name of Juan de Osorio who was as popular with the expedition's men as Mendoza was unpopular. Mendoza was jealous and when the fleet was at Rio de Janeiro, he ordered Osorio to be arrested. The lieutenant requested an audience with Mendoza to clear himself, but the governor was angry at their meeting and made a brutal remark which led his chief constable to consider it to be an order to slay Osorio. Chief Constable Juan de Ayolas, immediately drew his knife and murdered the lieutenant. Mendoza was more unpopular than ever now.

In the month of January of 1535, the Mendoza expedition sailed into the mouth of the Rio de la Plata and chose a most poor harbor for his chief city called Buenos Aires. There he considered, which were supposed to last twelve months. However, they were rapidly depleted, and Mendoza had to put his men on short rations. The game and fresh fish given by the Querandi Indians were insufficient. When Mendoza tried intimidation and try to compel them to provide more, the Indians reacted by cutting off their supply altogether. He sent his brother Diego de Mendoza out to chastise these Indians, but the Spanish were lured into a morass where they were ambushed and lost more than half of their force including Diego. Next the Spanish killed an estimated more than a thousand natives. Mendoza by this means had cut off the supply of food from friendly Indians who were now alert to them.

The vessels could not find anything along the coast and Ayolas disapproved of this failure. They ate anything they could. Soon the Indians set fire to the Spanish settlement and the small vessels in the Riachuelo. Fortunately, at this point, Ayolas returned with a supply of friendly natives whom Cabot had made friends with years before. These were the Timbu Indians.

Seeing the success of his chief constable and hearing he had left one hundred of his men in the Timbu country in a fort called Corpus Christi, Mendoza decided to move there. Next, he sent Ayolas to map out a trail to rich Peru. He waited one year, but when Ayolas did not return, he traveled north after him and established La Asuncion, which was to become the capital of Paraguay. The Spaniards continued to anger the Indians in the manner of Mendoza and the Indians turned upon them, until Domingo Martiniz de Irala made friends of them in Paraguay.

The failure of the audiencia in governing the Spanish possessions, let Charles V to set up a viceregal government in the Indies. It was a natural choice because viceroys had proven to be an effective way to rule in Spanish possessions and provinces in Europe. Spanish kings had ruled through viceroys in Sardinia, Sicily, Naples, Aragon, and Valencia, and Venetian and Portuguese rulers had used viceroys to govern in the Orient. In a country where orders came form above, it was a logical move to have authority in one man, especially in a land where conquistadors and their soldiers were difficult to govern, and could be controlled best by a strong man with prestige and a fitting representative of the emperor. The decision to create viceregal governments served the purpose of the crown well into the next three centuries. First to be viceroy in New Spain, Antonio de Mendoza was a fourth choice of the monarch, and had to be persuaded to take the post of 1528.

The Mendoza family of Spain was one of the most distinguished families in the country with genealogical claims going back to medieval Roman patricians and the Visigoth dukes of Cantabria. Kindred in the family had over seventy titles of nobility. Few people rank so high in the haughty Castilian aristocracy of western Spain. Among the specific claims of Mendoza were descents from the Cid and the lords of Biscay, but even more illustrious were ancestors who were Spanish king during the Christian reconquest of Spain. Long lines of ancestors fought in the battles against the Moors in the long centuries of wars and raids which returned the kingdom of Iberia taken by the Moors in the early eighteenth century. The original seat of the main line was one of the Basque provinces in northernmost Spain.

Spanish viceroy of Mexico, Antonio de Mendoza arose to a high level in the family tradition and in his position of government became the most famous of Mendozas. The viceroy's great grandfather was Inigo Lopez de Mendoza, a marques and second son of Diego Huntado de Mendoza, who had been grand admiral of Spain and the wealthiest nobleman of his time. Inigo was born in 1398 and was to be known internally and in the rest of Europe as a poet, statesman, warrior, and scholar, but still young he had to fight to preserve for himself the estates of his recently dead father and older brother. He earned the respect of robbing neighbors, the Court of Juan II of Castile, and the Moors in his various encounters and tournaments.

His third son was known as an honored general, ambassador, and scholar. This able man had one son who became a bishop, patriarch, archbishop, and cardinal in the Roman Catholic Church. Another, was Antonio's father Inigo Lopez de Mendoza, the eldest and inheritor of family estates. In 1486, he aided Pope Innocent VIII against King Ferdinand of Naples and played a major role in the war against Granada. Antonio was to inherit the governing ability of Inigo, whose handling of men and events and whose sympathy for people helped keep the peace, until a harsh Cardinal Xihenez intruded to force conversions among Jews and Moors there. Mendoza had to end the rebellion with promises of reform and hostages as a pledge of good faith.

Antonio de Mendoza was born in 1490 or 1491, and received a knightly education. Then he successfully led troops on the battlefield. Later, he defeated the Comuneros around Huesar and served as diplomat. He carried letters of credit to King Ferdinand of Hungary for the emperor. Despite the dangers of being waylaid, Antonio made it safely and quickly. Once in Hungary, he served as imperial ambassador and returned to Madrid in 1528. During the next few years, he served the queen and stated in 1529, he would be willing to govern New Spain in reply to an offer of the queen. A number of years passed until Charles V appointed him viceroy on April 17, 1535. Months later, he sailed for Mexico, which he reached in October of that year.

Meanwhile impressed by what he had seen in North America, Cartier enthused others with the importance of his voyage. He immediately wrote up a report to the king which inspired the French monarch. The report told of the falling of land to the southwest and the open waters to the west. It was immediately wondered where these waters led. Hopefully, there was a northwest-passage and the French may be on the verge of its discovery. On the last day of October, the king gave Cartier a new commission and three vessels. Some of the younger nobility were to go along on the French explorer's second voyage.

On May 16, 1535, Bishop Bohier held a service in St. Malo for the explorer and his sailors and three days later a gale of wind swept them out of the port and on the following day into storms and tempests. Separated, the three ships found their own way to Newfoundland.

Cartier continued with his explorations. Sailing into the gulf to the west, he named the body of water, the Saint Lawrence Gulf. Shortly, they saw a great number of whales. They also saw a number of capes, and then, walruses. Next, they met some tribes of natives. The reaction of many were to flee at first approach, while some ware aggressive and closed the big ship, until scared off by the guns they had never seen before. The ships were to be home in St. Malo on the sixth of July 1536.

Named governor of Santa Marta, Pedro Fernandez de Luco asked Gonzalo Jimenez de Quesada to be chief magistrate. His legal experience would be needed, but Lugo could not know that it was to be the military arts that would make Quesada famous for the ages. They all sailed from Santa Criez de Tenerife in 1535, and reached Santa Marta without event. There they saw the city that was destined to be wretched, a town of mud hovels thatch with reeds. Living in tents, they were plagued by dysentery. Since they were unaccustomed to tropical climates, fevers played great havoc among them. In an attempt to resolve the problem of scarce provisions, he forced some of the inhabitants to go into the surrounding countryside to plant, but these settlers were immediately attacked by Indians and had to return with loss of life. Civil troubles plagued Lugo. The sailors cried out for their pay and the colonists Lugo brought with him suffered because of terrible housing. Settlers in the Americas had great difficulties, especially in farming as opposed to plantations with many slaves.

Meanwhile, Pizarro kept his agreement with Pedro de Ovarado and the follower of Cortez visited the conqueror of Peru on the coast before Alvarado deported. However, Alvarado's uncle and brother, in keeping with their right to go or stay as they pleased attached themselves to Almagro. Several other captains who had distinguished themselves also sought their fortunes in Peru. At this point in time, while on the coast, Pizarro had founded what he called the City of the Kings, later known as Lima, and a seaport for Lima called El Calleo. Then on June 12, 1535, Pizarro and Almagro made solemn and inviolate friendship pledges by which they were to divide all future profits in conquering South America. With this warm agreement between them, Almagro began his march into Chile.

Francisco's brother, Hernando Pizarro returned from Spain on his mission for the conquerors as a knight of Santiago, with grants of kingdoms for Francisco Pizarro and for Almagro. The conqueror's province was the northern one to extend about six hundred miles where Almagro's province was to commence. Auzco was well within the Pizarro kingdom, but no one knew that for sure at the time, and this was to cause trouble. Pizarro decided nothing should be done until the arbitrator should fix the division. Meanwhile, however, the place was besieged by the Incas under Manco.

A besieged Governor Pizarro at Lima quickly sent to Santo Domingo and to Mexico for reinforcements and aid. These arrived very shortly, and the Indians were forced to withdraw from before Lima, the capital. Still cut off from Cuzco, Pizarro, concerned about his brothers and their men, sent Alonso de Alvarado for their relief and prepared an army to follow up this force.

While the Pizarro were fighting for their very lives, Juan de Herreda went to Almagro's camp with the news of the grants to the two governors. From where they were situated, the captains under Almagro considered Bolivia and Chile to be poor countries and Cuzco to be the most important city they could obtain. They took their opportunities and declared Cuzco to be Almagro's. Some also laid claim to Lima for him also. Almagro was swept along with this captain and turned his back upon the territories he was to conquering, and set out to obtain his prize from an exhausted army under Gonzalo and Hernando Pizarro, barely safe from the Incas.

However, the Spaniards under Almagro hoped to embark the Inca Indians under Manco Inca against the Pizarro before the Incas were pacified, leaving it to civil war to determine who should control the riches of Peru. Diego de Almagro left Captain Juan de Saavedra in Urcos with 250 Spanish troops, while he continued to the valley of Yucay. There it was agreed by letters, Manco Inca would come to him peacefully. The adelantado reached an Indian town called Calica. Its inhabitants, an Inca garrison, was led by a young Inca of the lineage of Han-Cizco, who was only kept from destroying them or making such an attempt by orders from Manco.

This became known to Pizarro at Cuzco that Almagro was going to Yucay to make an offensive treaty with the Incas against Pizarro. The Spaniards at Cuzco decided to seek out the Spanish at Urcos. They marched forth and avoided the lagoons and morasses, coming into conflict with the Indians along the way. The Indians, eager for the fray by which some of the invaders could be killed by an Indo-Spanish force, tried to set the two Spanish forces under Hernando Pizarro and Saavedra against each other. Learning of the approach of Hernando, Saavedra prepared his force to meet the Pizarro faction. He would command the cavalry and put Cristobal Ponce de Leon in charge of the infantry.

The marching Pizarros still could not believe that Almagro was plotting against them with Manco, however that was what the Indians, who believed that the ascendancy of the Spaniards in Peru was ending, were shouting at them. When the Indians began shooting their slings at the Pizarro army, the latter marched and caused many deaths among the Indians, watched by two scouts from Saavedra. Seeing this, Hernando was now convinced about what they had heard. Almagro had arranged some treachery for sure.

Word reached Hernando Pizarro in Peru that Callao was in revolt and that Villaoma had reached from Almagro's expedition where he commanded Indian troops. The Inca and Villaoma had plotted and on April 18, 1536, the two men left Cuzco for the great mountains of the district of Ares. Once there, they raised the flag of rebellion. Hernando Pizarro was informed of the revolt and made attempts to seize the person of the Inca, but he was well protected. Still in skirmishes in the region Peruvians lost their lives. However, they were reinforced by numerous numbers of their own people. The fighting was fierce, but when the Spanish reached the more mountainous area, the Peruvians began to prevail. In one battle, the Spanish were greatly defeated and had to withdraw from Cuzco. Pizarro regained the nearby fortress, but he soon had to abandon it and the siege of the city was undertaken.

The Indians set fire to the houses between the fortress and city. A great wind came up and the fire spread to the city with its straw or rush roofs. War cries abounded and the Indian attacked. Amid the fire and smoke, the Spaniard held their own quarters of the city in what soon became hand to hand battle. The battle continued for six days and the Indians with their large numbers prevailed so ably that the Spaniards were forced back to the great square, but it was retaken by Pizarro's men. Fifty horsemen led by Juan Pizarro left the city to attack the fortress outside. In the effort, he lost his life and the Spaniards had to withdraw. The Inca sent fresh troops to the fray, but they did not arrive in time from preventing the Pizarro brothers from gaining the fortress.

Villaoma had already fled and the Spaniards put the Indians in the fortress to the number of fifteen hundred to the sword. By this success, Cuzco was relieved from a siege that almost succeeded. In a mopping up operation, the Indians in each camp hit with all the Spaniards had and were defeated with a great loss of Peruvian lives. Meanwhile, the Indians near Cuzco stopped to make their sacrificial ceremonies and Pizarro had occasion to get a supply of maize into the city. Subsequent siege of operations failed, although a force attempting a rescue at Cuzco resulted in a massacre of some two hundred Spaniards by Indian forces.

Francisco Pizarro having lost contact with Cuzco and knowing the straits they must be in, was concerned also about Lima's safety. He needed more troops for both Cuzco and Lima and so he summoned back Alonso de Alvarado, sent to conquer another province, and wrote to Panama, Nicaragua, Guatemala, New Spain, Hispaniola. He even called for the aid of Alvarado of Guatemala, promising him Peru if the came to their aid. While theses appeals were underway, the Inca army began to invest Lima with fifty thousand Indian. Under Teyyupanqui, the Peruvian force advanced over the level ground and the Spanish had the advantage and killed their general and principal leaders. With this loss, the Indian lost their spirits and fled.

Now came a danger to both the Indians and Pizarro, when Almagro returned from Chile, with its lack of rewards, to Cuzco, which he claimed as his own. In his ambitions, Almagro over-reached himself. Under the guise of a truce, he entered Cuzco and over powered the Pizarros who were there. Alvarado found out what the situation was and notified Francisco Pizarro. At this point, Almagro attacked Alvarado. The latter was outnumbered and outfought and fell prisoner to the governor of Cuzco. Almagro sent Orgonez to attack the Inca. This was successful and the Inca was almost seized, losing a golden ornament to Almagro who give it to the Inca in his pocket, Paullo.

Negotiations were undertaken between Francisco Pizarro and Diego Almagro, but these were fruitless, so Almagro who also claimed Lima, marched upon Pizarro at Lima. While he was marching, Pizarro gathered together and form other parts of the Spanish empire and soon had one thousand men at arms. When Almagro learned this, he decided to avoid an attack upon Lima. He provided defenses in the valley of Chincha instead and listened to Pizarro suggest arbitration by the Provencial, Bobadilla, who decided in Pizarro's favor, and who gained a treaty leaving possession of Cuzco to the king's decision. All was not peaceful, because Hernando Pizarro forced the Almaristas to flee from the pass they occupied.

Next, Hernando Pizarro marched upon Cuzco most carefully because of a fear of attack and the crossing of swollen rivers. Almagro sent his men out of the city to encounter Hernando. The Almaristas were commanded by Rodrigo Orgonez. They met for battle near the salt pits near and between a mountain and a river. Orgonez disposition was most skillful. The fire of Hernando's arquebuses was very fatal and Gonzalo Pizarro' charge was the turning point with great loss of life to Almagro's infantry. Orgonez was killed and his army fled. Hernando Pizarro entered Cuzco after the battle of Salines of April 6, 1538. This was not the end of the matter because the defeated and impoverished Spaniards rallied around Almagro's son. At an opportune time they murdered Francisco Pizarro. Diego de Almagro was made governor, but Vaca de Castro, the judge, arrived and defeated Almagro in battle and assumed the government.

Meanwhile, Gonzalo Pizarro was appointed governor of Quito and explored the eastern slopes of the Andes in search of El Dorado. Returning to Quito in 1542, he later rebelled against the first Peruvian victory. In 1546, Gonzalo Pizarro and Blasco Nunez Vela, the viceroy, fought a battle in which the viceroy was killed. In 1548, the army of Pedro de la Gasca, sent by the king, defeated Pizarro in battle, whereupon the unfortunate Gonzalo

Pizarro was fined, condemned and executed as a traitor for his rebellion against the royal authority.

With the help of experienced officers, Pedro Fernando de Ligo led an expedition in Columbia toward Bonda, but it failed on the rock of native resistance. Reaching a mountain in the interior, Lugo found the Indians in a strong position up the side of the mountain. The Spaniards attacked anyway, and carried it, but with heavy losses. The Indians retreated to another strong position further up, which Lugo would not change with assault. This might have been fatal. He led his men into the native village but found nothing there.

Returning to Santa Martha, with his wounded, Lugo left behind his son Luis de Lugo to march along the coast and Captain Suarez to take a force parallel to Luis. When the captain met desperate resistance, he had to join Luis on the safer course. Together, they stormed a native stronghold and gained much gold but Luis absconded with the loot and was imprisoned in Spain. He did not stay long in prison. He was released because of his boldness and connections. His Adelantado father was awashed with the dishonor brought upon the family by Luis and the financial straits for which the gold was to be secured.

Chapter XVII

ALMAGRO

On April 6, 1536, Gonzalo Jimenez de Quesada commanded an expedition of eight hundred men with five large boats to ascend the Magdalena in Columbia with two hundred soldier and sailor of the total number. Quesada was chosen by Pedro Fernandiz de Lugo over lesser men. It was a good choice. The leader was born to inspire men and had great amounts of fortitude, resources, endurance, resolution and was an accomplished writer and lawyer. He and his men had a difficult march. Not only were the mountains hard to travel though, but there were no Indians to provide provisions until they reached a valley where Indians were harvesting their maize or corn. One hundred men were lost by the time the Spaniards were able to rest at Tamalameque. Meanwhile, the boats ran into trouble. One was wrecked at the river's mouth. Crews deserted two others. Other boats had to be sent, and they had to go through a gauntlet of natives in their canoes with their poisoned arrows. They joined Quesada in time for the most difficult part of the journey.

Continuing up river, Quesada directed his men along the riverbank. They cut through the dense jungle, through which no other man had probably traveled. The Indians always stuck to the river, but for a month, the Spaniards did not see any Indians. They suffered through heavy rains and from the dangers of mosquitoes, ants, hornets, snake, and wild animals like jaguars and alligators. Losses were heavy reaching one hundred once more. The captains wanted to retreat, but their leader told them that, that would be more fatal than an advance. They said nothing further and the Spaniards marched into the mountains where they suffered from the cold. From the heights they saw the kingdom of Chibcha in a vast cultivated plain which Quesada called "the valley of palaces." After the cold rains and subsisting on raw maize, the new sight was joyous.

At peace externally and internally, the people of Chibcha were enjoying a hard-earned prosperity. But they were alarmed when they saw the strange men coming down from the mountains and terrified by the horses, such arrivals they had never seen before. Because of their arms and animals, the Indians at the edge of the mountains propitiated the Spanish with provisions. But from a distance, their ruler Thisquezuzza knew no fear and noticed the small number of invaders. Militarily experienced, he had six hundred of his best warriors. Quesada was headed for the saltmine of Nemocon when the Indian force attacked his benefit of surprise the Chibchas were doing well but they themselves were surprised, in the rear and flank by the attack of the Spanish cavalry. The Spaniards overthrew the sacred memory of the Chibcha and caused havoc. This quezuza fled in the panic of his men. Shortly, he headed for a secret retreat. As Quesada advanced, he could find no gold. The cold tablelands ended one exploration past the Chibchas and the fierceness of warriors on ridge ended another.

In the period of 1536-1543, which we have entered, Zumarraga managed the Mexican Inquisition and oversaw the charging, questioning, torturing, confession and punishment of those who worshipped idols and demons. Heretics, relapsed Jews, blasphemers, and witches were treated in the same way. Many of those were Indians. The number charged were few considering the newness of the religion to the natives and the lack of instruction given them. The first denunciation was against, and truthfully so, two Indians in the encomienda village of Tanacopan.

Tacatetl and Tamxtetl served as native priests of the Indian religion engaged in pagan ceremonies. Confessed, the two men were exhibited through the streets, flogged, shorn, saw the various idols burnt, and were incarcerated in jail and remanded next to the monastery for awhile. Three Indians were tried and punished for sorcery. In 1538, three more Indians were found idolaters of note and made an example of, but they were soon reconciled to the church. A native witch was lashed to warn the other Indians away from that sin. Other idolaters were tried, but the natives would not reveal the hiding place of the idols.

An important problem of the Mexican Inquisition was that of the native dogmatizers. These Indians preached against what the missionary friars were teaching, and for a return to paganism by their people. One Marcos Hernandez Altaucatl kept concubines and would not get rid of them, but he denied criticizing Franciscan teachings and morals. Faced with torture, Marcos confessed and he and Francisco, another Indian, were banished. Cacique of Texcoco, Don Carlos, grandson of the great Netzahualcoyotl, had great prestige with the natives of that city. They listened to the ridiculed friars who prayed for relief of drought and plague. The Spaniards found caches of idols in one of his houses and learned he had criticized the morals and hearing of the confessions by the priests, who were the ones who wanted to hear them and not God. Carlos denied all, but he was condemned and strangled to death. His body was burned.

The Spaniards feared Lutheranism although it was never more than very minor in Spain and existed in the New World mostly through a small number of the European foreigners who came to Hispanic America. Of Slavic background, the Moravian jeweler Andres Aleman had traveled widely in Europe and came to Spain or Mexico. Aleman carried with him books in foreign languages in itself a suspected act and had made statements which were Lutheran in orientation. Not only was he deemed a Lutheran, but it was claimed that his ideas were linked with Erasmus. Aleman was interrogated and confessed of the sins of proselytizing Lutheran doctrine. He contended that excommunication was offensive to God, holding anti-image views, believing that priests should marry and criticizing the moneys accumulated by the church. He criticized the moneys accumulated by the church and contended that papal bulls, indulgences, and pardons were valueless. Also he doubted the truth and authority of the pope and favored an interpretation of the scripture versus reliance upon tradition. If he confessed rightly, he was indeed a Lutheran. Alaman was punished and went to Spain.

There were four other tried on charges of Lutheranism. Juan Nizard showed disrespect and refused to go to Mass. Maestro Pedro of Seville in the last years of his life, over seventy, thought it would be better to have married priests, and opposed the priests that kept concubines. The authorities also tried Alonso Delgado. Another foreigner, Juan Banberniguen denied the existence of purgatory. Francisco de Sayendro was tried for Erasmism in 1539. Other Lutheran and Erasman trials by Zumarraga were minor.

The Catholic Monarch had put emigration restrictions on the Jews and converts, but it failed in time because the Jews and converts had money to invest in colonial trade and could bribe their way to the New World under changed names. By 1536, there was a sizable Jewish community in Mexico. Earlier steps had been taken and two Jews had been burned at the stake. A third escaped death, because he had friends in high places. Zumarraga and his Inquisition continued the persecutions. Gonzalo Gomez was indicted on thirteen counts of heresy for insulting behavior towards Catholic symbols and ceremonies, as he had renounced God. He received mild punishment. Mexico City saloon-keeper Francisco Millan was accused and confessed implicating others to get off the hook himself. This lead to an investigation, but Zumarraga was unable to effect any result, and the Jewish community in New Spain grew. A later effort also failed.

There were other crimes such as blasphemy, sorcery, and superstition dealt with by the Mexican Inquisition. The cursing of God brought many Spaniards in Mexico to trial, with minor punishments and penance. Because of man's natural failing and the absence of sufficient numbers of Spanish wives and girlfriends bigamy, concubinage, and prostitution were inevitable. Questionable clerics were also tried by the Inquisition, called the Holy Office. Among sorcery suspects were many women.

At this time Alonso de Fuenmayor was president of the audiencia at Hispaniola. He learned of Pizarro's distress at Lima and Alonzo named his brother Diego to be captain of a force to go to the rescue from Santo Domingo. Diego de Fuenmayor led the more than 250 Spaniards from the island and reached Lima, where he raised the siege. He then went with Governor Pizarro to march by the coast road and go into the mountains to pacify the Indians. There were more than four hundred on this march. A confrontation of the Pizarros and Almagro was in the offering.

The two scouts sent by Saavedra fled before the force of Hernando Pizarro. His associate Hernando Ponce remarked to his fellows that no sight had ever been seen that their Christian friends should run away from them. They must found out the secret of this event before returning to the city. Hernando sent two men forth and these brought into camp the two scouts.

Saavedra's two men told of the happenings in Chile, the goodwill of Diego de Almagro, and that he maintained that Cuzco was within the limits of his jurisdiction. The Indians saw this and went to complain to Saavedra, who marched his force to tell Hernando Pizarro that he must stop fighting the Indians in what he claimed was his jurisdiction. Short of the arrival at Pizarro's camp, Saavedra sent forth two envoys. The men from Cuzco were astounded at what the envoys had to say. Next Almagro and Pizarro meet briefly. Hernando decided not to act first, but allow Almagro to break the lords of oaths to Francisco Pizarro. The Inca Manco was concerned about the friendship of the Christian faction towards each other and determined to destroy Almagro as well as the Pizarros. Manco sent fifteen thousand Indians to attack Almagro, but he forded the river in full strength in face of Indian hostilities.

Adelantado Almagro sent orders to Saavedra to march to Los Salinas where he would join him. He was to keep an outlook for Hernando Pizarro on his march. Almagro demanded of Cuzco to receive him as governor and would march towards Los Salinas with Cuzco on his right hand until he had surrounded the city of Cuzco. Once at the meeting place, Almagro and Juan de Saavedra marched together in unity. The Municipality of Cuzco could not agree whether to accept Almagro's claims and evaded the demands of Almagro. They decided to arrange a truce, but Almagro, with greed in his eye, would not agree to a truce and was determined to force an entry, if nothing else, with his superior force. However, when Almagro was told of his friends in the city, and the possibilities of them gaining the support of others, he decided upon a truce.

Pedro de Cieza de Leon wrote at this point in his chronicle that the great sin of the Spanish in Peru was the reason for God's punishment in misfortune and misery. They cared only for the wealth of the countryside, forgetting their hungry families back in Spain.

The city was subverted by those who felt they would gain more out of Almagro than they would out of the Pizarro. It was estimated that one half of Hernando Pizarro's 200 men were in favor of Almagro and the latter had 450 Spaniards. General Rodrigo de Orgonez, on the false rumor that Pizarro had broken down the bridges, and marched to the city. The Pizarros were undone and the Almagroistas were able to take Hernando Pizarro after a brief fight in which they set fire to his house. Francisco's brothers were now captives.

Pedro de Cardova was vicar of a band of monks in Hispaniola when they decided that the encomiendo or plantation was both a fraud against their monarch's will and destructive against the Indians. As we have seen, Antonio de Montesinos and then Las Casas undertook the abolishment of the encomiendo. The Indian must be segregated and kept away from the lay Spaniard altogether. This was the beginning of the idea of the mission. The first mission was a tract of land granted by King Ferdinand on the continent near Cumana, but unfortunately it was raided by pearl fishers who carried away the chief. Since the Indians blamed it on all the whites, they killed two of the friars. This idea had failed through no fault of the churchmen.

Relying no more upon the usual secular treatment of the Indians, Las Casas decided that the encomienda would not work and that Cordova's mission idea was the right way to proceed. He came out of retirement and wrote a thesis in Latin that persuasion converted best. On May 2, 1537, he entered into a contract with Alonzo Maldonado, lieutenant to Governor Pedro de Alvarado of Guatemala, that the wildest of Indians could be converted to Christianity and pacified and converted by persuasion. They picked a severe test of the idea. In Guatemala, in the province of Tuzulatlan were a fierce people whose land because of its warring nature of the Indians was a place of terror and war. Between 1537 and 1539, Las Casas sent Fra Luis Cancer who was very successful in pacifying and Christianizing the natives that he was soon known widely as the Lord of True Peace. There were no lay whites allowed except the governor and no plantations were to be created in the territory.

Meanwhile, in central Colombia, the Conqueror Quesada found the Chibchan emerald mine at Samondaco, but it could not be worked at the time. Because there was a scarcity of water, the earth could be washed only during the rains. Next, the Spaniards reached the lost Chilocha village to the east. There they could see the Amazonian forest stretching into the horizon. The territory to the west of the village belonged to the ruler of Tunja. This old man was conciliatory but would not reveal the locations of treasure. Greedy to an extreme, the Spaniards pillaged a very notable wealth and they were still insatiable and wished to take the Temple of Suano with its god, but the aged priest left in charge burnt the structure around him before the eyes of the invaders.

In October of 1537, the next chief led a well-disciplined army against the Spaniards. Tutama had heard of the sacrilege at Suaro. At the battle of Bonad, he fought long and well. Quesada fell with his horse, but was rescued. Tutama retreated his army into the morasses in good order and safety. Quesada also led his army from the battlefield and prepared a defense against further attack. Thirsting for more gold, the soldiers influenced Quesada to go across the mountains toward Neyva, but their guides escaped.

The Spaniards in Chilocha tortured two boys in the cruelest way they could. One, a brave Indian, died without uttering a word, but the other was finally forced to talk in the same process. He told them were his ruler could be found. Thus, the Spaniards of the sixteenth century show, as so often before, their criminality, and once again, stained Spanish honor forever. In a surprise attack, Quesada mortally wounded Thisquezuzza, but was badly defeated. Resistance continued, and Quesada had to retreat once again. With the help of Sagipa, the leader of the resistance gained Quesada's assistance against the Panchas. After the Spanish victory, the friends of Spain tortured Sagipa to death, but he said nothing.

Thus the invaders did not find out where the gold, if there was any to be found, which was the reason for the torture. On August 6, 1538, Quesada founded Santa Fe de Bogota and named his land New Granada. The Indians were no longer a prosperous and happy people but slaves under a crushing tyranny. Spanish cruelty continued in the godless lust for gold. Massacres and tortures were common.

Concerned about the Indians in the New World, Pope Paul III promulgated the bull Sublimis Deus that read that God loved the human race so much that he created them so that they might enjoy the good of life and the doctrine of the faith. Since the Indians are truly men they could become Catholics and desired to do just that. They were not to be deprived of their property or liberty even when outside the faith. They should not be enslaved. Any violation of this is null and to no effect. Furthermore these Indians should be corrected through preaching an example. Las Casas used this bull in working for the benefit of the Indians in the New World.

Las Casas also used the ideology of St. John Chrysostom who had declared that the men consider what we do and not what we say. Words will do harm when not backed up by action. During the time of the Spanish in America, there was much law and philosophizing about the fate of the Indians, but very little good treatment. Las Casas could preach to no avail, and get laws passed that would be ignored in action, thus leaving the so called Black Legend, a truer statement of what was happening than the laws from the court and bulls from the Vatican. Those that ignored the laws were in Hispanic America and away from Spain and its king. Las Casas could write of the peaceful virtues, but his life was devoted to an attack upon those who maltreated the Indians, and a fierce measure to change them. He succeeded in making enemies of some with a true antagonism and bringing opinion to those who cared for the Indians and supported his cause. He was not an objective historian, but was subjective in his history. His goal was to write for the benefit of the Indians in America, but he wrote with facts.

Back in Peru at this time of Las Casas' effort, Captain Alonzo de Alvarado was nearing Cuzco when he learned of the capture of the Pizarro brothers. Almagro sent negotiators to Alvarado, but they were imprisoned when they had their say. Alvarado sent to Francisco Pizarro news of what happened at Cuzco. Meanwhile, Almagro learned of the capture of Hernando and his brother, and went into consultation with his advisers. Rodrigo Orgonez wanted Almagro to execute Hernando Pizarro and march to take Alvarado. He believed they had friends in Alvarado's camp. Others agreed, but Almagro wanted to secure the government without any great damage along the way, and in fear of the emperor in Europe. Orgonez feared what Hernando Pizarro would do, should he be freed at any point. The Almagroistas acted at last, and defeated Alvarado in a confused night battle and captured the captain. With the lines of brother and friends at risk, Francisco Pizarro opened negotiations with Almagro.

With things at an impasse, Governor Francisco returned his army to Lima, where he and they were welcomed. He prepared his army, awaited reinforcement, and declared war upon Almagro. While there, Pizarro was joined by the able Captain Pedro de Vergara. Almagro recognized that Francisco Pizarro was in a position to gather more and that this meant Almagro must take Lima. He claimed that the city as his part of the territory which was to be delimited by an arbitrary of the emperor, but he never recognized that he should have awaited the arbitration before taking the lands before him. As it turned out, neither Cuzco nor Lima belonged to him. Neither side was disposed to await the adjudication from Spain.

Meanwhile, Almagro was interested in destroying the Indian force under the Inca Manco. The Spaniard ordered Orgonez to take two hundred Spaniards from Cuzco and subdue the Indians. Many were eager to go with him thinking that they could capture much gold in the process. The Indians were preparing to be attacked, moving into rugged territory, with plenty of defenses to be built after worshipping their idols and offering sacrifices. Rodrigo de Orgonez soon marched his soldiers toward the Inca stronghold. They found the way difficult for horses to trod and lost many over the precipices. The Indians could not withstand the crossbowmen at the first fort. The Indians fled and the captive Ruy Diaz walked out of his prison to tell of his maltreatment by the Incas. Manco fled and escaped the pursuing Spaniards, with a woman to whom he was greatly attached, but most of his men were captured. The Adelantado called Orgonze back to Cuzco.

The Captains Alonzo de Alvarado and Gonzalo Pizarro escaped from prison after Almagro had left Cuzco in the middle of September 1537 to ship the king's gold to him. In the ensuing weeks there were more negotiation between Pizarro and Almagro. The city of Lima was loyal to Pizarro, not wanting their share of the Indian laborers to go to he followers of Almagro. Negotiators would settle the legal facts of the case, but neither wished to relinquish their property as they claimed it to be. A truce was settled upon, signed on October 10, 1537. Soon the provincial, Fray Francisco de Bobadilla was appointed to be the judge in the dispute. His efforts required little time and once the observations were taken as to latitude, it was declared that Pizarro owned Cuzco and Lima, and Almagro had acted wrongfully. He declared that both armies be disbanded and the conquest against the Incas be brought to fruitation. Almagro had to back down and he released Hernando Pizarro from prison.

Before peace was to come, there was a big battle between Almagroistas and Pizarro's men. The Indians gathered to watch the battle from the ridges and hills, hopefully that each of the Spanish forces would kill the other faction, and would die themselves, until there would be no Spaniards left. Hernando Pizarro ordered an advance after Mass was celebrated. The two lines advanced upon each other. Many of the men under Almagro fled and threw his forces into confusion and Pizarro was master of the field. Orgonez had to surrender and his head was cut off right away. Almagro fled to Cuzco. The battle took part on April 6, 1538. Shortly, Hernando Pizarro sentenced Almagro to death, and had his head severed.

Chapter XVIII

DE SOTO

The explorer of the coast from Florida to the Mississippi, Hernando De Soto came to America from Spain, and by his courage and good qualities in soldiering, he became a cavalry captain and took part in the conquest of Peru. After a distinguished part there, he returned to Spain with a fortune, some of which the emperor himself borrowed. After living in luxury and marrying the daughter of a count, De Soto entered the second great adventure of his life. Charles V made De Soto governor of Cuba and adelantado of Florida. Before he left for the Americas, he met Cabeza de Vaca who had just arrived at court to tell his story of adventures in North America. This man had been shipwrecked and had a stay with various Indian tribes in what was to be Texas and a journey on foot across to the Pacific. The suffering he and his fellows went through was told in his account. Cabeza de Vaca responded to questions from De Soto and told him Florida was the richest country anywhere. At first the two men decided Cebeza de Vaca would go along, but they disagreed upon terms.

During April of 1538, De Soto made final arrangements and delivered his ships to his captain, commanding a fast new ship himself. One of the ships was given over to the Portuguese who were going on the expedition. Across the Atlantic to Cuba, the adventurers left Havana on May 18, 1539. They saw land seven days later. Landing on the 30th, they soon had a skirmish with six Indians, who had resisted. Next, the Europeans entered an Indian town six miles away and destroyed the Indian dwellings and their temple. They prepared housing for themselves and made ready for a night attack. On orders from De Soto, the soldiers leveled the ground within the distance of a crossbow shot. When the trees were downed, there was room for the horses to run and should the Indians approach, they could be killed by bows. The governor set the sentinels out.

Once he was ready for any necessary defense, De Soto sent out large patrols. Battasar de Gallegos led one to capture Indians. He had with him forty horsemen and eighty footmen. Captain Juan Rodriquez Lobill went into another direction with fifty infantrymen. Most had swords and bucklers and others carried crossbows and guns. After Lobillo's men passed through the swamps, they saw some Indian huts near a river. The Indians fled, plunging into the water. The men grabbed four women. Twenty braves attacked against the odds and fought so hard against the superior weapons of the invaders of the whitemen that the invaders had to retreat. Their quickness kept the Spaniards from drawing a bead on them, but the Indian's arrows were accurate and rapid, killing one of the Spaniards. The four women were taken back to camp.

The governor sent a force to a province called Paraoxi to search out the nature of the country and order ships to go to Cuba for supplies. Baltasar de Gallegos found the lord of Paracoxi. He and his men were interested in the gold they greedily expected. When the Indians told them that it was in the next province, a familiar ploy of the Indians, the Spaniards were overjoyed. Pressing forth into the land, they made a bridge of a tree across a river of powerful currents. They had to use a hawser to draw the animals across. With limited provisions, they found no precious metals. Further on, the country was wet with great woods and many ponds. They lived on watercresses and cabbage and were told of fields of maize that they soon found. It was now August of 1539, and they were in what was to be Polk County Florida.

Across the Caribbean, the Oidor Vadillo in Cartagena had a record of bad conduct in office and when he learned that a judge of residencia, or the usual examination of official conduct at the end of a service, was to judge him, he was stricken with a fear of the approaching justice. In that year of 1538, Vadillo used his manifold talents to undertake a great expedition which would make him rich and result in official reward in the place of the threatened loss of position and power, and as probability of punishment. With him, went Heredia's lieutenant Francisco Cesar and the nineteen year old Pedro de Cieza de Leon who recorded the events which are related here.

Cesar served as guide on the expedition from San Sebastian de Uraba into the Abibe Mountains covered with thick forests. The only pathway they could find were streambeds, which were tortuous and subject to mountain torrents. Cesaar was careful because he had once before tangled with tribes and barely gained a victory against Nutibara's people. Now as the invaders entered the Indians fertile land this time, they met with a hostile reception and were defeated by the natives fortified in a fortress, which was so high, that Spanish horsemen could not get near. Only a valiant defense led by Cesar at a narrow place on the retreat prevented the Indians from destroying Vadillo's expedition totally.

Skirting the homes of these Indians to avoid further battle, Vadillo continued his march. When they reached Nori they found another Indian defense, but the chief Nabuco then gave them some gold to get rid of them. Passing through dense forests to this province, they defeated the Buritica chief in his high fortress and burned the chief to death when he would tell them where the source of the gold could be found. A weary and sick Spanish force found rest in the next rich valley.

The natives who lived there fled to the mountains and the Spanish had a feast with native food supplies. Harassed on their further march, the aggressors had a great loss when Cesar died. The soldiers attempted a mutiny because Vadillo would not return. They forced matters and did arrive at Cali and safety. Their fugitive leader was returned to Spain and died in poverty in the midst of a lawsuit for his life.

Having put the affairs of Plata in good order, Governor Francisco Pizarro marched to found the city of Arequipa when he received news that the Inca Manco wanted to make peace. This was not true, but he did not know that and turned around to go to Cuzco to secure the Inca. Meanwhile, Gonzalo Pizarro was on the heels of Manco. Francisco's brother occupied a rocky eminence and destroyed two bridges and it seemed the Inca would fall into Gonzalo's hands. It was then that Manco sent the messengers of peace to Francisco to catch the Spanish off guard. Francisco did send Gonzalo to Quito in the north. The brothers took some followers by the royal road, determined to move into the land of cinnamon where there were supposed to be great riches.

Francisco then went to the valley of Yucay and sent messengers to Manco proposing peace talks. The Inca killed two men. Marquis Pizarro was angry and put the Inca's principal wife to death. While this was going on the Spanish under Garci Diaz Arias founded Pizarro's city of Arequipa. Francisco made a provisional distribution and returned to Lima.

Pizarro had sent General Lorenzo de Aldana, a just and human man, to be governor of Quito, Popayan, and Cali to replace Belalcazar who was gone to Spain. Aldana was a moderate man and charged his subordinate rulers at Timarrra and Popayan to protect the Indians from robbery and to punish those who robbed the Indians of possessions of land and other things. Looking at the large number of Spaniards who were in Cali, Aldana decided to colonize a place in the provinces of Anzerma with them on the river of Santa Marta. He wisely chose Jorge Robledo to found and govern the city. Robledo left on July 8, 1539. Next, Aldana made a division of Indian labor and lands subject to his city of Cali. Founding another town, Aldana sent to Quito to remain until the arrival of Gonzalo Pizarro.

Marching forward, Robledo passed through the village of Pescado on the banks of the Santa Marta after crossing with his baggage on a raft and in a very large canoe. One hundred Spaniards were with him. The Indians fled at their approach and hid themselves and their supplies. Robledo sent his swiftest men forth and they captured more than 200 natives. He freed the Indians with instructions to bring their chiefs for conference. This worked and peace was established. Robledo founded the town of Anzerma and was joined by an expedition from Cartogena. Under Robledo's direction, Indians were brought into the settlement, but Chief Ocuzca was held under guard. He escaped at night. All the rest of the chiefs submitted after the cruel Spaniards cut off hands and noses of certain Indians. At one point, the Spaniards seized more than 12,000 pesos in gold. For awhile, after this, the Indians threatened the new settlers of Anzerma, but an Indian girl told Pedro de Cieza de Leon of the plot and the Spanish were forewarned. There was no attack.

Jorge Robledo ordered the spoils to be returned and established a shaky peace with the natives. He next ordered Gomez Hernandez to explore a rich province to the north with fifty soldiers through rugged territory. They could not take horses with them because of the nature of the terrain and made their way through dense jungles to a place of undulating country. Unfortunately the cords of several crossbows were broken which put the Spaniards at a certain disadvantage during a battle. The masses of the Indians increased in the fight until the Spanish soldiers had to retreat. Most of them were wounded and they returned to Anzerma.

Ruy Vandgas forced the Indians of Pirso to come to peace terms, Robledo left him in command with a little over one hundred soldiers. Robledo explored the river of Santa Marta. Over awed by reports of the invaders, the Indians received them with provisions of pesos and gold. The Indians told them of a plain beyond the Andes called Arbi, where the Indians were hostile to each other. Robledo crossed the mountains and made peace with the various tribes. Robledo crossed the mountains and made peace with the various tribes. He used the old strategy of divide and conquer to take these regions. He did not always succeed, because he was subject to one, which he won, being wounded in the fight.

In revenge for this wounding of their captain, the Spanish resolved to kill all of these natives of Pozo. The Spaniards sent in their dogs to tear the Indians of Pozo to pieces. Those that escaped were killed by the Indian allies. Three hundred Pozo Indians lost their lives. The Indians of the region were so frightened that they gave their gold and surrendered themselves and their souls to the Spaniards.

Because of some lost pigs and a claim that they were stolen by the Pozo, Robledo became angry and once again forgot his humane policy. Three thousand Paucaranos joined a force of fifty men under Melchor Suer de Nava, the ensign, and they returned to kill, rob, and burn. Suer de Nava took some pigs and returned to his leader. The Paucuranos took with them bodily parts of the two hundred Pozos they murdered for their cannibal repass. Robledo later fought the rich people of Arma for their gold, but whose devils allegedly told them to fight the invading Spaniards despite the strength of the Europeans. The next group of Indians put up a strong front, but soon fled. Indians came in peace. Further on, a tribe was put to flight. By this time, the Indians of Arma hated the Spaniards so much, that they combined in a league against them, and stopped providing provisions for them, but the Spaniards left for greener pastures before the war could be undertaken.

While Robledo was exploring and conquering from the south, Spaniards coming from Santa Marta were exploring the province of Bogota. Word of the great gold and emerald finds of New Granada reached the provinces of Ecuador. Merchant Pero Lopez del Infierno, Captain Osorio, and others left Popayan for New Granada, trusting in the general peace of safety on the roads. Unfortunately, the Indians were intent upon rebellion. They decided that they would attack Infierno's band and Pedro de Onasco, another traveler separately. Anasco was warned by a friendly chief, but he would not listen to advice and merely went on the alert instead of heading for safer jungle. The Indians attacked before dawn and destroyed the Anasco group. Six miles away, Infierno and Osorio were also destroyed and eaten. "Anasco died a terrible and long death, having been taken alive and eaten, part by part. Juan de Ampudia sought revenge with a force of sixty Spaniards. He met the natives with horses, crossbows and dogs, and defeated them in one battle.

The next battle was harder and finally the Spaniards had to flee back to Popayan, with limited losses, but exhausted and completely defeated. Juan de Ampudia was one of those dead. Pascaul de Andogoya came into the provinces with papers proving himself to be their new governor, while Robledo explored the province of Quinbaya and founded the city of Cartago. When he learned of the Andogoya's presence, Lobledo left Cartago and went to Cali to report to the new governor. Andogoya married him to a relation of his wife to secure his allegiance.

Pizarro and his men were doing well, but the followers of the dead Almagro were in great difficulty. His son, Diego Almagro Jr. was forced from house to house. His men went from Indian village to Indian village, seeking food for their hunger and clothing for their misery. Ten or twelve of the former Almagro captains had to share one cloak among them. The marquis was warned that the Almagroistas would kill him, but he took no precautions.

Gonzalo Pizarro reached Quito, where he was received as governor. He was able to gather a large number of young bloods together because of reports of El Dorado in the Cinnamon Valley whose people wore clothes of gold and whose land contained no mountains or jungles. This was true fancy, but the Spaniards did not know this. They were so eager for great wealth that they would believe stories such as this. Everyone wanted to take part in the expedition of Gonzalo's and within a few days he got together 200 Spaniards. He sent Antonio de Rivera ahead with the vanguard.

Francisco de Orellana reached Quito with thirty men and when he learned of what was done, he followed the expedition to take part in the great riches many had foretold that Gonzalo Pizarro would find. First, all had to cross a range of mountains; during this transit over a hundred Indian men and women were frozen to death. The Spanish too suffered much from the cold, but none of them died. They next went through rugged countries full of rivers and well peopled jungles. They opened a road with axes and wood knives and reached a country of stores of provisions, ninety miles form Quito. Orellara caught up with Pizarro and was welcomed and made Pizarro's lieutenant-general.

The rested Gonzalo Pizarro band went on ahead under Gonzalo, while Orellara rested a bit before following. Because of the rough terrain, Pizarro could not take horses. Pizarro headed directly eastward with local Indians to guide him. The Indians responded negatively about the land they sought. When they were not given information, which they decried, that the rich land of cinnamon was just ahead, the cruel Gonzalo began torturing the poor natives. Some were burnt, while others were thrown to the remorseless dogs. The next Indian tribe they met, knowing what had happened, told the Spaniards lies of great and rich civilizations further on. A delighted Gonzalo Pizarro built a bridge across the river and crossed on, defeating Indians on the other side with firepower. Orellara came when called and the entire force was joined.

Francisco de Orellara was sent downstream on a tributary of the Amazon River to explore, but he and his men went forward on the Amazon, leaving Pizarro and his men behind. He went down to the ocean, returned to Spain, and took an expedition to the great river where he and his followers died miserably. Pizarro and his men also had a very hard time of it. Their lives were saved when they reached a yucca plantation. Further on, they were soaked with many rains and were also covered with sores, hungry, naked, and barefooted. Soon the Spaniards had eaten many of the dogs and horses.

Meanwhile, Hernando De Soto was leading his men through Florida, crossing rivers and eating maize. They learned that Panfil de Narvaez had been there. The news was old because Narvaez had been head since 1528 and the survivors of his expedition, after wandering for years had returned to Spain, notably, Cebeza de Vaca. De Soto knew this. They went through some villages and assaulted the Indians at one point. Indian deaths were high.

That night, the soldiers guarded one of the lakes because they could not guard both. The Gentleman of Elvas was to write that the Indians, in attacking to escape in the dark, would swim noiselessly to the shore under cover of water lilies, but the observant Spanish would watch carefully. If they saw a ripple in the water, they would dash into the water on horseback and force the natives to retire once again.

Both sides spent the night anxious and waiting with no rest. Juan Ortiz, the man who had been found among the Indians, called one that since escape was impossible, they should surrender. Twelve of their principal men preferred to die, but the Indians of Paracoxi swim into the water and pulled them out by their hair. One captive made an attempt to strangle De Soto and others began fighting the Spaniards. The rebels were subdued.

The Spaniards set out into the country and enslaved the Indians. They put collars about the neck and forced them to carry baggage and grind corn. Spanish soldiers would take the slaves into the woods or fields to cut wood, or pick maize, and from time to time, the Indians would kill the Spanish, although they still had their chains on. Others would use a splinter of stone and file at night on their chains to free them. Once the women and youth were taken from the country in which the natives lived, they became passive and did not seek to escape. They did their work and quickly learned the Spanish language.

De Soto led his men towards Apalache. The Indians fled from them. Crossing a forest river, they were endangered by the Indians who plotted to destroy the white intruders to prevent a passage, but the crossbowmen came up and dispersed the Indians. Later on they found a native village which the Indians had set fires to prevent it from falling into the hands of the invaders. They found a well-inhabited country down the way. De Soto met with the Indian lord of the province, and the Indians supplied maize, pumpkins, beans, and dried plums and told them that the sea was twenty-four leagues away. At the coast they found a large felled tree, stake, mangers, and skulls of horses which proved to them that Narvaez had been there. Ten days later arrived at their port and sent two caravels to Cuba.

Building a piragua, thirty men went to await the arrival of the brigantines and fought with the natives who traveled in the estuary in canoes. On Saturday the 29th of November, the Indians took advantage of a high wind and set fire to the Spanish town. The fire consumed part of the town. Almost one month passed and Juan de Anasco arrived. De Soto sent a captain of infantry named Francisco Maldonado to search for an entrance and others to punish bold Indians who came close in attempts to kill Spaniards.

On March 3, 1540, on a Wednesday, Governor De Soto left Apalache in western Florida on another trip. He had heard of Yupaha and provisioned his men with maize for a march of about one hundred and eighty miles of barren lands on foot and on horseback. Four days on the journey, they arrived at a deep river that was the Flint River. They built a piragua that had to be protected by a cable of chains across the water. On one occasion, the Indians killed one soldier and wounded three others.

Pressing forward through barren lands, they went from Capachiui to Toalli. At this last place, the housing of the Indians had improved. Dwellings had been covered with dry grass, but now they were roofed with cone construction like tiles such as were in Spain. The houses had clay sides built like tapia or mud walls, and in addition, there was a winter house that was heated, to the extent, that the Indians did not need clothes during winter nights.

Soon, De Soto was to meet an Indian chieftain who sent him along the way to another land. There, the Indians were very numerous and friendly, giving provisions liberally. The Spaniard explored further into Florida, fording the Great Ohoopee and Cannouchee rivers, and in succeeding days, searched out more territory. There were barren lands and mountainous country westward. Fortunately, they were not harmed or threatened by the Indians. The Indians of the Gulf coasted received them warmly. Usually the exploration party made fifteen or more miles a day. They were now in Alabama in and around the later Greene County. They had trouble in the area suffering an affray, and were saved by the arrival of the horsemen at the time the Indians were trying to unroof the house some were hiding in.

Their easy passage had ended. The Spaniards and Indian fought fiercely but despite the courage of the inhabitants of the land they were slaughtered. Eighteen Christians were killed while about two thousand and five hundred Indians perished. Victorious, De Soto and his men marched though barren country to a river, meeting more Indians ready to fight, but the Europeans passed on, without having to fight. It was snowing in the south and there were great stores of maize for the winter season. The governor captured some Indians and gained the friendship of an important chieftain. This leader came to visit the governor and generously offered De Soto not only the services of himself and his people, and the produce of his land, but used his influence to come to the Spaniards in peace. the two came with a gift of one hundred and fifty two rabbits for Hernando.

De Soto's friendly chieftain had an ulterior motive. He complained to the explorer, in the Gentlemen of Elvas account, that a vassal of his was rebelling, withholding tribute, and the chief asked for assistance. His aim was to have De Soto divide his force. He expected the governor to take half of his force to the attack and planned to destroy each half separately with his full force.

An unknowing Spaniard took the bait and let thirty horsemen and eighty infantrymen to the lower Tallahatchie River, which was in northwest Mississippi, after this supposed rebel. They discovered the town, but the Indians had set it afire. Because both forces of the invaders were alert and careful, the local enemy did not dare assault the Spanish. Some of the natives killed and stole Spanish owned hogs. They would come in the night. When the white man caught three of the raiders in the act, Governor Hernando De Soto ordered two to be shot with arrows. He sent the third away minus his hands, which were cut off

In March of 1540, John Phillips sailed the *Barbara* of London from Portsmouth and headed directly for Brazil. Early in May, the ship and its captain and crew reached the coast, where he traded with the natives and fought at times. He did not inspire the same trust of a Hawkins and had trouble. His hostile nature stayed with him, piratical natures surfaced when he sailed his ship into the Caribbean, and reached the south coast of Hispaniola. There he captured a Spanish ship with a cargo of hides and sugar. Because his old ship was leaking, Phillip ordered the ship abandoned and used the Spanish ship to sail home in. He took the ship, renamed the *Barbara*, and its cargo, to return home in, after letting the Spaniards ashore in Hispaniola. Back at Dartmouth, he was arrested for piracy because of the complaint against him by the Spanish ambassador. Few Englishmen suffered from their piracy against Hispanic shipping. The result of this trial has not survived.

Pedro de Valdiva was born in the little town of La Serena in the province of Estremodura of a family of gentle folk in 1500 to Pedro Oncas de Melo and his wife Isabel Gutierrez de Valdiva, taking his mother's name. He married Maria Ortiz de Gacte from Salamanca. A soldier at age twenty, Pedro junior fought at the siege and taking of Milan and at the Battle of Pavia. After a time, Valdivia went to the New World and in 1530, now Captain Valdivia, he distinguished himself in Venezuela which he helped conquer. In 1532, Pedro de Valdivia went with Pizarro on his second expedition to Peru and was a faithful soldier. After Almagro's fall, Valdivia fell heir to the conquest of Chile in 1538, and set out in 1540 by the coastal road with 150 men and a thousand Indians to use as porters. Almagro's veterans laughed for they said there was no gold in Chile, their having found none there on the way.

Founding a town called La Serena after his birthplace, he marched on. Next, on February 12, 1541, he founded Santiago. After heading south from this city he had to battle the fierce and intelligent Araucanians, unconquered by the Incas, but Mano had previously warned the Indians of Chile to hide gold and provisions from the approaching Spaniards. The Indians Valdivia had subdued and Indians to the south revolted. Divided into two forces, the Spaniards under Valdivia advanced to attack the main force, while the lesser moved upon Santiago and burnt it down. Then the ones under Captain Alonso de Monroy charged and caused the Indians to flee.

Valdiva sent Monroy back to Peru for more provisions and men. Monroy with five soldiers fell into an ambush and were killed or captured. Escaping while out teaching the chief how to ride, Monroy and his fellow captive soldier made their way across the desert of Atacama on a desperate ride. They left Valdivia with his troops for three long years, maintaining safety in the Indian siege of Santiago. Finally, recruits were found and joined Valdivia at Santiago, where they began settling the country while the Indians were in the hills. He did subdue the natives around the capital of Santiago however.

Chapter XIX

CARTIER

Once again, March had come. The De Soto expedition had stayed for sometime in the province of Chicago in Mississippi, as we have seen, and now the governor Hernando De Soto, felt it was time to move on. He wanted two hundred Indian for carriers. The explorers and conquistadors loaded their burdens on the backs of the poor Indians as much as they could. Because of their baggage and provisions, the Spanish needed these men, but the Indians had their own ides when De Soto asked.

De Soto had a premonition when he looked at the braves. They did not appear right to De Soto and he ordered his men to keep a careful watch that night. The master of the camp did not take heed or take precautions for a possible Indian attack. It was four o'clock in the predawn of the next morning. Suddenly, the Indians came up to the camp and attacked in strength on all four sides. They were discovered. At this point the Indian drummer beat his drum and the Indians shouted and ran into the camp. The three horsemen on watch ran and the attackers found no resistance. With the thrill of victory, the braves set fire to the camp and prepared to kill the Spanish coming out of the gates. The Spanish soldiers ran in all directions. The noise bewildered them, the smoke obscured their vision, and they were routed, fleeing the camp that was now on fire. Horses were burned in their stalls. Others broke their halters and escaped.

Confused and frightened soldiers ran to the best path of escape. No one fought back. The people of the land were masters of the field. Then, it was the attackers time to be confused. The Spanish horses were running in fright and in the dark that struck the Indian with fear that the invaders' cavalry was about the ride them down. Only the governor, showing his superior valor and presence of mind got mounted and struck with the blow of the lance, one native right before him, but he was thrown from the saddle. Because the saddling was done in such haste, it was not done right.

One woman had gone back to her house to get her pearl and was burnt to death when the fire enveloped the door. Others were burnt also. Fifty horses were destroyed in the fire and eleven Christians were killed. Four hundred swine were lost, and there were one hundred left. The Spanish began to recover, but they faced great problems. Many had fled from their huts naked, losing their clothing in the conflagration. The consequence of this was a miserable time in the cold. They had fires, but only one side of their bodies were warmed. When a number sewed dried grass mats for pads and blankets, the soldiers laughed, but had to follow their example. Fortunately, the inhabitants of the land did not strike subsequently on the second night. Licking their wounds, the Europeans made saddles from the ash trees and leaves. They had skilled craftsmen among them. The writer of the account praised their work. He said that they made saddles like the famed saddlemakers of Biscay.

There was another before dawn assault on Tuesday by the native warriors. They came once again on the 15th of March. The Spaniards were ready this time and De Soto led a force to meet them before the Indians reached camp. The governor defeated them and they fled. Some escaped when a friar stupidly and for no reason called out, "To the camp! To the camp!" De Soto headed there and the pursued Indians made it to safety. Native losses were heavy.

There was another battle with more Indians at a staked fort. Painted in stripes with feathers and horns, blackened faces, vermilion encircled eyes, fierce savage Indians rushed the Christian soldiers with yells and drums in the background. Juan de Anasco and his followers decided to abort a battle and retired. The governor was informed and he led the invaders in a charge resisted up to the point of the stake, but they fled and made their escape.

The scarcity of maize obliged De Soto to move on in the interior of the South, he marched during the next seven days in a wilderness of ponds, basins, lakes, and thick forests. At the next village of Quizuiz, they captured everybody in the dwellings, including the mother of the chief. When the Indian chieftain learned from a hostage messenger of the capture, he sent back to ask De Soto to release the prisoners and he would come to the Spanish explorer and recognize him as his master. Governor Hernando De Soto decided to make peace with the chieftain because of the need of his weary and weak men for maize. However, at the release of the mother and her fellow natives, the Indian gathered his braves and advanced to do battle. When they found the powerful Europeans prepared, the chief decided to honor his peace.

Once again, the lack of Indian corn or maize set the governor on the trail until he arrived at a town with maize, and a mile and a half further, the great Mississippi River. Near the river, he found timber for boats and a good campground where the Spanish built houses and settled. After gathering maize in the area and felling timber, they sawed planks for the construction of barges.

At this time, Indians came up the stream, jumped on shore, and told the Spanish expedition leader of their greet lord by the name of Aquixo. This superior ruled many towns and people on the western shore. He would bring his people to receive the commands of his lordship. This was done on the next day. However, this chief came with the aim of destroying the explorers, but when he saw the Spanish strengths and alertness, he would not land from his boats. When the natives moved off from the shoreside, the Spanish crossbowmen fired and struck down some five or six natives. The tribesmen and their chieftain quickly withdrew.

The Spanish soldiers had the four boats finished in thirty days following this incident. Four cavalrymen in whom De Soto had trust were put aboard each boat to secure a passage across the river. In the boats were crossbowmen of foot. The boats ferried the expedition across the swift and very deep Mississippi. Soon they reached Aquixo that was deserted by fearful natives, but the cavalry killed ten and captured fifteen on a plain near the Indian village. The governor sent men in the boats upstream and they traveled around the bays in the windings of the large river. The Indians raised their bows from ravines along the bank of the river. Since the current was swift, the boatmen had to stay near the land, and they were exposed although without loss. De Soto sent crossbowmen to protect the imperiled men.

After this, the expedition set out for a province in which they expected to find gold. There was a small river to cross and they had to march in water. Sometimes, the water was up to their knees and their waists. About this time, they came of believe that they would be lost all night standing in water, but they suddenly found solid land. They robbed Indian villages where the inhabitants had not heard of them. They noted the various trees, including walnut, mulberry, and persimmon. They reached the mouth of the Tyronna River.

Meanwhile terrible events were taking place in Peru. On June 26, 1541, the Almagroistas assassinated Governor Francisco Pizarro in a fight when they forced his house to murder him. They installed Diego Almagro as governor and the son made it to such a position as the father could not. Next, the ruffians busied themselves with robbery, and imprisoned the principal citizens of Lima. On his way to judge the affairs in Peru, the president, Cristobal Vaca de Castro was in Popayan. Vaca de Castro was very glad of his royal commission to govern the province. He looked forward to administer justice himself, in the event of the Marquis' death that now transpired. There was no justice in Lima however. There Almagro and Juan de Herreda had Pizarro's secretary Antonio Picado tortured to tell where the dead governor's treasure was hidden. Antonio did not know, but the tortured him some more. Finally, they had him executed. His head was cut off. Others were executed also.

In reaction, the banner of the king was raised against Diego Almagro. Pero Alvarez Holguin was one of the captains ready to rebel against Almagro. Another was Alonso de Alvarado, who believed that it was a great injury to the service of the king that Pizarro should be killed. Alvarado sent messengers to Vaca de Castro, urging him to come quickly for his forces and the masses would support the judge of the residencia of Pizarro. Vaca de Castro, when he was sure Francisco Pizarro was dead, ordered Sebastian de Belalcazar to come with an army to join himself. Belalcazar obeyed from fear. Word that Vaca de Castro was not the legal governor of Peru was sent out and the judge, and now proclaimed governor, decided to go on to Quito. Soon he learned that he was acknowledged at Quito and after that reached Quito where he gathered troops against the young Almagro.

Vaca de Castro called upon the people of Peru to join him against Don Diego for murder and usurping the government. The new legal governor was hailed along the way, as such, and gained recruits. Balalcazer was sent back to deal with a native revolt in his government. Almagro was determined to resist the decrees of Vaca de Castro, rightfully fearing for his life and determined on his usurpation. The followers of Almagro were with him in the field and cities elsewhere when Vaca de Castro entered Lima. After tending to things in Lima, the governor joined his army in the field where Diego de Almagro and his troops were waiting, and sought by letters, to justify their actions by blaming the Pizarro faction for the troubles, especially because of the murder of the elder Almagro. These two messengers were dispatched from Vilcas on September 4, 1542.

The two armies gathered on a spur of the Andes at Chupas and were exhorted by their respective sides to fight for victory. The coming battle was preceded by a thunderstorm and torrents or sheets of water. The soldiers on both sides had no protection. On the sixteenth, the Indians watched their enemies, the Spanish fight one another. Both sides fought hard, but the rebel artillery did not do it's part. By the time the sun was set, it was clear that Almagro was defeated and Vaca de Castro was proclaimed the true governor. Almagro was captured and executed.

Also in 1541, Jacques Cartier made a third voyage after a nobleman persuaded the king of France to allow him to return to that great river of the St. Lawrence with its fertile lands.

The captain and his shipmates were impressed by the hard life they had during the long winter of their second voyage. Because the French had found no gold and the winter was so harsh, the French king hesitated to encourage Cartier to return to Canada. At this point, an influential nobleman in Picardy by the name of Jean Francois de la Rocque de Roberval, who was very interested in exploration and French colonization in the New World, gained the support of the monarch to head the expedition with Cartier as captain general and chief pilot of the king's ships. Roberval gained permission from the king to establish a colony in Canada. Probably in May, Cartier set sail for North America.

Once again, he was there for a year. Roberval had not shown up so the captain-general headed back for France. When in the harbor of St. John's, he met the nobleman with his three ships and two hundred colonist, but he would not turn back. Roberval landed his men at Charlesbourg Royal. The French king had named Roberval to be viceroy of New France. Roberval sent out Jean Alphonse of Saintonge, a highly capable navigator, to search for a northwest-passage past Labrador. Alphonse met difficulties and risk from ice so he returned to France. Cartier may have made a fourth and last voyage, but it is certain that he died on September 1, 1557.

On November 3, 1543, the first viceroy of Peru, Blasco Nunez sailed for his post in a fleet of forty-nine ships from San Lucar, Spain. The winds were favorable and they quickly made it to the Canaries where they took aboard Diego de Cepeda, one of the judges to support the New Laws written to protect the Indian by doing away with plantations and peonage. Three days after Epiphany in 1544, the ships arrived at Nombre de Dios. Nunez and his people rested for over two weeks before crossing over to Panama.

The viceroy was to enforce the laws strictly, which would uproot the Indians once again and break up marriages and families. Some of the natives were happy with their new lives. These were to be sent back to their original homelands. Others of the natives were married to conquerors and these, according to law, were also sent back to their old homes. Those instructed in the Faith were sent back to native villages where they would lose their religion. Rectifying old mistakes by these new laws, as beneficial as they were at heart, caused other problems in the Spanish kingdoms. These new laws did not resolve much harsh treatment since they could be ignored and justice was often hard to come by.

The New Laws which were a benefit to natives under direct control of Spaniards in their jungles, plains, or mountain home were the result of the efforts of Las Casas and others. They provided for direct control of the Spanish kings and not under plantation or estate owners. The encomenderos had no authority over them except to collect tribute for the kings of Spain and could not benefit economically from their work. They took away much income from the conquerors and those they gave the lands to originally.

Former governor Rodrigo de Contreras in Panama came to see the viceroy and said that he could not believe that he would be ignorant enough about the alarm felt in the New World by his arrival to enforce the New Laws. The turmoil was not yet ended. Despite their just promulgation, the state of the country could not allow him to enforce them. He told the viceroy further that in this country the Spaniards were not of low degree but considered themselves great lords of noble bearing. They would rather die than submit to the New Laws.

Nunez took the hard line in saying most forcible that he could not believe what they were saying to be true, because good in preferable and that they were saying that evil is preferred to the good, and tyranny comes before loyalty, and if the king has no more taking the opposite side. His majesty's laws must be unaltered and enforce. The advisors would be treasonous to oppose the New Laws.

The first viceroy in Peru made many errors during the time of his rule, but the first took place when on a Sunday, September 14, 1544, he murdered the upright and popular factor, Illan Suarez de Carvajal. People were outraged and the judges, called oidores made charges against the viceroy and seized Blasco Nunez Vela. He was put on a boat with one of the judges and sent to Spain. In October, Francisco de Carvajal executed various followers of the judges and forced the judges to appoint Gonzalo Pizarro as governor and captain general of Peru to hold office until the matter could be brought before the king to decide.

The New Laws had great effect in reactions in Peru. Those opposed to the laws got behind Gonzalo Pizarro. He was living on an estate of his since returning from the jungles with his men. Now Gonzalo heard the call of the Spaniards in Peru and accepted the leadership of a developing rebellion in Peru against the new viceroy. In this, Pizarro was backed by Francisco de Carvajal, another man of humble birth and who had a good reputation in Italy, Mexico, and Peru.

Nunez Vela's path was clear to him. The people of Peru were audaciously rebelling against a royal order and he was resolved to fulfill the royal wishes, but his plans for action changed from time to time, to crush the rebellion in Cuzco himself or to defend Lima. Finally, the viceroy called the four judges to enforce the New Laws, telling them that they should take up arms against the rebels. The judges were anxious that the viceroy would assemble troops and start a civil war. Cepeda replied that they should wait until the bishop and regent of the Dominicans returned from peace talks. The other three troubled judges agreed. Secretly they were against the enforcing the New Laws, but the dared not tell the viceroy that.

Next, the viceroy prepared a loyal army headed by Alonso de Montemayor and Nunez Vela's brother-in-law Diego Alvarez de Custo. While the viceroy was preparing for war, Pizarro continued his preparations also; he could use the money which was in the royal treasury to revolt against royal authority in Nunez Vela's person, but the leading citizens would not agree, raising instead money in their own persons and their property. The bishop wished Pizarro to disband his troops. The soldiers with Pizarro in Cuzco began to have their doubts about attacking the royal will in arms, although they outnumbered the viceroy's force.

Pizarro advanced very cautiously and there was dissension behind him in Cuzco. The Inca Manco heard of the dissension once again and decided to send an Indian army against Cuzco, killing and burning. He did this and succeeded in getting within eighteen miles of the city, but because they were unprotected by armor the Indians would go no further. There was great fear in Cuzco for awhile.

Meanwhile in Spain, Charles gave to the wily spider in the service of the church, Pedro de las Gasca, the presidency of a royal audiencia or court-executive in Peru with board power to set things right in Peru. He sailed from Spain on May 26, 1546, and on the way learned of the Peruvian Battle of Anaquito. He was the bearer of that formal revocation and a general amnesty for the rebels, undermining the rebellion with this. Gonzalo Pizarro would not avail himself of a pardon. Retreating, he was followed by Gasca's formidable friend Diego Centavo who was ordered not to fight, but he had no chance. At the Battle of Huarina on the shores of Lake Titicaca on October 26, 1547, Centavo was badly defeated by the outnumbered Gonzalo, mainly because of the leadership of the stout Carajal. The defeated soldiers joined Pizarro's army.

President Gasca kept his head and went to Lima where eighty merchants loaned him 300,000 pesos of gold and where the recruited a fresh army of 2,000, twice Centavo's force. The audiencia president gave Gonzalo Pizarro another chance to return to his allegiance. Pizarro and Carvajal were still interesting in maintaining themselves and blamed Gasca for the harm they themselves were doing in South America. There was another battle in Peru's civil war. Because the royal force had cannon when Gonzalo said they had none, the rebel troops deserted in mass and the two leaders were captured. At the orders of Gasca both Pizarro and Carajal were beheaded on April 10, 1548.

A friend of the Indian tribes, Diego Alvares Correia worked closely with Jesuit missionaries in Brazil from 1549 to 1557 when he died. He especially helped Manuel da Nobrega. Known as Caramuru, he had been a Portuguese sailor shipwrecked off the coast of Brazil about 1510. The American Indians took to him and he was to serve as an intermediary and agent for logwood traders. Married to an Indian woman, he settled southeast of All Saints Bay and was granted land by Coutinho. He was of ideal benefit to Nobrega who in 1549 was chosen to lead the first Jesuit mission to Brazil in 1549.

The Jesuits decided to work hard for the conversion and protection of the natives, isolate them in native villages from the baleful influence of Portuguese laymen. They learnt the Indian languages helped by such as Caramuru. Nobrega was university educated in Portugal and used that knowledge as Jesuit provincial of Brazil. In 1553, he also opened a mission field to the south in the captaincy of Sao Vicente (Sao Paulo). He founded secondary schools and worked for the recapture of the Bay of Guanabara from the French. On October 18, 1570, Nobrega died, leaving behind the fruits of his services and two books on Brazil.

Chapter XX

THE FRENCH THREAT

The French threat alarmed John III of Portugal and he acted in 1549 to meet it and to establish his supremacy over the proprietary colonies in Brazil by centralizing government in Brazil. The crown had been overly generous to the colony and allowed the captain and lords ample powers. Now the Portuguese king begun taking these away. Viewing the captaincies as part of the whole, he weakened the rights in new charters to proprietors replacing old owners when they died. He gave full authority to his governor-generals, although some charters had not been renewed and changed yet. Next, the king established inspectors to go into the captaincies despite promises in the charters that this would not be done. One proprietor wrote the king on November 24, 1550, that all the people of Brazil were very upset with these changes but there was no action and reaction like that in Peru earlier.

One of the Portuguese missionaries of southern Brazil was the man Jose de Anchieta, who had been born in the Canary Islands. In Portugal for his higher education, he attended the University of Coimbra. After his studies ended, he shipped out for Brazil where he taught at the Jesuit college of Sao Paulo and served as a missionary in the settlements of the area. From 1577 to 1587, he was provincial of the Jesuits and led in education for the Indians. His Tupi grammar was published in Coimbra in 1595, two years before he died in 1597.

In 1550, Bartolome de Las Casas used his anthropological ideas to oppose Juan Gines de Sepulveda who believed that the Indians were natural slaves in accord with the dictum of Aristotle. Because they were slaves in law their property or service could be commandeered by Spaniards. Therefore war could be justly waged against them in the Sepulveda view. According to Las Casas, the Indian should be measured not by Spanish yardsticks but understood in his own culture. Human beings were in various stages of development and the Indian was in his.

Las Casas' idea astonished many Spaniards when he said these Indians compared favorably with people of ancient times and fulfilled standards for rational beings. They fulfilled every requirement put forth by Aristotle as required for the good life. In order to carry forth his theories, he even advanced them superior to the Greeks and Romans. Mexican Indians were said to be superior in working with their hands and in rearing and educating children. Their martial arrangements were reasonable and conformed to natural law and man-made law. He found many ways to compliment the natives of the Americas including agricultural and craft skills.

He wrote at length about Indian anthropology which were to be used by him to advance Indian rights. Las Casas even went so far as to state that the Aztecs in their human sacrifice were showing a high conception of their God. The sacrifices of human beings were the most magnified sacrifice available. Las Casas would go to considerable lengths in proving his point.

In the year 1552, Las Casas published his *Relation* in Seville and idealized the Indians as was his wont. He wrote that this infinite multitude of people was created by God to be without fraud, without subtlety or malice, to their natural governors most faithful and obedient. They served the Spanish well and were patient, meek, and fearful, and who lived without thought of revenge. Some were delicate and were not meant for labor. These generalizations were marked, but the fact was that the Spaniards were not always met with friendship although most of the Indians were submissive toward the conquerors once conquered. Unlike mainland natives, the West Indian worked little and indeed the harshness of the work forced upon them made havoc of their systems, but it was probably disease that mostly killed the Indians of the West Indies about whom Las Casa is talking, second only to murder.

Las Casas speaks of the Indians as lambs and the Spaniards as tigers, wolves, and lions who were cruel and inhumane in their butchery of the Indians. From three million to three hundred the population fell and the lands were desolate in the Indies. Many of the Indians were shipped out to work elsewhere. According to Las Casas, the Spaniards were equally cruel on the mainland and destroyed in their tyranny twelve million or fifteen millions, a number which might have been exaggerated. The right numbers could be ten millions. Exactly how many is unknown but it was very, very high. This extermination was achieved by the desire of the Spaniard to get rich quick. The Spaniard were so materialistic that they did no extend religion to those natives, now dead.

In Hispaniola, they were well received, these Spaniards, as if they came from heaven, but the Indians struck by Spanish greed were soon hiding their children, wives, and victuals. They fled to mountain to escape the murderous intent of these Christians who acted worse than pagans, slaughtering unborn infants as well as the born. Las Casas, who was there, records that the Spaniards spared no one of any age and killed women as well as men. This was the cruel intent of men who would dash infantile heads against rocks. They erected gallows, twisting the Christian living to murder in Jesus' name, by burning the Indians tied to gallows but touching the ground. They sent messengers to the mountains with their hands half severed to hang by the skin.

Las Casas wrote of other burnings of the natives by slow degree which he had himself witnessed. Next, they took hounds to the mountains to hunt the Indians out and exterminate the previously free wretches. When the Indians happened to kill a Spaniard, the rest of the invaders executed in death one hundred Indians. Las Casas had seen much of this with his own eyes and had heard the rest from Spaniards themselves. He had been there.

In Europe, Spain and France were at war and the French pirates were loosed upon the Antilles and Francois Le Clerc had led a squadron with ten ships provided by the crown to pillage Puerto Rico and Hispaniola. He struck the small settlements and small ports most thoroughly before moving to bigger game. During the year of 1554, Le Clerc hit Santiago de Cuba. He captured the town and took away a large booty. Le Clerc had a lieutenant, a French Huguenot named Jacques de Sores. In July of 1555, Sores and his men plundered Havana. This pillage lasted eighteen days. By the end, the people had nothing to pay a ransom with and the French cruelly burned the city to the ground. They left but another French pirate squadron and were eager for the prize of Havana. A few months after the sacking, this group arrived before the walls but found a blackened hull and had nothing to steal.

Two other French pirates had undertaken raids along the shore of the southern Caribbean in 1555. Pierre Beaguez made a visitation upon Santa Martha. Elsewhere, Jacques de Sores, seeking the wealth of pearls, landed his men on the island of Margarita and with the help of an inhabitant seized the town. He freed its slaves and extracted a heavy ransom, promising that they would not burn it.

The French action in releasing Spanish slaves was to be made often in the century. Both French and English raiders sought to turn the Indians and the blacks against their oppressors. It was clearly a means of undermining the Spanish empire that they coveted so much. Next Sores landed on the Main to pillage the church of Santa Martha and burn Carthagena. Sailing to the northeast, the pirates under Sores burned and sacked Santiago de Cuba and Havana. When peace came in 1556, the Spaniards could relax their fear of the French marauders.

Religious conflict and an interest in the Mediterranean and Levant kept the French form following up their aggressive activities in the New World. Although Frenchmen had explored and raided, the lacked the backing of their government. Officially France in the truce of 1556 accepted Philip's demand that only in the case of special licenses was the trade of Spanish America to be allowed. This, however, did not prevent the merchants and seamen of Normandy and Brittany from perusing their own way. The main exception to this was the official Coligny effort of 1562-65 in Florida that we shall take up.

The English were to claim that the Spaniards had no monopoly because although Columbus was the first to see the New World, the English thanks to Cabot was the first to visit the mainland. Whatever the exact merits of this observation, it became the corner stone of English endeavors and arguments for exploration and settlement. Of course they had claims to northern territories due to Cabot's voyages and other trips of exploration. Since Elizabethan England was basically Protestant and officially Anglican, the English would hardly have respected papal divisions of America. Their rejection of Hispanic exclusion was based more upon political, economic, and social views of the English, who would not be kept out.

On February 16, 1562, the skillful Jean Ribault of Dieppe set out upon an expedition of five vessels for Florida. Not only was the fleet commander an experienced sailor, but he had served his king in the field of diplomacy. He was picked by Gaspard de Coligny for the project. Both men were Huguenots and patriots, eager for a new glory for a France then in political and military decline. Martial ties which had been consummated between Philip and the French princess Isabella of Savoy were for naught. She was now devotedly Spanish as a loyal wife and queen of Spain should be and there had been no gains for France in an alliance. Now the French looked for overseas possibilities. Half of Ribault's crew of 150 men were arquebusciers and most of these were veteran soldiers. The French were prepared for a fight with Spaniard and/or Indians. They had a large supply of artillery, ammunition, and provisions. To avoid detection, the fleet had spent two and a half months on a more direct course, without the advantage of currents and winds.

Arriving on the thirtieth of April at a headland on the northeast Florida coast, Ribault coasted northward to discover St. John's river and to make friends with the Indians. He erected an engraved stone column to claim the land for France. Discovering by a careful eye the mouth of various rivers, the French Huguenots noted a large river which might have been the Board River given the description of a nine mile wide mouth. Ribault made friends with natives there and explored inland for awhile, before settling a colony of volunteers to hold Port Royal for their sovereign. It was then named Charlesfort after the then king of France.

He turned his ships toward France and because of the civil war in the homeland, no one returned to relieve or strengthened the colony and the French left the men to their fate. However, in the months ahead Ribault gained am audience with Elizabeth I of England. She would not help the Huguenot and his colony directly, but encouraged the colonizer to undertake the project with private means. However it was up to Stukeley the next year to do anything solid to implement the idea.

The closed system in Spanish America challenged foreign merchants and adventurers to find a way into the rich pot which was Mexico, Peru, and other dominions of the Spanish king. One Englishman thought he could drive a wedge for trade by selling much-desired slaves in contraband. John Hawkins of Plymouth was already a successful businessman and shipowner, a freeman of his town, and most persuasive and charming. His father was an esteemed West Country sea captain for Henry VIII. And now Hawkins junior was set to make his mark for slave trading in the Atlantic. It was autumn of 1562, when Hawkins sailed his three or four ships to the African coast at age thirty to buy slaves and take them to Hispaniola.

In order to finance his voyage, Hawkins had to talk business with finances for a variety of business transactions and projects. Going to the city of London, the talked with magnates like Sir Lionel Duckett and Sir Thomas Lodge in the richly paneled offices of downtown London. They knew him as a bold and reputable man and when the Englishman told them of his trading idea, the financiers listened. The sure and dazzling nature of his story brought them into the project and they formed a syndicate to exploit the slave trade.

He bought his slaves at Portugal's Sierra Leone. Before the Portuguese allowed the English to board four hundred, they wanted a show of force so they could tell their home government they were robbed. Portugal did not want foreigners in their trading area and might cashier any officials selling slaves to the English or French. When the English fleet had left, the officials stated that Hawkins had captured six ships with nine hundred slaves, ivory, and other cargoes. In Lisbon, the Portuguese sent word to their ambassador at London and told Whitehall in London their grievances about Hawkins and also against Martin Frobisher who had traded in Africa also. Both Englishmen were backed by Queen Elizabeth I.

In Hispaniola, there was the same problem. Spain's official, Licentiate Lorenzo Bernaldea, required that the English could trade only by presenting a show of force which Hawkins did with his ample guns, muskets, and pikes and fierce crews. After the sale, Hawkins paid the legal seven and a half percent duty on the deal and took his gross in gold, pearls, sugar, and hides. There was no piracy since Hawkins sent two ships with cargoes to Lisbon and San Lucar, where the cargoes were confiscated and the merchants in whose navies they had been shipped were imprisoned. One was a Spaniard and another was an Englishman. The Jewish convert Bernaldez was called home to answer to authorities. Hawkins had lost two ships and their cargoes and had profited greatly with the remainder. His city backers added to their great wealth and Hawkins bought a house near the Tower of London with part of his profit.

Meanwhile, in May of 1563, Thomas Stukeley was in the midst of arming his fleet of five ships. Elizabeth I had provided him with one of the vessels and Ribault with another. Further, the queen presented Stukeley with a royal standard to fly on the flagship. Ribault provided three French pilots who had been with him in Florida and which gave the expedition a valuable knowledge of the particular waters they were to enter. There were to be a three hundred-man crew and a plentiful supply of provisions, ammunition, and artillery for the journey.

The bishop of Aguila, Alverez de Quadra, who was then the Spanish ambassador to England from Philip II relayed the rumor that the Stukeley expedition was to attack Florida. He also told Philip that he heard that the mission of the fleet was to capture Spanish vessels on the way from the West Indies to Spain. Stukeley himself told the ambassador that he was urged on the undertaking by the government and that he intended to go into the service of Philip once he reached a Spanish port. Quadra replied that this was impossible because of the friendly relations existing between England and Spain. Then the English man lied that only a few Frenchmen had seen the destination, but that it was three days sail from Cuba. This land Quadra said was in territory granted to Spain by the pope. The ambassador thought this frankness was a cunning device to prevent a Spanish attack.

Then in an unexpected turn of events, English intelligence discovered that instead of leading a fleet to the French colony, Ribault and his French pilot planned to escape to France with ships and hostages. Ribault was seized, thrown into prison, and threatened with hanging. The three pilots were put into chains to prevent their escape. The English planned them to lead Stukeley to the French colony.

While this turn of events slowed relief, the French colonists at Charlesfort were enduring hardship and dangers in the Carolinas. First and foremost was the need for measures of safety. They worked day and night to complete their defenses and sought the friendship of neighboring chiefs. Time was also devoted to exploring the surrounding territories. They traveled up rivers and discovered swamps and forests. Like the Spanish, the French did not prepare for the future. The maize was not planted, perhaps because the season was late. Instead they relied upon generous Indians, but the native stores did have limits. The French colonists expected relief ships and lived for their arrival.

Soon, however, they found internal troubles from which their defense works could not protect them. One night after a colonial expedition had just returned from a trip up the River Belle, a fire broke out and burnt almost all of their possessions. They replenished their food supply. Captain Albert hung a drummer. His men thought that Albert did not have sufficient reasons for this drastic punishment. They were most unhappy when the captain banished a soldier to starve on an island. In order to protect their own lives, the colonists revolted and killed Captain Albert. They immediately rescued the soldier and elected Nicola Barre their leader, a fortunate choice.

When relief did not arrive from France, they set to build a ship. No one in the colony knew how to construct one, but they were desperate and achieved their purpose. Sailing forth without a navigator, they entered calm waters a third of the way to France. Their provisions ran out and they suffered from extreme thirst and hunger, relieved only by leather shoes, jerkins, seawater, urine, and cannibalism. Their vessel began to leak and a contrary wind almost swamped them. Finally an English ship rescued the shipload of crazed colonists who had seen land but were unable to make an effort to attain landfall.

Admiral Gaspard de Coligny wanted to undertake a second French colony for profit and Florida was the key. Because Ribault was still imprisoned in England, Coligny selected one of Ribault's companions, Rene de Laudonniere, to command the second attempt for a colony in Florida. Unfortunately the commander lacked Ribault's character and presence of mind, could not adapt to colonial conditions, and made enemies of the natives. With funds from

Coligny, Laudonniere equipped three vessels and assembled three hundred future colonists. On April 22,1564, they set sail by way of the Canaries, the Bahamas Islands, and the Florida coast near St. Augustine. Going ashore near St. John's River, he was joyfully greeted by the same Indian chief Saturiba whom he had met on Ribault's first visit. Saturiba showed him a pillar left by Ribault and uncovered by Marique. The commander went to the chief's village and explored the area.

Shortly, Laudonniere demanded that Saturiba tell him where the silver wedge given by the Indians earlier was. The Indian said it came from Timauga inland on the riverside and the home of the tribe's enemies with whom Saturiba was at war. The Frenchman promise aid to the Indian and had his men build a fort on a broad, flat knoll near the river and above the marsh. It was in the midst of a heavily populated region of Indian villages. Laudonniere launched the search for the source of the silver with a party of men led by Ottigny, which went inland for ninety miles and learned of a king with great wealth of gold and silver further inland. Of course none existed in Florida, but the Indians led them on with even more fabulous stories of the metal so greatly desired by the French and other Europeans that they never had enough of it.

One of the ships made a return voyage to France and the colonists worked to gain all the advantage they could with the least risk. Laudonniere would not go with Saturiba as promised and the chief made a successful Indian attack against the enemies of the tribe. When the French wanted to return the prisoners as a means of buying the friendship of the tribe's enemies, Saturiba refused until threatened. The French had earned their enmity, making a staunch friend into an enemy.

When a severe storm with hail destroyed the harvest and fields and destroyed the subsistence, Saturiba though it was a cannonade by the French. A stupid Frenchmen supported the idea, and the chief and his people left the neighborhood, leaving the intruders to a growing internal discontent, built by their leader's favoritism and disdain of the common soldiers in the colony. When the Frenchman attempted to murder Laudonniere, he had to flee to such protection as the Indians could give.

The chief reason of existence for the French venture was to have a base for preying upon Spanish commerce and Spanish colonies in the New World. On September 20, 1564, thirteen Frenchmen stole a bark and sailed away for a profitable encounter. Near Cuba they captured a Spanish ship with its golden and silver treasure and plundered a village in the vicinity. Taking the captured vessel, they headed for the harbor of Mantanzas, which they missed. When the ship was at Arcos for water, an impressed Spaniard escaped to give the alarm. The Spanish captured the French and imprisoned some in Spain and others in Havana.

Back at the French colony, sixty-six men had mutinied and seized Laudonniere who had returned from his place of refuge when Captain Bourdet arrived from France with reinforcements. These mutineers took out in two boats on the eighth of December to raid the Spanish. Again more pirates were loosed upon the Spaniards in the West Indies and mainland of the Liberian colonies. The ships became separated, but both captured Spanish vessels separately.

After successes one group was captured in Jamaica and all were hung as pirates, while another group made its way back to the French colony, where four ringleaders were shot on orders of Laudonniere. Soon after these events, the colonists began to suffer from famine. Seeing these, the Indians began to lose their fear of the French and abused them. Laudonniere seized the Indian chief Outina and held him for ransom of food and gained some food supplies as the weeks wore on.

Suddenly on August 3, 1565, they were rescued by John Hawkins and his ships on the way back from the West Indies. The French then introduced the Englishmen to pipes and tobacco. Hawkins offered Laudonniere passage for his colonists to France, but a suspicious Londoniere refused the idea and his men became angry at their leader. The English privateer sold the French a small ship, provisions, and some artillery, powder, and a note. Soon after this the colonists prepared to return home with the next favorable wind.

In the midst of a flow of information about the French on the eastern coast, Philip II of Spain considered what action he could take to prevent French and English intrusions and expel any foreigners in what the Spanish called Florida. The Spanish king sent orders to Governor Diego Mazariegos of Cuba to send a ship along the coast to remove and destroy the columns of claims set up by Ribault. The commander of the expedition would take any possible action to expel or capture the French settlers, bring back all of the artillery, and destroy the forts.

Hernando de Manrique de Rojas was selected and set out in a frigate with only 25 men in the latter half of May of 1564. A Spanish search for the column was fruitless in the central coast of the future state. At what they called the Rio de las Corrientes (possibly the St. John's River), Manique learned from Indians that three Christian vessels had been there and headed north. The commander was elated and sure he was on the right track.

Further to the north he heard about other bearded white men but could not find the expected fort of French settlers on the banks of the Santa Elena. Whether it was the same river as the Santa Elena of European reports can not be known, but it is doubtful a French fort had been erected there. This part of the coast was heavily settled and if the French had built a fort there, the Indians would have said so. Although he had by now fulfilled the specifics of his orders, he was determined to pursue the hunt further north.

Six harbors later, Manique learned from the Indians that a vessel with thirty-four white men aboard was there recently. One member was left ashore. This person turned out to be a seventeen ears old French lad named Guillaume Rufin. The boy dressed in Indian clothes told Manique through a French sailor serving on the Spanish ship that the was a colonist at Ribault's Charlesfort. Then he showed Manique an empty thatched hut in the midst of the works and the columns. The Spanish burnt the shelter and took the column back to Cuba with him.

Chapter XXI

HAWKINS

On October 18, 1564, John Hawkins made his second voyage to Africa and America with four vessels. First there was the *Jesus of Lubek* with 700 tons burden, the *Solomon* of 140 tons, the *Tiger*, a bark of 50 tons, and the *Swallow* with its 30 tons with crews of 170 men, a lean crew for better health facilities. He had ordinance and rituals suitable for his undertaking. Ten leagues out to sea, the ship ran into ships of Her Majesty, being bond for Guinea; one of these, the *John Baptist*, joined the Hawkins fleet. A storm arose on the 21st and Hawkins lost the company of the *John Baptist* and *Swallow*, but was rejoined by the latter. Bad winds forced the fleet to put in at Ferroll in Galicia, the northwest corner of Spain, for five days.

They sailed on for Tenerife to repair his ship. The *Minon* that had led the *John Baptist* joined them. It had found the *Merlin of London*, which sunk after en explosion on board her had set the ship afire before the eyes of the sailors of the *Minon*. They were separated once again and Hawkins reached Tenerife after some trouble in finding the island. From there they deported on the fifteenth of November at night. Ten days later Hawkins reached Cape Blanco in Africa, where they fished and gained other necessities. They took in a Frenchman living on the coast and went to Cape Verde.

Hawkins captured a number of Sapier who had been made slaves of the Sumbas, who had conquered them from the interior. Next, he went twenty leagues up the Callousas River and gained two caravels loaded with blacks. The Portuguese traded with the English and complained to their government, that pirates had taken the slaves in order to protect themselves from punishment. With information from the Portuguese, the English attacked a native town, Bimbia, but when the English raiders broke up their formation to look for gold, they were at a disadvantage and narrowly escaped massacre. They took only ten natives for slaves at the coast of seven Englishmen killed and many wounded. Another raid was made up the Caceroes River in January. At this point, Hawkins took by force some sixteen or seventeen Portuguese ships with 600 blacks, a lot of ivory, and some gold. No one was killed, suggesting apprehension on the part of the surrendered ships and/or trade under the table.

On January 29, 1565, the Hawkins fleet departed from the Sierra Leon for the West Indies and were caught in a calm on the ocean, rescued by the winds or Almighty God as they claimed because they were the elect. They reached the Cannibal Island or Dominica Island on the 9th of March for water. About the Indians, an Englishman wrote in the account that the cannibals there in the area are the most desperate warriors in all of the Indies. The Spaniards could not defeat them. From there, they went through the island chain. After some of this, the

English found fresh water for their ships from a small Spanish community. Also, they received supplies from the Indians.

Sailing westward upon the Spanish Main or the northern shore of South America, Hawkins reached Barburata on the third of April. The governor there was Alonso Bernaldea. Hawkins had a letter of introduction from his uncle Lorenzo Bernaldea of Hispaniola or Santo Domingo, but the governor was not home and the people thought the English were French pirates and privateers and fled. The governor's lieutenant said he had no power to allow trade, but he supplied Hawkins with food. The inhabitants hoped to trade because they were in need of many things. Hawkins used threats that could be used as an excuse for the Spaniard to allow trade. Alonso let the English trade.

After one month, Hawkins went to the next port to trade, using the same methods. At Rio de la Hacha, he had to fire one gun in his artillery to gain compliance from the small force there. Soon he sold all of his wares and headed north by Hispaniola where he hoped to buy hides to finish out the long voyage, but the current took him off course and he headed for Florida. There he left foodstuffs for the French in Florida, on a bill never discharged. He sailed home, having yielded a good profit.

In France, during the early months of 1565, Coligny decided upon a third French expedition to relieve the settlement in the land called Florida. The French admiral was greatly concerned over reports he had received from the French colony on a vessel that arrived sometime before from the New World. Being an austere man, Coligny was indignant because Laudonniere had with him a woman on such a dangerous and distant colony. Jean Ribault was back in France and Coligny chose him to take a fleet of seven vessels to replace Laudonniere and develop the colony. This expedition included adventurers, soldiers who refused to pay for their lodgings, and a number of artisans complete with families.

On May 10, 1565, three hundred colonists embarked on the ships and Ribault had them underway only after what were to be fatal delays for supplies, detention by a storm for news, and finally by a lack of a favorable wind. They reached Florida at the same time Laudonniere was about to sail for France.

The Pedro Menendez de Aviles, who was to make a success of building a Spanish colony in Florida, was born in the seaport of Aviles in the Asturias on February 15, 1519. His boyhood so near the ocean developed in him a strong love of the sea, expressed throughout his long life. Several of the early Spanish kings were buried there. Pedro's ancestors had served the kings in Austurias. He was of the noble and ancient house of Oviedo in the northwestern mountains. When his father died and his mother married, a second time, the chosen foster-parents affianced Pedro to the ten year old Ana Mario de Solis in an attempt to keep him from running away to sea, but Menendez enlisted in an armada against French corsairs anyway. Following two years of service, he sold part of his inheritance to buy a warship to adventure once more against the pirates of the Spanish shore.

There was adventure to find. A French ship and three small frigates used cars in the calm t0 capture a maiden of rank destined for a husband. She had more than sixty relatives aboard and all were taken. The brave Menendez wished to join in a rescue effort with the three ships but only his fifty men would follow. He took the vessel, made his demands upon the French and when he pretended to flee, two of the corsair vessels pursued. When one of his two was ahead of the other, Menendez and his men turned about and took the pursuer and then the other. Next in his own ship, and the two captured frigates, he headed for the final French ship and it's prize. It fled and left the prize to be rescued by Menendez.

This daring rescue was heard of by the regent Maximilian and he ordered Menendez to take some French corsairs that had captured eighteen Biscayan ships. With no lost of time, the Spaniard went straight to the coast of Brittany and captured five of the prizes and seized the French captain responsible for the original capture of one of them. Because of contrary winds, he was anchored when French authorities forced him to give up the prize with a promise that these authorities would punish the corsairs.

His actions commended him to Charles V and Philip II. The later named Menendez captain-general of the Fleet of the Indies. Corsairs almost captured him on a trip to Seville on orders from the king. His first major action was clearing the Spanish coast of enemy corsairs in April of 1557. During his time in high office, he served his king under great difficulties and on complicated missions. He proved one of the most expert mariners of the age. After this, he and his brother Bartolome were imprisoned by the Casa de la Contratacion on charges never proved. Finally Philip II had to order the two men freed. The jealousy of the Casa had resulted in twenty months in prison for Pedro and twenty-five months for Bartolome.

Philip II told Menendez that he was sorry because Menendez had had such trouble and hardship and he would help Menendez search for his missing son, if he would explore the Florida coast and make careful charts. Many ships had been lost because this had not been done. Treasure and lives had been lost. The admiral told Philip II that he would be zealous in the enterprise presented to him, more so than he had in all his previous efforts in royal office.

Menendez set sail for Florida on June 29, 565 with one galleon and ten ships. It was a large expedition of 995 sailors and soldiers served by four secular priests. For the colony to be founded in Florida there were 117 tradesmen including locksmiths, millers, silversmiths, tanner, and sheepshearers. The new adelantado or governor of Florida financed sixty percent of the sailors and soldiers and all of the rest. Menendez's expenses were high in the service of the king. Bad weather caused great grief off the Spanish coast and the fleet had to return to Cadiz for a time. The Spanish had more storms west of the Canaries. On the 28th of August, the Spaniards sighted the coast of Florida.

Because he had sighted land on St. Augustine's Day, Menendez was to name his Florida settlement San Augustine. But first things must come first. The Spaniards knelt to praise God with the ancient Christian hymn used for the occasion, to repeat their prayers, and repeat their prayers, and entreat God to give them victory in all things. One morning, they saw Tomous Indians on shore. Menendez sent forth his campmaster with twenty arquebusiers, not wishing to frighten the natives by disembarking more men. When the Indians retreated into the woods, the campmaster did not follow, fearing an ambush. He was wise. However, because one of the soldiers had committed a crime, the campmaster chose to risk his life and go to the Indians without arms but with some presents. The Indian greeted the officer and were reassured. When questioned, they told the Spanish that the French were twenty leagues to the north.

A happy Menendez sailed north. He discovered a harbor that was to be the site of the settlement and on the next afternoon saw four French galleons. He decided that these were the relief sent from France. His captains wanted to return for other ships to attack, but Menendez thought that the French would be awaiting them and preferred surprise. Moving in, the armada was fired upon by the French, but Menendez sought surrender. The French fled and the Spanish followed for a time. The Spanish sought the French fort by land.

As brave as usual, Menendez led the advance marking the way with blazed trees across the marshes. On the fourth night, the Spaniards got soaked by a rain that wet down powder, wicks, and biscuits. This was too much for the effort for his officers who became abusive of be troops. Their leader persuaded them to try their fortune and led them to a surprise attack on Fort Caroline with swords and took it. Menendez oversaw massacres of the French before and after Ribault and his fleet fell into the hands of the founder of San Augustine. The cruel slaughter was on account of them being Huguenots or French Protestants.

Also in 1565, in Europe, Malta was besieged by the Turks who were endangering Western Europe. Soleiman the Magnificent had inspected the Turkish fleet on March 29th, and it was soon underway, to come back to Constantinople with only one quarter of its numbers and those wrecked by sickness and wounds. To Europe that failure of the siege was a matter to celebrate and word of the Christian victory passed over the seas to America.

Jean Parisot de la Valette, the aged Grand Master of the Knights of Malta had commanded the defense and saw heavy losses among his knights and warriors from his outnumbered force. He had two advantages, he knew the secret Turkish war plans before the attack, and his men prepared to fight to the death, and did. Behind strong fortifications, they were protected. This enabled them to outfight the Turks, who lost more men than did the Christians. Their victory was a turning point to blunt the Turkish drive to the west, to be topped by the Western victory at Leponto six years later.

The Chichimecas were a major burr in the Spanish saddle in northern New Spain or Mexico. News of their warfare against the Spaniards had reached the king in Spain and he wrote to the Viceroy Villamanrique that he was informed, that the cruel Chichimecas were waging a more formidable warfare than previously and the cost of the war was increasing. Present action to reduce and pacify with military action and the building of presidios or forts was no longer working. Another course was necessary.

There were different suggestions on what should be done. Some would establish three or four towns in the pass to Chichimeca lands. These would keep the passes closed and end the warring on these lands. Other suggestions included three or four monasteries of friars in the pass with the towns to attract the Indians by a more gentle method. The king would settle these towns with peaceful and allied Indians, and create inducement for settlement.

Hawkins had poor relations, but with the same high respectability of his family. One of these kindred families was the Drake family, and in that family was Francis Drake who got off to an early and good start. His grandfather and grandmother were John and Margery Drake at Crowndale, in the parish of Tauistock in Devon, running a farm on each of Gedord's estates for which they paid four pounds rent every year. Their son Edmund was married and he and his wife had Francis in 1542, named after Francis Russell, later earl of Bedford and godfather to the auspicious young man. Edmund was a sailor, drawn by the closeness of Plymouth Sound and by the Protestantism of his day.

When the Cornish peasants rebelled against Edward VI and his prayer book, the Drakes fled to live in a hulk in the Midway near Chatham Dockyard, the king's main naval base. They survived Mary's reign and three or more of Edmund's twelve sons became sailors and were staunch Protestants. They lived in a hard world where if they were made prisoner by the Spaniards, they faced lashings and cruel galley service sentenced by the Inquisition as did one of Drake's friends whom he had converted from a Cardiff Catholicity.

Going to sea at the conventional age of ten or twelve, Francis quickly learned the mariner's trade from a fond elderly skipper with a ship which was barely seaworthy. The old man and the boy made friends and when the former died, he left it to Hawkins, who sailed it for awhile before selling the tub and going to better things at about twenty years old. The years were exciting ones and his profession, one of the great opportunity in an expanding world. He sailed far and furious in his days and in 1563 at his majority was third officer in a Hawkins ship, stopping where there was a profit in the ports of the Gulf of Gascovy and the Guinea Coast.

In the month of November of 1566, Drake sailed with the four ships of the expedition of Captain John Lovell to Atlantic and Caribbean waters. The total tonnage of the flotilla was 350 and it was navigated from Plymouth to the Cape Verde Islands. Just off the islands, Lovell and his men captured five Portuguese ships. Circumventing the prohibition of trade, the flotilla commander took the goods and slaves of these ships and captured two Spanish merchants who were relieved of 1,500 pesos and given slaves in return. it seems that the trade had been contracted for on an earlier Hawkins voyage. Lovell attempted to effect another transaction off Rio de la Hacha on the Spanish Main and although he and French corsair Captain Jean Bontemps allowed themselves to be driven off by a band of sixty Spaniards and Lovell left ninety slaves. The slaves were sold for the king's account. Hawkins later wrote to local treasurer Castellanos that he had not been given the purchase money as he expected. Despite this loss, the overall profit of the voyage was good for the investors in the venture.

One day in early 1567, in a city busy with the making of money, in London of course, two Portuguese adventurers visited Admiral William Wynter of the Navy Board. Antonio Luis and his friend, Andre Homen told him a tale of great opportunity that was to inspire the interested high government officials and the queen herself. There was a fantastically rich gold mine in Africa which was still in native hands and nearby could be found a good harbor. It was a likely tale, better than most rumors which had their beginnings in imaginations of the sixteen century, but his one caught the interest of normally ungulliable officials in England. Such a gold mine in English hands would be worth going after. Wynter, and then Lord Treasurer Burghley thought it was a good idea. Elizabeth I was impressed also. She ordered plans to be quickly made for a large expedition to secure this fabulous gold mine before Spain or Portugal should find and seize it.

Hawkins sailed his ships out of the Thames to Plymouth. Lovell and Drake were not with him because they had not arrived back home from the Caribbean, but they did arrive during the wait at Plymouth, when Hawkins sailors were all at church. Hawkins asked Drake and some others to come along on the adventure. There was already trouble before they left. Flemish admiral Alphonse de Horugogne, Baron de Wachen failed to dip his flag to the queen's ship and Hawkins fired upon them until they did so. The Flemish admiral made his exploration and was given a gift of beer and chickens.

At this point, a Spanish galley was raided by masked men who freed some Flemish men condemned to literally row their lives away in the most inhumane subjection. Hawkins was found responsible although he blamed the baron of freeing his countrymen. Then suddenly, the Portuguese pair disappeared in a boat for the French coast, thus unmasking the swindle. Some said that they knew the truth all along. Elizabeth decided that instead of looking for the discredited gold mine, Hawkins should collect slaves off the Guinea coast to sell in the Indies.

On October 2, 1567, the flotilla set out southward and soon were in the midst of a great gale, from which they barely emerged to reassemble at Santa Cruz in Tenerife. Surviving Spanish hostilities there, Hawkins took the fleet toward the African coast where Portuguese authorities and local African chiefs refused to sell him slaves. When Hawkins insisted he and his men were attacked with arrows. Hawkins among others was wounded and they were offered an antidote for the poison, probably at a price.

It looked as if the venture would fail, a fate for which Hawkins would have suffered to some degree and the hands of a success orientated queen. Then there was good news. They learned that a local African king in Sierra Leone needed help in a siege against a walled town named Conga. Hawkins took his force, everyone who could be spared from the ships, against the objective. His command and incendiaries set forth a large fire in the town and it fell to the English and the king. He gave Hawkins 260 blacks to sell in the slave market and killed the rest. It was suggested that the dead survivors be eaten for dinner. They found a like amount elsewhere and took the Atlantic trade winds westward with his ten ships. Drake found himself captain of a new ship.

Bearing down upon the island of Margarita in the Caribbean Sea near the mainland, and a Spanish possession since its discovery by Columbus in 1498, Hawkins made contact with the officials. The Island was a narrow one, forty miles long from east to west with a mountain series in the east and in the west, connected by a lowland center. Most of the economy of the island was off its coast. Pearl fisheries were important in the sixteenth century and, as George M. Thomson noted in his Drake hook, the Spaniards had a great need for slaves to dive for pearls because those on hand were worked to death harvesting them. Hawkins had a strong fleet, a cargo of slaves, and needed fresh food for his men and the slaves abroad so it seems foreordained that some trade would follow.

There was a rough fair for eight days while trade was underway. Since Hawkins had plenty of English cloth aboard, that was exchanged for meat and maize, and presumably slaves were given for pearls received. During the trading, Hawkins and the island officials had their own exchange of hospitality and friendly chatter. On the ninth day, Hawkins sailed his fleet for Borburata on the mainland some three hundred miles to the west, nearer to the capital of New Andalucia.

The governor of that province in the winter of 1567-68 was a member of the nobility of Spain, indeed of the grandee class. A man of maturity and distinction, Diego Ponce de Leon was well educated and had experience in the colonial service. Belonging to one of the four landowning families of Spanish Andalucia, he could be counted upon to uphold Spanish policy, at least on the surface. Hawkins must have expected that much, but it did deter the Englishmen. In a polite but pointed letter, John let the noble know that he wished to sell some sixty slaves and some English goods to pay his soldiers, leaving the Spaniard to think that this was a veiled threat. Unpaid soldiers might ravage Ponce de Leon's province on the Spanish Main.

Diego was busy making an inspection tour and seeing a recently founded city to be later called Caracas, near the sea, but over one half miles above sea level. A saddle shaped mountain overlooked the place, selected by its builder in 1567. Diego de Losada founded the city. While, he awaited Ponce de Leon's answer, Hawkins ordered his men to set up shop and to take the slaves from the ship to give them exercise on land and thereby improve the condition of his live cargo and show them off to potential buyers at the port. Spaniards bought and sold until a letter arrived from the governor. With orders that trade was not allowed, however regrettably this might be, Hawkins then prepared for his next step.

Withdrawing to his ship, Hawkins conducted more trade and the governor said nothing. Ponce de Leon decided to wait and the likelihood of a rebuke because he did not act. Hawkins in his ship were too strong to tangle with, but the governor could have asked to restrict traders and buyers of slave from keeping their purchases. The Englishmen gave two slaves to the local bishop in exchange for a testimonial and Diego was not likely to take these slaves from him. Deciding that now was the time to move on and trade in the westward, Hawkins gave orders for his fleet to proceed.

Chapter XXII

DRAKE

When Hawkins sent Drake ahead with two ships for Rio de la Hacha to reconnoiter, he was probably aware of the revenge Drake might be expected to exercise for the treatment that Lovell and Drake had received in losing the prize of ninety blacks on the previous voyage. There, Drake expected to find Miguel de Castellanos, the Treasurer. Arriving at the town, Drake asked for water for his ships and received gunfire. Captain Drake directed two shot into the treasurer's house and waited for the rest of the fleet to arrive.

Up the coast came Hawkins' ships and Drake reported what had happened including his kidnapping of a Spanish captain under arquebus fire. The flotilla's leader demanded that the Spanish allow the English to sell sixty blacks, and reassured, that any armed Englishmen ashore would leave upon request. Angry and belligerent, Castellanos told Hawkins by envoy that he was armed and ready to fight. Hawkins decided to use force since talk would be useless.

What had worked with Ponce de Leon, would not suffice for Castellanos. The gunners fired upon order while Hawkins landed his force two miles from the town. Outnumbered Spanish troops fired upon the English, lost their ensign, and retreated into the woods. Hawkins took Rio de la Hacha and a fire broke out destroying part of the town. Castellanos said he did not care if everything was destroyed to which the English leader said that the treasurer could talk, because he had sent his belongings to a safe haven and would not be hurt. Unhappy at being in the woods, the Spanish rebelled. Disloyal slave eager for revenge, showed Hawkins where the government bullion was hid and Castellanos was undone. He spent four thousand pesos of government money for slaves and bought twenty for himself at price of one thousand pesos. Local planters bought 150 black slaves and many rolls of English cloth. Castellanos and his officials told the king that the money went for ransom and that the treasurer was valorous in battle.

By the time Hawkins went to Santa Marta to force trade under English guns, the whole of New Andalucia was warned. Word also came of corsair action in Nicaragua and San Bernardo. The commander at the famous port of Cartagena, defended his town with five hundred infantry, some horsemen and a few thousand Indians. Hawkins proved that force enough existed and was discouraged. War against that walled town would be too costly. It was time to go home, but the winds were adverse and the English were driven to the Florida coast and then across the Gulf once again to Yucatan. A Spanish captain was detained and the Spaniard advised Hawkins to go to Vera Cruz where the treasure ship would be assembling.

On September 15, 1568, the much battered ships of Hawkins' fleet sailed into the roadstead of Vera Cruz with the fortification of San Juan de Ulua. His crews were hungry and the situation was made more delicate by the arrival of the galleons of Francisco de Luxan with mercury of the operation of Mexican silver mines. Further the highly placed viceroy-designate Martin Enriquez was in the fleet, which had set sail at San Lucar in Spanish Andalucia. Hawkins was faced with a severe dilemma since it would almost be an act of war to prevent Enriquez from landing at Vera Cruz and Queen Elizabeth did not want a war at this time. This was made clear to Hawkins before he left England so long ago.

Quite logically, Hawkins decided to negotiate with and equally hard pressed Enriquez who risked wreck in the waters outside, but who did not plan to deal with the English in good faith. Hawkins wanted both fleets to rest peaceably in the roadstead. Enriquez wanted to seize the English fleet. This of course was unknown to Hawkins. When the agreement was made the Spanish entered the roadstead. Then Enriquez sprung his trip. The Englishmen on the island, drinking heavily with the Spanish, were almost all killed and their cannon captured.

The Spanish took the *Minion*, but Hawkins regained the ship in a fierce fight. One Spanish ship was blown up and the Spanish flagship caught fire, but continued the battle at the bottom of shallow waters. An attempt to set a fireship against the English failed, but there were only four ships left for the English. Then Captain Bland lost his ship. Finally, Hawkins escaped the roadstead in two ships. His young nephew did not make it, was captured, and married well in Mexico.

Because there was a lack of food on board, Hawkins men died one by one or were put ashore in Mexico until only fifteen men of that one ship arrived in Cornwall. Drake also arrived with his ship of fifty five men. The expedition was a disaster for Hawkins. He had lost hundreds of men. There was a rich haul in the hold of a value of 13,500 pounds making the voyage a financial success, but at what cost.

One of the foundation stones for the short lived Spanish Jesuit Mission in Virginia was an Indian, a youthful native who evidently claimed to be a chief, or brother of one, in what is now Virginia. The Spanish named the area Ajacan, an approximation of a word used by the Indian's tribe. He was picked up along the coast near his home. Because he was sponsored by the viceroy in Mexico, the Indian was called Don Luis de Velasco at his baptism.

Philip II took an interest in the native as he did in even small details, and after a number of years in Spain, the Indian was sent by royal orders back to Spanish America in the company of Dominican churchmen. In Spain, the king had clothed and educated the young man, but in America he served no great purpose for awhile. He lived on various islands before being brought to Havana, and meeting Father Juan Baptist de Sequra and opening the way for his place in history.

At the time, the Spanish authorities had heard rumors of French intrusions to the north of Mexico's silver mines and an interest in forestalling the French in the north encouraged the Spanish to expand up the coast. They would need Don Luis' help in settling the Chesapeake Bay which they believed led northward to "a large bay" that they had heard about. This particular bay had a basis in the Great Lakes that they believed was separated by only a narrow band of land from and arm of the Pacific, which of course had no basis in fact. To the north was a landmass to be known as Canada, and north of that, was the famed and much sought for strait of Anian, ice bound as it actually was. Because of this belief in the importance of the Chesapeake that the Spanish called the "Bahia de Santa Maria," the Spaniards were interested in what Don Luis could do for them in Virginia.

Menendez, Segura, and Don Luis discussed establishing a mission in Virginia. The missionary was enthusiastic, believing that the Indian would be as valuable to his as Timothy was to St. Paul. Using the discretionary power that he had received from Jesuit general Francis Borgia, Segura proceeded upon his mission with later approval from Borgia. Because the fruits of religious effort were so scarce in Florida, Borgia felt that his missionaries should go to another field to which their hearts were better disposed.

On August 5, 1507, Father Segura and his missionaries with Don Luis set sail without the soldiers which the missionary felt would have set a bad example and stir up trouble such as had been the case in Florida. Storms delayed the ship, but in early September, they saw the bay, and moving up the James River landed near where Jamestown later stood. Because the area had suffered a six-year period of famine, Segura took a special concern to send the ship back for foodstuffs for the mission because the Indians had so little. He also asked for grain seeds for the Indians to plant. The Spaniards built a house. Don Luis lived with the missionaries for two nights, but moved off. Segura censored Don Luis for a native way of life and stated his need of Don Luis as an interpreter, but the Indian had returned to his beloved former life. Low on flour, the missionaries went into the woods for roots and berries, and traded for corn from the nearby Indians.

Tragedy soon followed when an ill Segura sent three brothers to Don Luis. The Indian was cordial and promised to return. However, on the fourth of February of 1571, the Indians killed two of the missionary brothers and wounded a third with their bows and arrows. The wounded missionary escaped into the woods but was discovered the next morning and dispatched. Don Luis led an attack on the rest and killed all but the boy, who they spared because of his youth despite his pleas to kill him also. Soon afterwards, a Spanish relief ship arrived, and when attacked by Don Luis and his Indians, retired to Havana. A punitive expedition in 1572 captured the chief of the Indians and five leaders and eight braves and offered their return for the boy Alonso. The natives hesitated, but Alonso escaped to the ship and the expedition returned to Cuba.

Drake, a hater of Catholicism and Spain, formed vast schemes and was most venturesome in their applications. On May 24, 1572, he struck out on his own in command of two vessels, one small at seventy tons (the Pasche of Pasco) and one smaller still at twenty-five tons (the Swan) with crews of 47 and 26 each. It was a young ambitious bunch of sailors. All except one was under thirty and the ships belonged to Hawkins and Drake and brothers. He had as second in command John Drake, another brother.

There were great numbers of weapons of artillery on board and other weapons hidden in saltwater free casks below decks. Remembering the starvations of the earlier voyage, Drake had enough provisions for one year. He was headed for a cave he had earlier picket and clearly knew what he was aiming for. The recent victory at Lepanto established Philip's Spain as the premier naval power. Spain was at its peak, but Drake had a clear notion of its weaknesses, and was brave and resolute.

Unseen in five weeks, Drake and his men passed into the Caribbean Sea between Dominica and Guadeloupe and fished on a deserted rocky island. The fresh fish was relished by the Englishmen and the water replenished the casks aboard the ship. They sailed westward along the coast and saw the mountain range behind Santa Marta. Since he wished to gather no attention, Drake did not come within thirty miles of the shore. Drake found his cave that seemed like paradise indeed with a deep harbor full of fish, a forest of large trees and wildfowl.

Trouble was expected when Drake found a lead plate with a message from John Garret warning him always. Garret had left five days earlier. The Spaniards knew about the place and Drake's goods left there earlier had been taken. Brave Francis Drake did not fear the Spaniards and set his men to build a fort. Suddenly an English ship captured by James Ranse sailed up. Now Drake was sure. Too many people knew the place. Ranse joined Drake and it was decided to attack Nombre de Dios on the Caribbean side of Panama as Drake had planned.

This town was at the crossing point for the gold shipments from Peru, vital for Spanish strength. Drake would strike at this point. Philip needed money to pay his soldiers and sailors. Drake learned that he might have allies in Panama itself because there were black former slaves in the interior, who raided at will and had almost taken Nombre de Dios a few weeks later. Shortly, Drake struck the city in the dark of night. At the time, it was about as large as Plymouth back home. It was a complete surprise until a gunner left his solid stand over the cannon and warned the town. Nevertheless, the attacking force carried the day. Drake's brother came from the other way and the short hard fought fight ended when the Spanish fled. The silver treasure was captured at the governor's house. A Spanish fighter had wounded Drake, and without his strong leadership, the attack was aborted. The Spanish did not follow the retiring English.

Later, Drake did capture a Spanish cargo ship after recovering from his loss of blood. Before returning to England, the English pirates waited out the alarm. Drake was in no hurry to return and he began raiding farmers and ships. His brother John Drake made contact with the blacks in the backcountry. Two told him of a supply of metal they had over the years stolen. It was useless to them and they only wanted revenge upon the Spaniards for their enslavement. Because it was under the riverbed and it was the rainy season, Drake would have to wait five months. He would wait and his men built a fort, then raided near Cartagena. Since he did not have enough men, he could do little, but the Spaniards had no power to harm him although they tried. Drake sailed his ships away and captured a ninety ton Spanish ship and found the food he so desperately needed. Returning back to base, Francis learned that his brother John had been killed. Next, Joseph Drake died of disease. It was a heavy loss for the family, but life was a great chance.

The blacks, or as they were called the Cimmarrons, reported that a fleet had arrived in Nombre de Dios from Spain. It was January of 1573 and the English were eager for action. In order to verify the story, Drake sent out one of his pinions, the *Lion*, which fell in with, and captured a frigate laden with maize, hens, and pumpkins, and carrying thirteen Spaniards for the Panama province port. Drake's Cimmarrons wanted to kill the prisoners, but the English leaders persuaded them not to do so. Deciding to make an overland attack on the city of Panama, he asked the black what would be needed for the trip. They stressed that the slaves would be most needed because there would be many rivers to cross with hard stones and gravel in their beds. Doubtless, an attentive Drake took the advice.

His force had been cut into half by death and illness. Twenty-eight of his original crew had died of fever or were sick, five more were left to guard the prisoners, and others were killed in the earlier fight with the Spaniards. Drake took eighteen Englishmen and thirty Cimmarrons for the attack. The blacks helped carry provisions and supplies. The journey was hard, but there was a plentiful supply of fruits, plantains, and potatoes, and the black hunters brought in wild pigs, and an otter at one time. They stopped once at a walled Cimmarron town, clean and pleasant, where they were welcomed by the fifty households. Reaching a summit on the fourth day, Drake was able to see both oceans at one view, a moving sight and he decided that he would sail the Pacific Ocean one day. On the day down from the ridge, the divide, he saw grass that could grow faster than the cattle could eat it.

A spy went forth to Panama and came back to tell them the treasurer of Lima was about to cross the isthmus with a mule team with eight mules of gold and one of jewels. They set forth on the ambush, but a drunken Englishman named Robert Pike ran toward the train, and gave the attempt away. Next, a frustrated Drake attacked the village of Venta Cruces and then returned by land to the ships, where depressed Englishmen told of their failure, and an ever enthusiastic Drake planned other ventures. They came in with a pirates' ship, commanded by a Huguenot captain, Tetu, who told them of the slaughter of French Protestants in France. The two pirates joined forces and seized in ambush some silver and gold. Spaniards in Panama feared for the safety of the isthmus. They recovered some of he silver, but Drake escaped, but not all of his men had returned. Tetu had been killed. The French and English went their separate ways and Drake and his men were in Plymouth on August 9, 1573. This adventure made his men well-to-do, at least for a time, and Drake independent of his Hawkins kin.

Chapter XXIII

FROBISHER

Martin Frobisher and his fellow Englishmen were interested in extending English discoveries and about 1575 noted the significance of what Cabot, Cortez, Reales and others had found in a memorandum. The writer of this historical note believed in a water passage to the west into the northern Pacific on the way to China. Mentioning Labrador, he noted the southside of that land which was a broad bay lying towards the west. It had such breath that it seemed to be a great sea. Cabot, he noted, had said earlier that in the sixteenth degree there were mountains of ice and snow covered islands. In the vicinity of 66 to 68 degrees, he marked a narrow sea first discovered by the Polish pilot, John Szkolny, in the service of King Christian II of Denmark, who supposedly landed on the coast of Labrador in 1476. This was before Cabot and even before Columbus had made their epic voyages.

The English note of this poorly verified voyage, also mentioned a Spanish voyage out of New Spain 1541 which had found the south side of the northwest-passage. Another document had urged these profitable voyages to claim lands that the English king and her subjects could enjoy. In the Arctic there were lands not already possessed or subdued by any other Christian Prince in Europe as could be seen by the charts and descriptions. The writer of the manuscript sought to prove the exploration was possible, because of what was known by geography.

Englishmen had the means. There would be well-prepared ships and enough experienced and acknowledgeable mariners who knew the coasts of America. The westcountry of England was the best launching place for ships in Western Europe. The British had plenty of cloth for trading which would increase well being at home. Religious considerations were important. Elizabeth would be honored by increasing the faith and her dominions. They would preach to the naked barbaric Indians a religion. The writer dreamed of great discoveries of gold, silver, and pearls. Englishmen would enrich themselves with a low capitalization. Expenses would be very low in comparison with profits. Because the English would buy their own spices in the East Indies, they would not have to pay the Portuguese and Spanish, who charged such high prices for their own enrichment.

The businessman writer answered the arguments put forward by the gainsayers. There were those who warned of the dangers of torrid climates, but he answered, Magellan and the Portuguese had been there many times without harm. Englishmen had been to Guyana in the heat. Some warned that England would be depopulated by sending its people to new lands. He answered that in England there were more people already than could be well provided for. More ships could be easily built. A true defense system would gain from navigation to foreign ports and drain on mariners at home would not endanger England. Her majesty could regulate the usual according to the needs of the kingdom.

The English did not seek places which the Spanish and Portuguese had already subdued and colonized, but did hope to trade with those colonies. Ships from England were not endangered on the high seas, on which any country could sail. Furthermore, the voyages already undertaken had been lawful. He noted the French activity in Florida and Brazil despite the papal grant of those lands to the other Catholic people on the Hispanic peninsula.

Proposed English voyages need not cost the government anything, because there were gentlemen adventurers who would willingly provide the necessary sums. Elizabeth was therefore petitioned to grant letters for franchise and privilege required. Such would provide for government and authority for colonies and ships as well as men to direct the event.

Another discourse considered what was known and its effect on the voyages. Because Greenland was known to be an island, there must be passage to the west. America and China, they believed were not connected, and so there was a continuing water passage to Asia and northwest of New France. There was another way by sea up the coast of western America to the opening. From hence this writer discussed the distances involved. The name of the northwestern passage to the north of western New Spain was the Straits of Anian. Because the north was navigable only three months in the year, the expedition of discovery must be timed right. The passage would be made easily found on the southern trip rather than northwest of England, considering the dangers of the latter. A reply suggested that the northwest route must be pursued, because it would be shorter by a ratio of 6 to 15. The way was open for Frobisher.

Sir Martin Frobisher was born into a well-established family in Doncaster. Francis Frobisher who was probable his father (there being no records available for the period of his birth), who was mayor of Doncaster in 1535. The parish church does not register Martin's baptism until 1558. Other ancestors were men of note in their towns. Martin father bred in him the sea, so Martin had the necessary training in his early years. One of his early trips was to Guinea in western Africa and about 1566 while living in Normanton in Yorkshire, Frobisher was examined by authorities, because they expected him of having fitted out a ship for the purpose of going to sea as a pirate.

In a materialistic age, in which Frobisher and his fellow Englishmen saw becoming ever brighter, the thought of gold and its possession drove men at a furious rate and underlay their view of the world and of philosophy. George Best opened his account of Frobisher's first voyage with the idea that man was born to serve his own term and help those of his kinfolk, friends, and the commonwealth for profit, and his hand with the fruits of his labor. There was a wide variety of beneficial activities. Solon and Lycurgres gave laws, Aristotle gave philosophy, Cicero and Demosthenes provided excellence in rhetoric, and Euclid enlarged arithmetic geometry. Astronoid observers provided a celestial knowledge for taking mankind's pains and rest. There were soldiers for defense and just conquests. Men in arts and sciences and their practical application brought pleasure and profit.

It was in this latter age that Captain Martin Frobisher sought his fame. Being such an experienced sailor, he was well suited for his undertaking. Frobisher believed that the northwest-passage could be a shorter way to China than Portuguese South Africa's Cape of Good Hope. After preparations that he could make himself, Martin conferred with his friends. He convinced them too that not only was the northwest voyage possible, but could be easily performed. He could go himself, contacting various merchants. Frobisher worked to gain support for his great undertakings. Next, he went to the royal court and with the aid of Ambrose Dudley, earl of Warwick, achieved his designs.

Queen Elizabeth's privy gave Martin a letter to take with him on his visit to the offices of the Company of Muscovy to the effect that he discovery of a route to China by sea would be greatly beneficial. Because the company had a fur trade license already issued, the government referred Frobisher to that trading company with Russia. The corporate directors considered the matter and appointed a committee headed by George Barn, then Sheriff of London. Since the members of the company thought that they would soon be able to proceed further to the northeastern passage and soon be in China, they were not interested in Frobisher's ideas and his way westward. However, the company readily granted license and privilege for him and his associates.

On June 15, 1576, Martin Frobisher set out to the northwest with his two small barks and a small boat with crews. One of the ships was twenty-five tons and another was twenty-ton. The small vessel had a ten-ton burden. The *Gabriel*, he flagship, was the larger and the *Michael* was the other. All had enough supplies for twelve months. Frobisher and his voyagers sailed northwest from England, having left Blackwell. On the first of July, they caught sight of a high and ragged land surrounded by ice and mists. In a storm he lost the small ship with its four men and the sailors of the *Michael* had doubts and left secretly to return to England with claims that Frobisher was cast away.

Indeed, the captain was troubled by a mast that sprung, and a blown top-mast. The last was blown overboard in the foul weather. He persevered to the northwest, knowing that the sea would at length have a certain ending. Should there be no land immediately ahead, this might mean he was in the famed passage, but he expected to see some land along the way. He had sight of land on the twentieth, a high land which he called Queen Elizabeth's Foreland, and veering off to the north, he discovered more land and entered a bay in passage. Because of ice and contrary winds, he could go no further. With high hopes, he explored and thought he was between Asia and America and named the straits Frobisher, thinking he had the same honor as the great Magellan.

After moving sixty leagues, Frobisher went ashore and found a place where a fire had been made. When attacked by moose, Martin fled in a narrow escape. This time the usual defense of diplomacy would not save his life. Next, he discovered some men in small leather boats, whose friends got around him and almost cut off Frobisher from his ship. The curiousness of the Indians led him into conference with the Englishmen. Frobisher watched the natives eat raw fish abroad the *Gabriel* and show their skills at knots and ropes with strong arms and nimble bodies. The Indians traded coats of seal and bear skin for those various bells, looking glasses, and other toys.

English sailor went ashore, blinded by the friendliness of the Indians, were intercepted and disappeared. In reprisal, Frobisher caught a native, who was to die of a cold in England which he caught on the trip back. Returning to England, Frobisher reached home in October of 1576 with the native and a piece of black ore. Indeed welcomed, Frobisher cheered the people with his statement about the great hope of a passage to China and they excited them when the ore was said to be gold. Because of his ore find, many were eager to finance his next voyage. Frobisher visited the queen at Warwick's house in Essex. In actuality, the ore was not gold but the multitudes never knew that.

Everyone in England was sure that Frobisher had found a short way to China, India, and their great wealth. Cosmographers drew maps showing the supposed passage. One important promoter of exploration gave in a state paper his reasons for supporting Frobisher. First, there was a great hope that English seas opening into the seas of East India for an exchange of merchandise. Along the way were many people who had furs, hides, wax, tallow, and oil to trade much as was true in Lapland, Russia, and in adjacent lands. This trade was sure, while the assurance that land did not extend to the North Pole. Trade was trade!

A new company was formed named the Company Cathay. Frobisher's chief associate in England, Michael Lok was named to be governor of the company, having worked hard in politics and finance to arrange for the captain's first voyage and this second one. Lok was a leading mercer in London. Their grant from Queen Elizabeth provided in considerable detail for the administration of the company and its settlement or quarters in China. Because Lok had been out much time and money, he was granted one percent of all wares, goods, and merchandise brought in from the trade. Since the Queen and her people expected great wealth and trade would flow, when the explorer reached China, which should be done in the second voyage, that one percent would add greatly to Michael Lok's fortune.

In the second voyage beginning on May 31, 1577, the captain had besides the *Gabriel* and the *Michael*, a third larger ship the *Ayde*. All together, Martin Frobisher had one hundred and twenty men for mariners to merchants to man the ships. The *Ayde* was a 200 ton ship belonging to the queen commanded by Frobisher and his lieutenant George Best. Sailing around Britain, Frobisher anchored in Saint Magnue Sound in the Orkney Islands, scaring the people of the island. Underway again, the ships passed through the Sound brown by the winds and passing familiar scenes off Faroe Islands with their small birds and abundant fish. Of special interest were the "islands of ice," reaching up from the depths of the ocean. They did not taste of salt.

Troubled by the mists and the danger of grounding, they sailed on. On the open seas the voyagers sailed into a storm, in which the steerage and topmasts of the Michael were broken. Seeing floating ice on the sixteenth of July, they felt that they were close to land and soon reached Hall's Island and on other islands, killed a young seal, some fowl, and found some eggs, all of which they brought aboard.

Frobisher took a party of forty men of gentlemen and soldiers on shore of the larger island. After leaving a sufficient guard on the boats, he led his group about two miles to the top of a high hill which they called Mount Warwick, in honor of Lord Ambrose Dudley, earl of Warwick, with appropriate ceremonies and progress. They left a column or cross of stones, and retired from the barren and ragged land. However, in looking back, they saw some natives on the Mount, waving a flag, and making a great noise. Frobisher had his men reply. The noise of the English trumpets pleased the Indians and they skipped, laughed, and danced for joy.

A parley was held and a trade of possessions was effected, but neither trusted the other enough to go into their village nor on the English ships. When the English tired to capture two natives, they had to flee for the boats without them. Frobisher was wounded in the buttock with an arrow. A Cornish footman of Warwick's Nicholas Conyer then captured one of the men. The explorer's were plagued then with a stone and a troublesome fire on board the *Ayde*.

In one storm the English risked destruction with the great mountains of floating ice on every side. Some ice foes scrapped the ships. Only the skill of their sailors saved the explorers in the storm. The next morning brought an end to the tempest, and they sailed discovering a bay on the 21st of July. Within what they called Jackman's Sound was an island called

Smith's Island with a mine of silver. They thought they were on the American continent the 23d and thanked God on their knees. Next, the explorer's discovered Bear's Sound and Leicester Island, before discovering a tomb with its buried fish, various articles of life in the North Country, and learned from their captives that the natives used great dogs to pull sleds and little dogs for meat. Five leagues from Bear's Sound, they found another bay and named one island Countess Island after Warwick's wife Anne. Further on, the Englishmen found a deserted Eskimo village with whalebones in the place of timber, of which there was none in the Arctic country.

Captain York discovered a new sound, named after him, and also, a deserted native building of tents and some of the apparel of the last five men of the voyage. Their captive had been of these people and knew about the fate of the five. In his explorations, there was an encounter and a hot skirmish between the Indians and the English. The explorers also discovered the Strait of Sutherland and Queen Elizabeth Cape. There was another meeting with the natives. Because the season was so far advanced, Frobisher ordered the return to England in late August.

Once back in England from his second voyage, Frobisher hastened to Elizabeth's court at Windsor to tell the queen about the prosperous and successful voyage. The English monarch welcomed Frobisher and many noble men swarmed around to hear of his adventures. English quickly took an interest in the ore he had brought back and the Captain was courteously entertained and heartily welcomed. Elizabeth named the lands Frobisher had discovered Meta Incognita. Hope increased the preparations were begun for another expedition, and plans laid for the building of a fort in those new lands, to be staffed by forty mariners, thirty miners, and thirty soldiers. Among the soldiers, would be gold finders, bakers, and carpenters.

In late November of 1577, the astrologer, mathematician and geographer John Dee gained an audience with the queen at Windsor and spoke with Sir Francis Walsingham, her secretary of state and spy master and Sir Christopher Hatton, her leader in the parliament. Both men were leaders of the expansionist school in her council. They were patrons of seamen and colonizer in the Elizabethan council and they had much in common with Dee. A Welshman with the personality associated with that people, Dee was touchy and suspicious, was acute and imaginative, original and haphazard with an inborn tendency to go over the borderline of reality. He certainly saw ahead and dreamed great visions of English power-- except he always called it British" and implemented the phrase frequently to be used, "the British Empire." In his day, the term generally used for those two western continents, "West Indies." To Dee, this was misleading. American should have been known as Atlantis.

There were discussions about establishing English colonies in America in which Dee was drawn. These resulted in Humphrey Gilbert's patent and in Dee's being called upon to advise Elizabeth about her title to North America. He went further back than Cabot, he declared that the monarchy of England had Welsh based claims to America before Columbus since the Iceland, Greenland, and Labrodian lands to the west had been established by King Arthur and that the Welshman Prince Madoc had discovered America eight centuries before in the twelfth century. Then Dee told this to Richard Hakluyt for use in his work.

Dee had had a troubled and varied career because of his interests. In his youth, he showed great intellect. When he had taken his degree as a Master of Arts at Cambridge in 1548 in astronomy and geography, he stayed on. Later, in that same year he was accused of being a sorcerer because of his quiet interests and had to leave. He returned later, but was imprisoned by Mary's government because he drew up a horoscope more favorable to Elizabeth than

Mary. Shortly after Elizabeth became queen, she had Dee decide a most favorable date for her coronation. He was frequently at court, and when he was ill, Elizabeth sent him her own royal doctors.

Elizabeth selected Francis Drake to stir up trouble on Spanish American shores and circumnavigate the globe. Perhaps, he could find the western end of the northwest-passage to the Orient. This all was probably understood for there was no record of the talk between queen and pirate. More certain is that Drake was to have a great deal of leeway on his voyage. The royal body could be sure that Drake could cause Philip and his people a great deal to trouble. Further, it would be, hopefully, a prosperous voyage, which laid claim to any new lands that Drake might find, and perhaps much else besides. Drake was ambitious and daring and if his previous actions were any indication, he was hungry for the great coup that had previously escaped him. He was daring man of his day and Elizabeth picked him well, when she found him to accomplish that above which a single man whether it be Hawkins or anyone else could achieve given the same resources at hand.

With royal support behind him, Drake received financial backing and began fitting out five ships and four pinnaces, taken part, and showed in the ships. He has as his own flagships named the *Pelican* with its eighteen guns and weighing more than one hundred tons with a supply of weapons, a forge and equipment for a smith, shovels, axes, saws, and other useful tools for diggings, cutting timber, and building. Previously Drake had a year's supply of food. This time with a long voyage in mind, he had food and beer enough for eighteen months. All was well packed in his ship.

The four other ships were the eighty ton *Elizabeth* under John Wynter, the *Marigod* under John Thomas, and once again, a new *Swan*, fifty tons, and very small *Christopher* of fifteen tons. All five were manned by about 164 men, which included sailors and soldiers, and an apothecary, a shoemaker, a tailor, and a preacher. Also, one must count ten gentlemen adventurers who had come along having paid on the expenses, and expecting part of the glory and profits of the expedition.

The Spaniards had spies in England, but they were unable to learn about the Drake expedition, and so, Drake sailed from Plymouth in December 1577, unheralded. Sailing for the west coast of Morocco, Drake stopped along the way some Portuguese prizes from which he took need or desired provisions, but they hit pay dirt when they captured a forty-ton Portuguese smack. The fine fabrics, sherry, and modera were fine objects of cargo stealing. Also, they could use charts, astrolabes, compasses, and needles, still more valuable. What made it such as prize however was Nunez da Silva, an accomplished sailor who was a pilot who had been in Brazilian waters. Drake took him along and sent captives home in the *Christopher*, exchanged for the Portuguese ship. He had not time to ransom the rich men aboard, but might have considered the exchange in ship compensation for ransomed passengers. The new maps replaced a map bought in Lisbon some time ago, and Drake needed the new maps for his voyage.

On April 1, 1578, Drake sighted the coast of Brazil and had six ships. Drake sailed them south, and there was a trial after which Drake executed one of the gentlemen in what would have amounted to a mutiny. They reached the Magellan Strait and sailed through the uncharted body of water, but when in the Pacific, they were struck down by a storm for three weeks. The *Marigold* went down with all hands abroad. None survived from the ship's company. A separated Wynter sailed the *Elizabeth* back to England. In the midst of the storm, Drake was first to discover that there was a passage south of the straits. The channel separated islands from South America and the passage to the south was different. He discovered Cape Horn.

Chapter XXIV

ENGLAND

Meanwhile, the third voyage of Frobisher set out from Harwich on May 31, 1578, down along the south coast of England and at Cape Clear rescued the remnants in a small boat who had been attacked by the French and decimated. Frobisher and his ship sailed along the same paths as they had in the two previous voyages, and on the last of June, on Monday, they saw many great whales. Two days later, they reached the Queen's Foreland. There was some ice that prevented them from going everywhere they were interested in exploring. An iceberg struck the *Dennys* and sank it within sight of the fleet that rescued all the men from the vessel.

Frobisher met with other problems, ships became separated, he became lost, and the straits were frozen over. Further there was snow in late July. However, a port was established and a fort started. As August ended, the masons finished a house and an oven therein, and baked bread. Having to return home with the port unsettled, and expecting to be back the next year, the expedition returned home. They could not stay, they wrote, because of insufficient food and water.

The third was his last voyage. The ore did not prove to be gold. Since he never returned there was no further attempt to found a colony. The straits he discovered were no straits at all, but this was not known in the sixteenth century. Almost three hundred years later, in 1860, further explorers identified it as a bay, a large bay, 150 miles long, and from 20 to 40 miles wide. The maximum depth is 400 feet. Frobisher did however open the way to further explorers, notable among them John Davis.

Before the end of December of 1578, Drake was in the Golden Hind on the coast of Chile with only eighty men left and trouble erupted when previously friendly Indians, launched an ambush and all the English were hit. Drake barely escaped with his life with three arrows stuck in him. Two were captured and two were killed. The surgeon had already died and his assistant was back in Wynter's ship on the way to England. A ship's boy was the only substitute. A recovering Drake had to scale down his plans with only seventy-six men, but he did not explore up the coast and lost another man to Spanish horsemen. An alarm was spread then. The feared Drake was on the west coast! A scared and elderly governor of thinly settled Chile, Rodrigo de Qiroga took to bed and died. Shortly Drake captured a sizable amount of silver bars. He did play some havoc in the port of Arica.

A captured Flemish captain did not mention a treasure ship, but Drake learned about one from another source. They caught the treasure ship, but the silver had already been hidden inland with a strong guard. Another ship had already landed as Drake missed it too, but he did manage to alarm Lima's port of Callao. Unfortunately, he was unable to rescue his friend, John Oxenham in the dungeons of the Inquisition six miles away. Sailing northward, he sought after another treasure ship, while a warned viceroy in Lima put on his armor, and sword, and armed the subjects of the Spanish king in Lima. Drake had disabled the ship in the harbor and could not be quickly pursued.

Behind the English privateering and colonization was the desire for an enlarged volume of English trade. They sought to capture treasure ships for the economic value of gold and goods. They confronted the Spanish Empire to cripple and siege and to open up trade by barter. The closing of the Spanish colonies to foreign trade with foreigners was a mistake because of the great need of the colonies for goods and slaves, which the English could manufacture, transport, and provide. Mercantile Spain sought gold and control. Mercantile England was also a closed system. Colonies existed for the benefit of the homeland.

No attempt was made for specific areas to grant to colonizers until the English grant to Humphrey Gilbert that granted him specific territory. The English crown gave him authority in 1578 to expel all persons already there and to seize ships that were trading in the land grant area, and their cargoes for the enrichment of Englishmen. Although they deplored the merchantilistic theory on Span's part, the English saw nothing wrong with that of their own country. It was a long way to the free trade England of the nineteenth century.

There were several requirements for colonists, but a larger number of freedoms. Ownership in the soil belonged in full to the owners, but only gold found in each foundation was subject to condition, that one fifth would go to the sovereign. They were free to enjoy their personal and political rights, but they were to support religious doctrines professed in the Church of England. The economic benefit to England was manifold. Colonists would buy vast quantities of English woolen goods and sell great amounts of navel stores for use in building ships. The people who were idle at home could be useful in America and there was always the hope that gold mines would be discovered. Because it would increase trade, it would enlarge the number of ships that would increase the size of the navy in times of war.

Meanwhile, Drake sailed the *Golden Hind* as fast as he could to overtake the treasure bearing *Nuestra Senora de la Conception* that he had learned about. Still making progress, the pirate captain sailed into Paita, where he learned that the ship was now only two days ahead. He got in the pinnace keeping close to shore and four miles out, he had the *Golden Hind* sailing parallel to the coast. He promised a golden chain to the first man to sight the treasure ship

One day later, a ship was found, and although it was sought by his ship, Drake found some 18,000 pesos of silver aboard and took it to his ship. Sailors did find a large gold crucifix, with long emeralds, which soon was to grace a crown for Queen Elizabeth. In order that the captured ship when released, would not outsail Drake's ships and warn the quarry, Drake and his men wrapped the sails around its anchor, and dropped them into the sea. The English captured another ship a week later north of the Equator. They captured 15,000 pesos in gold and learned that the *Concepcion* was not far ahead.

About noon on March 1, 1579, Drake's ships caught of Anton's ship and by late in the evening caught up with it and boarded it after a brief fight. Drake found 400,000 pesos in silver and gold. This booty he transferred to the English ship. The English pirate gave presents to the Spanish captain and crew and a safe conduct should Wynter, whom he thought to be behind him somewhere, captured the *Concepcion* later. Bereft of the treasure, San Juan de Anton sailed to Panama to report the loss and what he now knew of possible plans by

Drake, and the English pirate went forward to the northwest for New Spain's western coast stopping at an inlet to clean and trim the *Golden Hind*. On Saturday, April 4th, Drake captured a ship with a cargo of Chinese silver and porcelain on the way to Peru from Acapulco. Next Drake took Guatulo on the Mexican coast and released Nunez da Silva, who was questioned by the Inquisitor before he was free to return to Portugal.

The English pirate went north farther than that of any European captain to a point in sight of Vancouver Island. His long sought for strait was obviously farther, much further because the coast at Vancouver Island was now going to the northwest. He named the rich country "New Albion" and set sail to cross the vast Pacific Ocean on a landless journey of sixty eight days, until he neared the famous Spice Island and pursued unsuccessfully a Portuguese royal galleon. He then joined forces with Sultan Baber of Ternate, who hated the Portuguese, and was royally received. The two leaders signed a treaty of alliance and Drake bought six tons of cloves. On December 12,1579, the English sailed westward once again for England. They hit a reef and Drake had to throw overboard eight cannon, provisions, and half of the cloves cargo to release them. This was the last great peril on the way to England. They were home once again.

It was a rich haul the official pirates brought into England and the queen suitable received Drake in a private audience and later had him knighted. There had been a division among the counselors and his life hung in the balance, but Elizabeth was sure in her own mind and Drake was not in danger. Some of the treasure went to bribe the royal advisors who had been in opposition to Drake. After the cost of the voyage was defrayed, the survivors were well paid, then the queen and others received their share. The investors received 47 pounds for each pound invested. The Crown was free from debt for the next year as a result of the haul. She invested part in the Levant Company whose profits later financed the East India Company and laid the basis for England's financial base. From this, there was capital and profits for England for centuries to come.

When the kingdom of Peru, or as it correctly should be called, the viceroyalty of Peru, was newly in the hands of the Spanish, a young friar, Reginaldo de Lizarraga, about the time of Drake, traveled its length and breadth. He observed its people, its lands, and later wrote his book of geography and history for people to read finally in the twentieth century, after gathering dust in manuscript. This land was long and narrow from Puerto Viejo in the north to Chile in the south. It was abundantly blessed with fields of wheat, corn, and other fruits of the earth, cows and sheep, and horses. The land's temperature was warm, but in moderation, refreshed by the air of the Pacific Ocean. The rain was good, but not heavy. Indians of Puerto Viejo made good sailors as suited this busy port. Many products moved thorough its portals. Following further on, we find the Cape of Santa Elena. There are few or not Indians there and it is a point to take water and find a hostelry not far away. Also, one finds a source of liquid pitch and gum.

To the south is the second Spanish town, that of Santiago de Guayaquil. It is very hot being away from the sea breezes. The plaza there is very small. The river that provides a beach is very copious and large. That river is navigable, but ships can only enter it during the floodtide and exit the river with the ebb tide. There is a great deal of velocity and violence of flow between the two. At this time, Guayaquil was bothered with many pests. In season, the town was troubled with mosquitoes. Guayaquil is the port city of Quito, supplying to Lima a large amount of very good wood. It is not wheat country, but maize is abundant as are oranges, limes, and fruits of the earth, including watermelon. Quito is almost two hundred miles inland from the sea. Some seventy-five miles of the journey was traveled by the river and the rest of the journey was undertaken by land. It took four or five days in the summer. Indians tribes and settlements could be seen along the way. Lizarrago discussed the converts nearby and entered into the valley of Chicama.

Fray Vicente de Valverde was the first bishop in these reigns. He was the religious leaders for all of Peru from Panama to the southern advance of Chile. He was reputed in that bishopric to have great treasure found where the Indians had concealed it. The Marquez Pizarro was sent from Lima with a few people who had discovered it and taken it.

The next port is Tumbez, where there is beach and wild coastline, and river and a supply of good water. The river cannot be entered because of the sea of falls and waves. Fishermen lived along its coast. Down the coast there is a river of Matape with a port of the same name, and beyond is the port to Paita and the city of San Miguel de Piura, the first that the Spanish built in this realm. This country produces large numbers of insects. The valley of Jayanca is very fertile. In it are many Indians and many encomiendas, where the Spaniards are served with expensive silver ware. There are also many mosquitoes and pests to plague the people, both Indians and Spaniards. Further on, one must be careful of quicksand.

In this area of the viceroyalty of Peru, there are many fruitful and wide valleys. These lands have been irrigated. Behind the valleys are the high mountains of the Andes with their year around peaks of snow. These mountains run commonly 17 to 10 leagues of the sea. Most of the Indians are concentrated near the coast. The Indians of these areas speak two different languages.

Two leagues or six miles from the coast is the port for the city of Trujillo, a rich city whose conqueror neighbors were very friendly to the travelers who came that way. They take you to their houses, regale you, and help you on your way in this inn-less country. On the coast are Indians adept at swimming and fishing. The area is noted for its buried treasure. Lizarrago writes here of the large and well fitted stone walls and foundations built without picks, strong cutters hammers or carpenter's squares to labor the stone.

Next to the south is the valley of Sonta with its port and irrigated fields. It grows large and round pumpkins. Beyond which are man other valleys with more Indians to serve their Spanish masters. Wheat and corn are grown here as well as sugar cane. It supplies Lima to the south. Lima is the seat of the viceroys, the audiencia, the Inquisition, and the University. It is on a large river draining part of the mountains.

To the south along the coast is the valley called Pachacamad, a narrow one of two leagues at its most wide and having fertile soil. At the entrance of the valley is an ancient Indian tomb dedicated to its creator-god. Nest is the valley of Chilca in corn and fruit country. There are a number of valleys further to the south until one reaches the valley of Canete. It raised corn, wheat, grapes, olives, and fruit. It had ancient irrigation systems. One valley to the south had 30,000 tributary Indians when the Spanish came, but now the inhabitants numbered less than 600. In the Chincha valley, there were the usual religions, noted over the countryside worshipping God in their own way. To the south, was the port of Arica.

Lizarrago now reaches the silver mining districts, and the southern Quito, followed by the valley of Riobamba, unpopulated by Indians. The Spanish raised wheat and cattle in the country. They entered hostile Indian territory in Chile and the city of Santiago de Chile. To the east, is the country of Tucuman, which is now part of Argentina and the land port of Peru. Inland also is the rich Indian capital of Cuzco and in Upper Peru, the mining districts of

Potosi, La Paz, and La Plata. Upper Peru became modern Bolivia. Quicksilver in these districts destroyed many Indian laborers. It was from this land that Drake's treasure came.

Half-brother of Sir Walter Raleigh and the son of Sir Otho Gilbert, Humphrey Gilbert, born into a noble family, studied at Eton and Oxford, and served as a servitor of a captain under Sir Henry Sidney and the governor of Munster in 1569. He was knighted in 1570 as a reward for his services in Ireland. During the next year, Gilbert entered the parliament and the next was an officer in the Netherlands fighting the Spaniards. Because of his interest in western discovery, he had petitioned "Queen Elizabeth unsuccessfully in 1566 to seek the famed northwest-passage, and wrote a tract about the sea road to Cathay, which was published in 1576. On June 11, 1578, Elizabeth gave him his famed royal patent to discover and possess land in America. He met with disaster on is first expedition of seven ships.

With five vessels, Sir Humphrey Gilbert departed on June 11, 1583, and reached Newfoundland to claim that island to be within the scope of his patent. He dominated the fishermen who were there from other countries and appropriated their fish and food for his own men. In return, Gilbert gave them vague promises of future benefits. His Saxon miner, Daniel found some ore to take back for assaying. Refusing to accompany him further, two captains and a considerable number of men set out on their own and he left a ship behind to transport some sick men back to England, when they recovered. With three ships, Gilbert headed for Sable Island where the Portuguese were raising swine and cattle. Gilbert met disaster in the wreck of the *Delight* and lost a large number of men. Then the Englishmen returned home. Traveling in the smaller of the two ships, Gilbert was lost at sea with his great dreams, to be unfilled by himself; but which were to the developed greater than his expectations in later centuries.

The preacher, Richard Hakluyt, was the most influential European bound promoter for the movement for English expansion in the world. Although he never went on ship to the New World, Hakluyt had more influence in the sixteenth century than any of the violent pirates, dauntless explorers, and success motivated merchants of England. He labored behind the scenes with steady resolution, using the pen for propaganda for colonial expansion and for exciting discussion of the development of scientific geography. In his profession, he preached for colonies and maritime enterprise and claimed this action in was God's plan for the universe.

As a student of Westminster School, he was connected in a mystical sense to the science of geography, and this conviction was the treat of his life, and this vocation as a preacher promoted his intellectual calling. At Christ Church, Oxford, Hakluyt studied religion and fulfilled his Protestant duties. When his duty was finished, Richard read whatever books on geography he could find in the library and books stalls at Oxford. Various learned men and students aided him in the young man's scientific studies. Earning his bachelor's degree in 1574 and his master's degree in 1577, Richard took holy orders and gave up-to-date public lectures in cosmography with reformed maps and gloves and geographical instruments. Many preachers, including Richard, preached an anti-Spanish imperialism and swayed the public into the imperialistic camp of Walsingham, Essex, and Raleigh. They wanted an attack upon the Spanish colonies, but Queen Elizabeth I pursued more cautious policy allowing Englishmen to take individual action in raids of piracy.

Richard wrote a book promoting settlement in North America. In this 1582 publication, he stressed the humanitarian settlement of petty offenders, who were in overcrowded English prisons, and felt that they would be eager to undertake honest and useful work in colonies north of Spanish Florida. The English could serve God's course by advancing Christianity. This book was later read by the directors of the East India and Virginia companies.

Although he really wanted to go on Sir Humphrey's expedition, Hakluyt went instead to France in the autumn of 1583 to serve five years as chaplain in the English embassy in Paris. Besides his religious duties, he talked with learned men and sailors and studied maps that the best geographers of Europe had created form information from explorers and geographers. He had thoughts on the evangelical efforts for the Indians and the settlement of English Protestants overseas. He also advised French Protestants, while keeping up with the religious threat of Spain. He left France for England and a religious post there. It was time, he thought, for a Protestant empire for French Huguenots who were being persecuted in France and for other Protestants in Europe.

There was a great deal of interest in overseas matters in the opening months of 1584 and many preparations for expeditions. From his Paris post, Richard Hakluyt was making plans and during the spring was trying to get English merchants in Roven to invest in one of his ventures in the west. Sir Humphrey Gilbert's Newfoundland enterprise was subject to development. Sir John Gilbert and others had an interest in northern American land with plans whose details are lost to us. Christopher Carleill set out on an expedition, perhaps for New England but which got no further than Ireland. In February, the queen gave the patent for the northwest discoveries to Adrian Gilbert as the logical successor to Sir John Gilbert. Parallel to that was a patent to his half-brother, Walter Raleigh.

By letters dated March 25, 1584, Elizabeth granted for the benefit of herself and her heirs and successors to her well beloved Walter Raleigh, and to his heirs, a license to discover and search remote countries and territories not actually possessed or inhabited by Europeans. He would have certain prerogatives, commodities, jurisdictions, royalties, privileges, franchises, and preeminences. She allowed travels to the west to inhabit and posses the land and such cities, towns, and villages and other places. The queen reserved for herself one fifth part of all the gold and silver gained there.

Raleigh made his April, 1584, voyage to North America with two vessels, a ship and a smaller vessel. Two gentlemen in his service, Philip Amadas and Arthur Barlow were captains of the two vessels. He gave them orders to discover the land that lay between Norembega and Florida. They were deemed to be the discoverers of Virginia in their own time. On April 27, 1584, the two men departed from Plymouth with written instructions from Raleigh back on the banks of the Thames where the ships were prepared for their voyages. All did not go well. Contrary winds delayed them and they did not reach the Canaries until the tenth of May. They made average time for the long journey to the West Indies and were at the island of Puerto Rico on the tenth of June. Sailing northward, they made contact with the mainland about midway between Cape Lookout and Cape Hatteras. Off the sandy beach the Englishmen found a land full of grapes, wild life, and woods.

On the third day, the travelers spied a small boat with three persons aboard. The Indians rowed toward them. They landed and one man walked on the sandy beach and without doubt or fear communicated with the Englishmen who had come up. Being brought aboard, the Indian received a shirt and a hat and other things. He tasted the English meat and wine with a liking for both. Departing, the Indian went to his boat, caught many fish, and went through a ceremony of unknown significance to the captain and their sailors. They were later visited by the native king's brother and a handsome and goodly party of forty to fifty men. The king was recovering from war wounds received in a battle with a neighboring king.

With the passage of a day or two, the English and the Indians began trading. Each got those things they lacked; English merchandise was plentiful in England and of low value there, and the same could be applied to Indian goods whatever the English dollar value there, and the same could be applied to Indian goods whatever the English dollar value. After observing, visiting, and learning about the country, Amadas and Barlow directed the ships back to home in England.

Chapter XXV

RALEIGH

Before Amadas and Barlow had returned, Raleigh had requested Richard Hakluyt to lay the way for the English occupation and settlement of the coast. In July of 1584, the penmen of English colonization, Hakluyt, began writing his *Discourse of Western Planting* to propagandize the Raleigh colonial idea. It was only part of an elaborate plan to move Queen Elizabeth I to sponsor settlement. Hakluyt argued that such an endeavor would embarrass Spain, strengthen England's position in the world, solve English unemployment problems, and develop English commerce and industry.

When on October 5, 1584, Hakluyt presented his manuscript to the queen, she and the English people were still interested in Amada's two Indians, skins, and pearls. The explorer's glowing report of great American resources and commercial opportunity, and of the strategic possibilities of Virginia were backed by Richard's arguments, but Elizabeth was normally slow to act. She rewarded Hakluyt however, and he returned to Paris where he was the embassy chaplain.

Sir Walter Raleigh was encouraged by the queen and he had a bill drafted for Parliament to confirm his legal title to lands discovered by his endeavors under the patent terms previously mentioned. The Commons passed it but when the parliament wanted to make additions, Raleigh had it dropped after its first reading in the House of Lords. The committee for its consideration in Commons, was made up by those interested in America, namely investor Sir Christopher Hatton, supporter of western ventures, Sir Francis Walsingham, Sir Philip Sidney, Sir Frances Drake, Sir Richard Greenfield, and others.

The Indians, Manteo and Wanchese, brought to England in September, interested the English and were rapidly learning English. They had a major role by their mere presence in the country, of promoting Raleigh's idea of settlement. It has been suggested that Thomas Hariot in Walter's household was the one who taught them English, because in the next year, he had special responsibility for Indian relations in the voyage of 1585. Hariot had been teaching Raleigh mathematics and teaching pilots and masters for the journey's navigation.

Queen Elizabeth supported the voyage of 1585 and invested in kind in the venture for royal profit beyond her fifth of any gold and silver found. On the Twelfth Day at Greenwich, she knighted Raleigh. She then gave the adventurer authority to name the new territories "Virginia," for the Virgin Queen, in her honor. Next, she gave him, as some of her part invested, gunpowder from the Tower, lent him one of her ships the *Tiger*, and released Ralph Lane from service in Ireland to help Raleigh with his voyage.

On April 9, 1585, Sir Richard Grenville sailed Raleigh's expedition of seven vessels from Plymouth. Simon Fernandez was the chief pilot of the fleet carrying about six hundred men. The queen's *Tiger* was the flagship. They made their way southward and near the coast of Portugal met a storm which sank a pinnace and scattered the squadron. Grenville reached Puerto Rico and landed on one of the neighboring islands to refresh his men. At Tallaboa Bay, which was probably the rendezvous, Grenville ordered construction of an elaborate encampment with earthworks, a swamp, and a stream as defenses. It was made strong to protect the English from Spanish strength nearby and as a more or less permanent base for English activities in the West Indies. Thomas Cavendish arrived in the *Elizabeth* on May 19, 1585, to the relief of Grenville.

Governor Diego Menendez de Valdes of Puerto Rico had received reports about the *Tiger* since it first appeared and ordered a watch upon the English. He thought that they meant only to take on water and leave, but when the English remained, they were visited by patrols of Spanish horsemen. Suddenly, Grenville decided to leave and to lay in wait with his ships for the Spanish. He took some prizes. When Lane was exposed on shore to gather salt from salt mounds, he rejoined the *Tiger* and quarreled with Grenville about the incident. His anger was to last through a series of disagreements and wrecked the harmony of the voyage. With five vessels, including those captured, Grenville traded with the Spaniards.

By the time the authorities stopped the exchange, the English had sailed on the twenty-ninth for the northern shore of Hispaniola, where they found the Spaniards around Puerto de Plata used to trade with the French, and eager to exchange with the English. Grenville and a party enjoyed an elaborate entertainment given in their honor with feats and a bullfight. This trade enabled him to go forth for the proposed colony on the American mainland that they sighted in mid-June.

At the future harbor of Beaufort, North Carolina, the *Tiger* ran into trouble and was beached. All of her corn, salt, meal, rice, biscuit, and other provisions were destroyed or damaged by the salt water. She had a large part of the supplies of these provisions. Grenville led an expedition of the mainland and visited the Indians. After establishing a colony, Grenville sailed forth leaving Lane and 106 other men there. The ships captured a rich ship with a large cargo of sugar, hides, spices, gold, silver, and pearls. On October 18, 1585, Grenville was back in England with his fleet. A happy Raleigh made plans to supply the colony in Virginia.

In May of 1585, Spanish officials boarded some English ships in the harbors of Spain and arrested and imprisoned the captains and crews. Next, they confiscated the cargoes. Only one of the ships escaped. The *Primrose* of London quickly set sail, with the arresting corregidor aboard, a captive of those he wished captured. This ship reached home and spread the alarm. Englishmen learned about this piracy of legal traders and grew angry. The merchants who had lost the goods clamored for redress. This they got.

In July, the Lord Admiral examined the claims and issued letters of reprisal for the capture of compensating Spanish goods at sea. Elizabeth did not go to war with Philip, but his actions added to the crises at hand, and there was now a private naval war on the high seas, an escalation of that which already existed in the exploits of Drake and others. Soon a large number of Englishmen who had not suffered loss joined the volunteer force at sea, gaining fraudulent letters of reprisal, and Admiralty license form his court and person, or letters patent from the queen. Others failed without light. This was to become "a common traffic."

Meanwhile, Davis had already gone on his northwest journey of exploration. John Davis was a few years married when he undertook his first northwest voyage in 1585. His son, Gilbert was two years old and a daughter was or had died in infamy. Having proved himself at sea and with the right contacts, Davis was available to conduct another enterprise for the finding of a northwest-passage, believed by his countrymen Frobisher to be already found, and which John was to advance. A number of gentlemen and merchants of court and country, of London and West Country, desiring to advance God's glory, and to seek the good of their native country, consulted together, but met with, by unlooked for problems, resolved to provide financing and a chief conductor for this effort. William Sanderson, a London merchant, was given the overseers task and he picked Davis to undertake the voyage.

After all things were prepared, Davis took his two ships out of Dartmouth on June 7, 1585, the *Sunshine* of London, and aptly a smaller, the *Moonshine*, and sailed to Falmouth; and five days later, with the right winds were underway again. They had to stop at the Scully Islands because of contrary winds. Twelve more days passed. In July, they saw porpoises and whales. Nearing Greenland in the fog, they reached the southern part on the twentieth. The fog raised. When John saw the deformed rocks and mountainous lands, he called it the land of Desolation. Soon the ships sailed around the cape and headed northwestward.

While exploring off the Greenland coast, they enticed some Indians to visit, and on the next morning, the thirty of July, men in 37 canoes came to call. The natives played for them on their seal skin drums, more like a timbrel, but beaten with a stick. Englishmen and Indians became good friends on the visit. Davis' men bought five canoes and articles of apparel. On August 1, 1585, they sailed with a fair wind. They explored further and found a mount which Davis named Mount Raleigh. Shortly, they saw their first white bears and killed one, who almost escaped in the water, wounded but defiant. They killed a second and explored further in the strait between Greenland and the western shore, before returning home. On the 30th of September, they came into Dartmouth.

In their exploration of the North American coast, the English discovered that the land was good, with forests and Indian-clearings of a fertile ground. They had spent the period from July 1585 to June 1586 on the American coast and therefore the winter on their voyage gave them climatic knowledge of the land. They had experienced winters with less cold temperatures than that they were used to in England. Although, they were to soon settle Ronaoke Island, this tract of land had limited resources, being without great agricultural or mineral attractions and lacking in good harbors. What was there was subject to severe coastal storms as the English discovered.

Some explorers had gone further to the north and found the region just to the south of Chesapeake Bay to be more open and fertile, and the natives friendly. When they learned of an inland sea, the English of that party went north and observed the southern shore and the open area to the southern tip of the Virginian eastern shore. A storm prevented a later trip by Ralph Lane to explore the great bay that he too had heard about.

In the autumn of 1585, the ship the *Black Dog* of London left England and went to the West Indies. The captain pursued a conventional strategy by sailing along the north coast of Cuba seeking prizes. There were forty men on the voyage and they succeeded in capturing three Spanish ships according to Richard Hakluyt or some eight or nine according to a deposition about the voyage. At any rate, these prizes yielded hens and victuals being sent to supply the galleys at Avand plus pipes of Spanish wine. One enemy ships had iron, horseshoes, wrought iron, cloth, olives, and not much else.

Then came trouble when they met up with an armed ship they could not force to surrender after an extended fight. Instead, the Spanish captain asked for peace talks or parlays. Several Spaniards came on board the *Black Dog* for the negotiations and entertainment, then quietly departed. Next, the Spaniards invited some Englishmen to visit their ships. This was done, but the Spanish captain and his men stabbed and killed English pilot Roger Kingshod and some of the privateers, while the rest leaped overboard and were rescued by an English boat, wounded but safe. The expedition was soon ended and the *Black Dog* returned to England.

With a well-organized and efficient fleet, Sir Francis Drake sailed forth once again on the 14th of September of 1585 and captured ships to the southward as they sailed. One Spanish vessel provided a cargo of dried Newfoundland fish. Others had jewels and leather. Sailing along the Spanish coast, they avoided a countryside's vengeance. He missed the treasure-bearing flotilla he sought so diligently. Next, he took and burned some Cape Verde towns, which were left by the Spanish undefended.

Misfortune struck when a malignant fever which they picked up in their stay ashore killed three hundred men in Drake's fleet, but undeterred, Drake attacked Santo Domingo from the landslide with aid from Cimmarron in the mountains. This third city of the American Empire fell and the Spanish governor had to ransom a partially demolished city. The English captured many slaves of Turkish, Moorish, black, French, and Greek birth. To leave was most advisable because the city was in an unhealthy position and the losses to fevers during this voyage had already been great. When Drake was to return to England with the news of these two successes, it informed the whole country with a desire to go to sea as privateers.

With a royal ship the *Victory* and others manned by about four hundred sailors, soldiers, and gentlemen, the earl of Cumberland made havoc of the French ships and Portuguese Azores in the summer and fall of 1589. On June 21st, three days after leaving Plymouth Sound, Cumberland captured three French ships as prizes. While two were sent to an English prize court with their French cargo of fish, the third was sent back to France with the men of all three. If Cumberland had kept them as prisoners, the French would have only been in the way.

English ships were met along the way and given victuals. They captured next a fleet of eleven ships off the coast of Spain with little resistance. After taking a cargo of pepper and cinnamon, the earl released the ships and their crews. Since this shipment belonged to a Lisbon Jew, it was considered a lawful prize, but the rest belonged to German merchants and were not taken. Seven of the men aboard the eleven went with the English, interested in the possibility of great profits in the pirate life.

At the easternmost Azores Island of St. Michael, they came in at night under the Spanish flag. Silently they reached the ships in the harbor and severed their cables. One was the *Falcon* of London, but the others were towed away for their cargo of wine and oil from Seville, Seeing their own ships dragged to sea the Spaniards leaped overboard, and with loud cries swam ashore. The town was alerted and its people cried out. Gunners in the castle fired into the darkness and the Scots in the *Falcon* fired into the air, making the Spaniards think they were enemies of the pirates. Days later, the English privateers captured a ship with thirty tons of good Madiera wine plus a supply of woolen cloth, silk, taffeta etc.

As August passed, Cumberland and his men captured in a fight, a Spanish ship whose captain was Juan de Palva and gained a ship with its large cargo of sugar, ginger, and hides from delightful San Juan de Puerto Rico. The pirates then went in under the guns of the castle and took five small ships with various shipments of hides, elephant teeth, grain, coconuts, goat skins from Guinea, wood and dogfish. John Davis and Markesbury aided their ships in this particular capture, having joined Cumberland sometime before. Raleigh owned Markesbury's ship.

On his second voyage, John Davis had four ships, two others in addition to *Sunshine* and *Moonshine*. They were the 120 ton flagship the *Mermayde* and the pyrne the *Northstar*. Leaving Dartmouth on May 7, 1586, Davis discovered Cape Farewich on the fifteen of June. Because of sleet and snow, the English explorers were unable to land. The shore had ice protruding leagues into the strait. They reached a point near Gilbert Sound. Later, they were warmly greeted by the Indians and went to their villages with their seal skin tents set up with timber and stores of dried small fish. On the fourth of July, the English found a multiple grave with a cross of some tragedy known only to God.

The English later wrote about the natives, who had by now become most friendly and helpful when Davis and his men were climbing the rock strewn slopes of the high hills. Both peoples engaged in wrestling matches with each other. The natives were strong and nimble with such skills in wrestling, that, the English wrote, they won over some Englishmen who were good wrestlers. However, the explorers could outleap the Indians. They worshipped images and spun incantations. Because the English thinking this was sorcery and sacrifice, because of the words and gestures used destroyed the fire. The Indians asked Davis to enter the smoke, but he thrusted a native into the smoke and had an Englishmen tread out the fire, and throw the operation into the nearby sea. The Indians had such a desire for iron and other items, they stole such until the English were forced to withdraw. Furthermore, they had dart weapons and some slings, bows and arrows, and used nets to catch the fish they ate without cooking.

Continuing to explore, Davis and his men found nothing but mountains along the rugged coast and into the interior. There were many sounds and inlets that required a mountainous noting. Looking for the continent, the English found nothing but island, Indians returned and were well treated, but during the night, the Indians threw stones with their slings. There was no peace with them. Such was the case with many of the American tribes. They would make mischief, or make war with many of the American tribes. They would do so and then sue for peace to avoid punishment. At 63 degrees and eight minutes, Davis found a glacier that astounded the Englishmen. Soon ice clogged the seas preventing further advance, but they discovered a current that they thought might be the desired passage.

Back to the south, Davis discovered geese and other birds and forests of fir, pine, apple, alder, jew, wither, and birch and a black bear. There were also great schools of fish. Indians attacked them, but fled when the English fired their guns. Davis had some losses to native arrows. After another storm, Davis gave orders with the right wind, they headed home and arrived in the West Country in the beginning of October. Davis brought home large numbers of sealskins.

Sir Walter Raleigh's second undertaking war made in 1587 under the leadership of Governor John White to place a colony to the south shore of Chesapeake Bay. There was a possibility the English thought that this settlement would become the base in North America for English shipping. People in the expedition were seeking new lives away from crowded and plague ridden London and economic depression in the agricultural lands of England. They sought great opportunity such as the offer of five hundred acres for each adventurer. Such a grant would make them rich in sixteenth century terms. White played the role of promoter and leader. A member of a smaller craft company in the city, the Painter-Stainers, White found the support, probably using Raleigh's name and connections once he had Raleigh's agreement. Raleigh assigned a company of adventurers the lands he had been allowed under the queen's decree en bloc. White and his twelve assistants were made gentlemen with grants of arms.

White and his Portuguese chief pilot often quarreled on the trip from England, beginning on April 26, 1587. He left his colonists who were settled on Roanoke Island. The people needed the friendship, but found hostility because Ralph had had the native chief killed in June of 1586. Indians had killed several of Grenville's men. Soon after the colonist's arrival, John Whittier's granddaughter, Virginia Dare, was born on the island, the first English child born in British North America. White returned to England and made a return voyage that was attacked by pirates and barely made its way to England. Finally, in 1590, White was able to return to his colony, only to discover, it had disappeared having left the settlement. No one knows what happened, but there is a possibility that Powhatan was directly responsible for their murders, based upon a confession of Indians to Captain John Smith and Indian descendants. The base of this claim further are those of the Indians who wanted to have white ancestors who "could talk in a book."

On August 5, 1589, John Chidley embarked from Plymouth with three ships seeking achievement of a trip around the world like Magellan's and Drake's *Lion*. The English decided to seize the riches of Arauce on the coast of Chile, but they were never to make it. All ships kept company to the Canaries and Cape Blanco; twelve days after leaving this point, *The Delight* was separated from the other two ships and their two small Pinnaces. *The Delight* kept course along the coast of Brazil and passed the Riber Platte before being struck by various diseases which killed sixteen persons. They landed at Port Desire on the coast of Argentina and recuperated for seventeen days. There, the captain hoped to make contact with the other two ships.

Next, the captain of the ship sailed it toward the straits and arrived there about the first of January. Needing the additional food, they killed penguins from Penguin Island and salted certain hogsheads or barrels of the bird, but found out they would still have to eat them soon. Tragedy struck again when they sent a boat with fifteen men to the island for the rest of their provisions and were suddenly struck by bad weather. The boat and its men never returned. Further into the Strait of Magellan, they met with a single Spaniard who was sole survivor of four hundred Spaniards, now dead from famine. These had been sent there to guard the passage in 1582 and keep out foreigners. Another colony had also been wiped out. Later, five Englishmen were killed by Indians. All in all, the *Delight* was six weeks in the straits, but because of contrary winds, they never reached the Pacific. On February 14, 1590, they set out for home. They had a miserable trip back by the coasts of Argentina and Brazil. They were driven onto rocks in Normandy to be broken up by the Normans in search of plunder. Four Englishmen reached England to find the other ships had survived the passage and were in port.

Chapter XXVI

CARIBBEAN

An optimistic Davis set out on his third voyage on May 19, 1587, in three ships and had an encounter with the savages one month and one day into his voyage on an island. Next, they were met with a dangerous leak. They saw some whales and later traded with the natives. Sighting Mount Raleigh, they searched further in Davis Strait, with as many islands. It was a fairly event filled voyage and the ships were back in Dartmouth on the fifteenth of September.'

In the afternoon of Wednesday, the tenth of September, the earl of Cumberland and his privateers reached Fayal road and called upon the Spaniards there to give way without resistance, but the Spaniards on the fortifications replied that it was against their allegiance to the king to surrender without fighting. Cumberland sent his men ashore and then took the town and its fortifications without a struggle; the Spanish soldiers dispersed and vanished before the English; all under fire from the ships. That town was ransomed for two thousand ducats, mostly paid in expensive church plate. Later, the island of Fraciosa was not so easily gained, although the English only asked for water, wine, and food from the island of the Azores. This ended in a truce and supplies for the privateers. Difficulties increased while they sailed among the islands.

While involved with the preparations for the Armada, the Duke of Medina Sidonia came across a report which claimed that the English had made a settlement on St. John's island near Newfoundland. This concerned the duke because it would provide the English with an efficient naval base which could interfere with Basque fishermen off Newfoundland, who were an important supplier of Spanish food. He ordered a naval expedition to take out this settlement.

Governor Pedro Menendez of Florida sent two fast vessels captained by Vicente Gonzales, but ordered it to proceed only to the thirty-ninth degree of latitude above Chesapeake Bay, which Pedro himself had discovered in 1573 and named the Bay of Santa Maria. At the time, the island of St. John was believed by the Spaniards to be at 43 degrees latitude, Menendez was not interested in this target, but in attacking the French believed to be of the coast of South Carolina. Gonzalez could not find any Frenchmen and one of the ships returned to San Augustine. The Spanish discovered a port in Winyah Bay where Gonzalez talked to an Indian chief who was wearing ear pendants of beaten gold, which the native said came from Indian tribes in mountains three days journey to the west. The captain thought that New Mexico must be just beyond these mountains.

There was, the chief stated, a passage to the Pacific held by the English. Of course, the chief did not know what he was talking about meaning to please the Spaniards. He could know nothing of a great ocean to the west and about a passage, but he based his statement on word reaching him about the English colony of Roanoke. Next, on his search, Gonzalez and his sailors sailed north and explored Chesapeake Bay, which they reported back was fabulous.

One of the most successful of English privateers and pirates in the Caribbean and Gulf of Mexico was the relatively unknown Captain Christopher Newport. He sailed in a number of raiding voyages before he became captain on his own. Newport plundered the shipping and coastal towns of the West Indies on a regular basis from 1588 to the end of the Anglo-Spanish War and went to the Indies to trade for years later. Newport was born in 1560 and later was on an expedition to Brazil. It was an ill-fated voyage, marred by jealousies and divisions among the merchants and the sailors. Because of the hostilities of Portuguese authorities, unity and more was needed, but there was no agreement among the Indians. In a quarrel, Newport and two other seamen left the ship for shore and settled for some time on the Brazilian coast. When the Portuguese attacked, the English captain had gathered a crew and ship to sail away. Two years later, he was a English seamaster and got married to Katherine Procter in 1584.

Newport was a master-mate in one of Drake's privateer ships on his attack on Cadiz. With the defeat of the Armada in 1588, he remained prizehunting on the coast of Spain and then took a privateering cruise. Next, he was captain in a fleet in the West Indies. They were just off the Cuban coast to the northwest, not to far from Havana, when they tried to capture two Mexico treasure ships. A quick blow to his right arm took it off, but a now one-armed Newport survived. Every year for four voyages in succession, he raided in the West Indies. In 1595, Newport traveled to the Mediterranean and came back with the capture of two Spanish ships, although he was supposed to be on a trading voyage.

In February or March of 1590, Captain William Irish, a man in the household of Sir George Carey, sailed the *Bark Young* from England for the Caribbean. Arriving off the south side of Santo Domingo in May, Irish and his men captured a Spanish ship with a load of sugar and hides. Irish had related to Puerto Rican officials that he was bound for Florida to pick up some two hundred Englishmen castaways from an English ship. Historians had suggested that the ship mentioned by Diego Menendez de Valdes in Puerto Rica was the ship *John Evangelist* sent out in that year by John Watts, but this ship was still in Dominica at the time Menendez de Valdes or his compadres talked with the English off Puerto Rico.

Irish probably knew of the Watt's ships mission and talked of that as being his own in order to provide a cover. The captain of the *Bark Young* had apparently been off the coast of Florida in 1587. There was subsequently other captures of prize ships for Irish with the aid of the *Falcon's flight*, a ship of Barnstaple owned by John Norris, a merchant promoter of numerous privateering undertakings. There was a clash with even French ships laden with dried fish off Newfoundland on a northern excursion later that year. The French captured the Spanish vessels that had been captured and sailed by the English. Irish and his men lost their prize cargo of sugar and hides with this French success.

Numerous corsairs swarmed the Caribbean by June of 1591, more it seemed to one Spanish official than was usual for the season. English historians counted eleven English privateers in the West Indies and there might have been more. John Watts and his various partners sent forth five ships as raiders, Sir George Carey launched three, and there were another three sent out individually. two ships and one ship separate. Watts' expedition of five ships was headed by the *Centaur* under Captain William Lamb, an experienced seaman who had already sailed in reprisal voyages for five years. He was also an able merchant and a member of the London Clothworkers Company. Watts himself belonged to this company and they had known each other for a long time.

The other four captains were unreliable as events turned out and three of the four were later to be suspected of embezzling prize goods on this voyage. There was dissension among the captains and several were on bad terms. Michael Geare had twice been to the West Indies. He had raided for six years during which he was turbulent and a leader of the problem seamen of his age. Watts was the major shareholder, and one the lesser holders of stock in the venture was Sir Walter Raleigh.

Captain William Irish was once again leader of Carey's expedition to the West Indies. The other captains were Ralph Lee and Nicholas Iisle. Lee was a minor gentleman, adventurer who had worked Sir George Carey's livery for some forty years and had been on reprisal raids for Carey four or five times. Before these they had done sea service for the Prince of Orange and the Prince of Corde. Irish's master, William King was to prove himself and in the following year to head an important expedition. Our Christopher Newport was to lead the two ships to Barbary for trade before going to the West Indies. Captain John Oker led the other, the single ship, forth.

Carey's Irish sailed his three ships in mid-spring and towards the end of May had reached the Caribbean. Watt's Lane took his five ships out of Plymouth, but the *Hopewell* lagged behind and never rejoined the fleet. The logging ship took a prize southward of the Canaries on the third of May and encountered Carey's expedition near Puerto Rico. Lane left behind another ship that Lord Thomas Howard was in. It has been suggested that this was intentional. A few days passed. They were westward of Cadiz when they captured a Spanish vessel with a cargo of hides, bullion, precious stones, other goods, and some money. Michael Geare and Stephen Mitchell conspired against Lant to squabble violently over the rich loot and shortly they reached Tenerife where they sold the prize and set course for the West Indies. With his two ships, Newport sailed off the coast of Hispaniola at La Yaguana and in combination with three other ships, possibly Watt's fleet took as its prize the *Nuestra Senora del Rosario*. The other three ships took three prizes.

On June 13, 1591, a Spanish patrol was sent to Cape San Antonio at the western end of Cuba to meet the incoming fleet from New Spain and escort to Havana on the north side of the island, but met instead Irish's three ships and the *Hopewell*. Diego de la Ribara commanded the Spanish naval escort fleet that was much superior in fire power and size. It was five o'clock in the morning of the thirteenth when the English described six Spanish sail. Four of the six were seen to be armadas of six hundred tons and seven hundred tons off the Cape de Corrientes to the east of San Antonio. Here was a chance at first glance to take some fine prizes. Then the Englishmen knew that it would soon be a fight from the signals to Spaniards made to each other.

After prayers, the privateers prepared themselves for battle. There was a first fire of three hours. Having the worst of the fight, the English sought escape, but this was delayed. The men of the *Content* were led by Lisle and Kind in a desperate battle until almost midnight. Eventually, they made it away, but the *Bark Barr* caught and blew up. Most of the men of the *Bark Burr* lost their lives. Irish and sixteen others were taken aboard the *Swallow*. Separated from the other English ships, the *Content* escaped.

The *Hopewell* and the *Swallow* returned to Cape Corrientes where they found land and five ships and joined them on the nineteenth. A number of these took three prizes bound for Havana to join the main fleet. The three carried hides, sugar, and ginger. Next, this fleet of eight ships and three prizes went along the northern coast pass Havana without trouble. Off the coast of Mantanzas, they sent the *Prudence* and the *Lion* to take the prizes home, and of the remaining fleet, Watt's four ships and the *Swallow* sailed back to western Cuba to hunt further prey. They thought of "wintering in the country," but success was to dictate their return to England.

In mid-July, the *John* and the *Pegasus* pursued and captured the stray *St. John* of Seville, a good prize with a cargo of hides and cochineal. After removing the cochineal, the English sailors burnt the vessel with its hide cargo. Later that day, four more Santo Domingo men fell captive. One had a supply of sugar and hides while the other was laden with turtles. On of the following day, they took the rich *Trinity* from Navarro's fleet with silver, cochineal, and hides. All in all, there take was so valuable, they left Cuban waters and went back to England. All eight prizes made a fine haul, worth about 40,000 pounds after pilferage and theft.

Lord Thomas Howard sent out four ships under the command of Captain Benjamin Wood ranging from the *Challenger* at 120 tons, the *Mineral* of 100 tons and the *Pilgrim* at 90 tons, to the *Flight* at 50 tons. Two of the four captains were in the livery of Howard, but Wood had no lasting connection with Howard. The vessel Flight had been a French ship, which Ricard Vavasour had captured in the preceding year. Later, it was taken or "arrested" in a French port and returned to its former owners. There were about two hundred men aboard the four ships, all dreaming of the great plunder that awaited them on the high seas. Wood sailed his ships out of port in April of 1592, passing various English privateers off the Canaries and reaching Trinidad, where he bartered for water and fruit. They moved with the winds off the Caribbean coast of South America. Two ships of the four disappeared in storms and Woods now had two ships and insufficient supplies of food and water.

At Hicacos Point, Wood met the two small vessels of John Middleton, followed by a prize of some 30 tons, taken off the coast of Spain. This was the fourth trip of Middleton in this same *Moonshine*. London merchant John Newton owned the vessel and fitted it out for reprisal voyages in 1586, 1590, and 1591, and then this year. They joined forces and attempted to capture a frigate run aground. Not only did they fail, but thirteen of the landing party were captured. Spaniards killed many and others were drown. The prize vessel taken by the *Moonshine*, mentioned above, capsized and sank. Alonso de Bazon captured Middleton. Leaving the disaster, Wood and his fleet joined other English privateers and sailed along Cuba's coast without result. The fate of Wood is lost to history.

Newport sailed several ships, headed by his flagship the *Golden Dragon*, down from London in late January and with a prosperous wind sailed them out of Dover Road on February 12,1592. They got water and fresh food on the Barbary coast of Africa, passed the Canaries, and reached Dominica on the fourth of April. For the space of one or two days, Newport's men bartered with fierce Caribs of Dominica, providing goods in return for the tobacco, hens, and potato roots the Indians had to offer.

Spreading their sails before the wind, the sailors of the expedition made their way down the coast to a watering place on the other side of the cliff and captured a Portuguese ship of 300 tons. This ship was from Guinea bound for Cartagena with 300 Negroes of varying ages to sell to the Spaniards. Next the English privateers made their way to San Juan in Puerto Rico where they tried to trade without success. In the hope of selling the slaves, they had landed the Portuguese merchant but he betrayed them. They could not keep the slaves any longer so they landed them some thirty miles away from the town to make off on their own, hoping instead to take out their value in plunder later on in the voyage. The Portuguese ship was sunk.

Later, in the month of April, Newport landed his men at two islands for pork, potato roots, and wild game. Along the south coast of Hispaniola to the west they chased and captured a frigate on the way to San Juan to buy wine. They took off twenty-two jars of copper money from the frigate. Two more captures added nothing of value to their plunder.

On April 15, 1592, Newport and his men sacked the town of Ocoa. There they found a sugar mill with its products abandoned by the Spaniards. The people of the town had fled to the mountains, but they ventured out to ransom their community with herds of cattle and two loads of sugar, while Robert Freed of the *Margaret* was at work across the bay. He captured two frigates for the sugar trade. The English sailed away.

After watering, they reached the northwest portion of Hispaniola and sighted Yaguana in the night. Two hours before daylight, they landed. A frigate, with its victuals for sale in Cartagena, had alert sailors who saw the invaders and gave the alarm to the town. The Spanish were up in arms and fielded 150 horsemen. The English required two hours to reach the town with a guide. The cavalry were aided by a few snipers in the low valley, but being unable to win the fight, drove cows against the invaders. Evidently, the English turned the cattle for they switched directions and ran into the defenders. The hardy and valorous governor fell dead in the fight. Although they seemed victorious, the English had doubts of getting away alive and retired to their boats and hence to their ships. When the inhabitants of Yaguana went into the mountains with their possessions, the raiders came and fired the town and a small village called Guava.

Newport and his ships sailed away from Yaguana and entered the Bay of Honduras on the ninth of May of 1592 and took a Spanish ship, subject to fire from a castle. Learning of the presence of three ships at Puerto de Cavellos, they went to the port, delayed by a calm sea during part of the time. When the vessels moved away, Newport landed his men before a withdrawal of the people into the mountains seeking safety. The English seized 5 or 6 tons of old sack, sheep, young kids, great stores of poultry, some store of money, and good stores of linen, silks, cotton cloth, and other items. They raided the church for three bells and destroyed the Catholic images. They did not burn the town however, but went to Trujillo and captured what was left of a Spanish ship lit by the Spanish. Newport and his men took what they wanted from the cargo of hides and sunk it. Calm seas made the eastward voyage slow. Later, stormy weather hit Newport's expedition.

Off Cuba at last, the privateers met a trip of Indians who welcomed them and showed them where to get water. The Europeans traded old hatchets and knives for pieces of gold and silver. Newport and his men found these Indians more civilized and modest than the Caribs of Dominica. Next, the English chased and caught a frigate and lightened it of its tobacco and hogs. On the way back to England, they captured the mighty Portuguese carrack called *Madre de Dios*. Newport sailed this ship to England with the expedition and they arrived in Dartmouth. The date was the seventh of September on 1592.

Meanwhile, there was another expedition in the area of the West Indies. William King sailed the *Salomon* of 200 tons and the *Jane Bonaventure* of 40 tons with 126 mariners. Coming south along the coast of Portugal undeterred, he had some encounters near the Canaries. They took a number of ships in the Caribbean, one with 270 Negroes from Guinea.

The privateers stole from the harbor of San Juan one English ship with 60 tons of Canary wines. It was a busy voyage with good winds and many searches and the capture of a number of other vessels of various sizes. The good cargoes added up but there were no great prizes. King had one fight for a short span near the forts of Havana and returned to that port to chase a ship losing four chests of gold when the Spanish captain had them taken on shore and spirited away. They were back at Dover about the tenth of November in 1592.

One of Drake's captains in the 1587 raid on Cadiz, Captain William Parker undertook a number of successful raids in the West Indies, but little is known about the captain himself. With small forces, Parker achieved surprise attacks in his expert manner. He made eight reprisal voyages from 1590 to 1597.

Another privateer in the West Indies was Sir John Burgh, born into a noble family and soldiering under Sir Walter Raleigh in 1592. On this expedition in 1592, he commanded the land forces that resulted in the great carrack capture of that expedition. With his letters of reprisal, Burgh sailed his fleet with the flagship of 300 tons, the *Roebuck*, with Christopher Newport in the *Golden Dragoon*. In this raid of 1593, Burgh landed his men on Margarita Island but had to withdraw them from an attack. Their goal was Asuncion but the did not get far from the coast. With more strength and determination the English might have been able to sack Asuncion as they wished. The time was October of 1593.

In his privateering expedition to the West Indies in 1593-4, James Langton beleaguered Santo Domingo or over two months. With limited resources, he could not take the island of Hispaniola or even this city, but he did capture prizes and make a through nuisance of himself to the alarm of the Spaniards there. His plundering trip caused damage and concern along the coast. Laving England with the *Anthony* of 120 tons, Langton had the Spaniard Antonio Martino to guide him. This pilot had lived long in the Indies, and was well acquainted with the coast. He did a good job for the English in the Indies. Langton's next ship was the *Pilgrim*, weighed at 100 tons with Francis Slingsby as a captain and Diego Perez serving as pilot. Perez was not as well acquainted with the Indies as Martino. The other vessel was but a boat of twelve tons, the *Discovery*.

Sailing along the coast of Spain, Langton made for the Canaries and the islands of the Antilles to water and refresh the expedition. The privateers agreed that they should take the pearl fishing villages on the island of Margarita. Because the pearls were so portable and easily hidden, it was necessary that they should land in the night and achieve complete surprise if they would capture anything of great value. Since the pearl fishers moved from fishing site to fishing sites, the English needed to check each out from the easternmost to the westward. The first town was empty and so the privateers got back on their ships. Village number two was also vacant, but the captured a Spaniard and two Indians and learned of the whereabouts of the pearl fishers five leagues west. They decided to go by land.

The day was hot and the Englishmen could not find water along their line of march. By the time they were within a half a mile of the village, some of the men began to faint, but they made it. Langton achieved great surprise. The Spaniards in the town heard the alarm, but thought it to be a trial or false alarm. When they learned it was real, they fled into the woods to safeguard their lives and regroup. The English pillaged the town and grabbed some two thousand pounds in pearls. Next, they broke all the Spanish weapons they found. Unfortunately, the Spanish guides escaped the English, but the Spaniards did not attack and the English ships came slowly and carefully down the coast of the island. After the Spaniards ransomed the town for two thousand ducats in pearls, the English boarded the ships, but towns were now guarded and the English sought elsewhere for plunder.

Langton took his ships south to Cumara on the Spanish Main, a city in the province of New Andalucia or Venezuela. The English reached the place on the thirtieth day of August. Governor Francisco Videz was gone to pacify the Indians of Cumanagoto province, but his lieutenant Francisco Gutierrez Flores set out lookouts and prepared the city for an English assault, certain Portuguese who had been with the English said was coming. He then prevented their landing when they sailed up. The privateers found another place to land, but the able Spanish lieutenant governor directed a defense so hot and heavy that the English retreated to their ships without actually landing, taking some loss. The captain sailed his ships away to Rio de Hache, but the Spanish were ready for them there too. Since the English needed the element of surprise, they were not at a disadvantage. The privateers weighed anchor for Hispaniola.

This expedition plundered the coast east of the city of Santo Domingo and besieged the port with whose few vessels he was a match for the Spanish on the seas. There were rumors of large fleets of forty ships from Cumberland in England and twenty from the dread Drake, with 2,000 musketeers, now that the English were abandoning the harquebus. Meanwhile, the English robbed, ransomed, and burnt what they wished before returning for England.

Chapter XXVII

THE FAR EAST

Sir John Hawkins gave his son Richard Hawkins counsel and help in preparing a voyage around the world by way of the Straits of Magellan into the Pacific Ocean to determine the geography and economy of peoples in the Far East. The English wanted to know what commodities the country yielded and what English products they needed. Once the Armada was destroyed in 1588, Richard turned to this project and set shipwrights to build for him a vessel of between 300 and 400 tons burden. At the launching of the ship, Lady Hawkins was allowed to christen and name the ship the *Repentance*. Richard changed his decision to use this ship and his father hastened to buy it for his own use.

After long delays,, Richard Hawkins prepared to set out on his voyage to the Far East. He was set to leave in early March when the visit of Sir Robert Cecil, principal adviser to Her Majesty, and Sir Walter Raleigh postponed the start. It was a great honor for the scion of the Hawkins family. Finally, he set sail from Blackwell, but the elements made for more delay and still more. Once underway, the fleet came across a Danish ship loaded with Spanish salt and let it pass.

About the end of June of 1593, they sighted Madiera and on the third of July, they passed the Canaries. Next they passed the Cape Verde Islands to cross over toward the coast of Brazil and Cape Saint Augustine. They had reached the perilous waters of the Bay of Todos Santos and the port of Santos. There Hawkins' captain sought authority to trade. While waiting he got 100-300 oranges and lemons and a few hens to treat his men for scurry. Instead of waiting further, Hawkins ordered his three sips southward down the coast.

By the eighteenth of December of 193, they were directed toward the Straits of Magellan. They chased a Portuguese vessel brining slaves from Africa to Argentina, where they were marched to the mines of Potosi. In February of 1594, the passed through the straits. Once thorough the passage, Hawkins sailed his ships northward along the Chilean coast, where they gained some gold to be divided in part with the crew. He then reached the area of Quito and was about to sail from South America when the Spanish fleet came around the point. Hawkins was overmatched and although he fought a hard battle fled a sinking ship to fall into the hands of the Spanish, where the remained for nearly eight years.

Puerto de Caballos was especially exposed to the privateers because its long beaches gave the raiders plenty of places to invade hand made the settlement harder to defend and because there were insufficient men and arms to oppose a landing. The raiders thought it such an easy prey that they repeatedly assaulted the town for several years in a row. Langton and

Newport hit it hard. William Parker and his French consort Jeremias Raynard together and then separately issued forth with their privateers. The Spanish tried to defend themselves there in 1597, but the large numbers of Sherley and Parker overwhelmed them. What little development that was moved out and Sherley called it later that year the poorest and most miserable place in the West Indies.

In May of 1594 when Parker and Raynard came into the seas nearby and would have captured Trujillo if the Spanish had not been averted there. They did however capture messengers from Caballos carrying news about earlier raids and a request for help. Still the governor of Caballos and his men were surprised when the privateers landed a force of fifty-five men with prior knowledge of where to attack. The town fell and fourteen days later the English and French carried away substantial stores of hides, indigo, money, and bullion. Spaniards had had valuables secured away during Newport's raid so he did not get them, but had been brought back to town since. The booty was lost to everyone when the two frigates with most of the plunder sunk before the privateers left the West Indies.

Since his seamen struck going to Pernambuco, Brazil, on the last leg of his oriental trip, Captain James Lancaster arranged to get three good ships fitted and victualled for an expedition to that city as a privateer. In October of 1594, he sailed his there ships from Blackwell and followed the coast around and down to the West Country in England, where buffeted by storms they had to delay to have a new mast put on the middle ship. The last of November they put forth from Dartmouth. There was another storm in which the last two ships were lost. Lancaster's the *Consent* with a burden of 240 tons survived and kept on course to the Canaries.

They caught sight of a sail and manned their boat for a fight. The Spaniards of the sail, which was towing two boats, attempted to flee, but the Englishmen captured both the ship with its eighty tons of Canary-wine and the Spaniards. Next, they caught another ship, this one with forty tons of wine aboard. Soon they meet their smallest ship, the *Virgin* whose crew informed them that the Salomen lost its mast the second time and had to return to England. The crews of both ships were concerned over their small numbers. A determined Lancaster said that they would no doubt meet the missing ship at the appointed places and could continue their mission. They were satisfied and shortly they did meet the *Salomen* and things looked bright once again.

Reaching Maio, they discharged their wine cargo and burnt the Spanish ship. Here they were joined by four sail. Meanwhile the ships carpenters built a galley for the attack. One midnight they came up to the harbor of Recife, the port of Brazilian Pernambuco. They prepared for an attack under the direction of Lancaster. He would first take the harbor and then the town, but as day came upon them, they were delayed by the tides until they could attack at two in the afternoon. The Dutch in the port got out of the way and when the governors of the town asked the occasion of his visit, Lancaster stated that he wanted the carrack's goods.

Lancaster led his galley into the harbor and the rest of the ships followed. The Portuguese fired his guns. The English ships roamed the coast and the Englishmen landed without casualty from the misfired guns except for one man's loss of arms. When the English ran up to the fort, the Portuguese were frightened by their resolution and left the fort to the privateers. The ordnance was aimed at the high town of Olinda where the greatest danger was expected and marched to the low town of Recife and took its stores of Brazilwood, sugar, calico cloth, pepper, cinnamon, cloves, mace, nutmeg, and other valuable property. Nothing was pillaged or spoiled, but there was need of provision besides the immense stores.

The English made friends with the Dutch in the port and fought off a combined force of Portuguese and Indians with hail-shot. They soon retreated. French ships of war came into the harbor ready for purchases and Lancaster gave the French commander the supplies he needed for which service the French kept watch. The British ships were unloaded with the merchandise they had aboard and loaded them with Portuguese goods as named above. Portuguese colonists fired some ships and sent them down upon the English, who took precautionary movements which foiled the Portuguese and fire ships burnt out without doing any harm. The Portuguese also tried a variation of this theme in burning rafts. Finally while the Portuguese were readying a third fire attempt, the English sailed out of the harbor after thirty-one days there. They sailed for home and reached Blackwell in safety, after en explosion abroad one of the ships caused a fire that was put out.

The young Robert Dudley was the out-of-wedlock son of Leicester, that powerful courtier of the queen, by the widow of John Sheffield, second Lord Sheffield. The lady was born Douglas Howard. She was first cousin once removed to Elizabeth I. Anne Boleyn was a granddaughter of Thomas, second duke of Norfolk through an earlier wife than the ancestress of Lady Douglas Sheffield. Young Robert's aunt, Douglas's sister Frances Howard also loved the masculine Leicester, Robert Dudley Sr. Because the earl of Leicester was in attendance on the queen in Bristol, he received news from a messenger from the lady's household of the birth. Leicester raised the boy himself and was fond of him.

Dudley took an early interest in the sea, this being natural for a young man in a family which had contributed three grand admirals of England. Although as a favored youth, he had held a colonelcy in the English army, he was most determined to enter the marine forces that were so important for the greatness of his country during his early lifetime. At the age of seventeen, Robert Dudley studied navigation, marine discipline, and war. He dreamed of combined naval and military enterprise in such exotic lands as India and built and manned ships of war with the best pilots he could obtain.

When at the age of twenty he prepared an expedition which would emulate Drake and Cavendish in the South Seas or Pacific, he was taken back by the queen's veto. Once recovered he decided to take his expedition to adventure in the ocean seas. There were four ships fitted out with Dudley's money. His flagship was the *Bear* (called by Wyatt the *Peregrine*) which was a large ship of 200 tons built at Southhampton with thirty guns. Ship number two was the *Bear's Whelp*, of eighty-two. Next were two small pinnaces named the *Earwig* and the *Frisking*.

On November 6, 1594, Dudley sailed from Southampton, but with trouble they were forced into ports, set forth for Spain and driven back in a storm. Off the coast of Spain finally, Dudley with the *Bear* and one pinnace once again suffered from the weather. The smaller ship was swamped, but eager for adventure, Dudley sought vessels as a privateer, giving chase every day. They sighted Galicia, the northwestern Spanish province, and went down to Cape Finister. The trip had been of great misfortune for Dudley since the ship he chased off Galicia turned out to be friendly. Meanwhile, the other two ships sailing separately had taken two prizes and returned to England so that when the young commander reached the Canaries, he could not rendezvous with his vice-admiral. However, Dudley did take two caravels under the calms of Tenerife and Palma and now had a fleet of three sails.

Next, he went to Cape Blanco in Africa, hoping to meet the *Bear's Whelp* and gain victuals from Portuguese fishermen, but they had been frighten off by the French. He was there for two days and walked ashore to view the waste and desolation of the sand and stone, the black lizards and wild beasts, and the tawny Moors, before setting out for Trinidad in the West Indies. They found a mine of false gold nearby and Indians to trade with. After a time, while the Cimmarrons traded with the English, the Spaniards became rather friendly. On February 17, 1595, Dudley sent forth his two caravels to seek fortunes in Spanish lands.

Dudley took an interest himself in the empire of Guyana, desiring to discover it and asked the Indians about it. They described the lands and the inhabitants and the green stones (Amazon stones). Verifying the reports of great wealth in Guinea, the Indians assured him of a gold mine in Orocoa. On this fourteen men were set forth on a trip of discovery into the mouth of the great river, the Orinoco. These men learned of a nation in the interior that supposedly sprinkled their bodies with gold powder. This was the land of Eldorado that excited Englishmen. The actual name came from a great town far beyond them, named El Dorado. This trip took sixteen days and covered above 250 miles. Dudley was eager to go forth, but his suffering men would not go with him.

Like most of his compatriots, Sir Walter Raleigh was more interested in the Spanish domain than in the vast and then unattractive North American continent. Intrigued by Spanish wealth and power, he wished to use raw force against that empire. He believed that the English could and must destroy Spanish power by taking the Empire in America. It was believed at the time that were its commerce intercepted at sea, the power of Spain would whither on the vine, but English strength was insufficient for the task. Viewing the recent history of the effort against Spanish America, Raleigh was disabused of what seemed so much success and no longer thought that possession of the Panama Isthmus was a sure means of achieving the aim of crippling Spain.

Raleigh's solution was to match Spain's advantage with gold from America by discovering other sources by Englishmen. Since Guinea was neglected by the Spanish and Portuguese that would be the place for the English to locate. Richard Hakluyt might have been the one to bring Walter's attention to the area, believing Guinea to be the great place for gold, pearls, and precious stones. English and French merchants and privateers had already begun trading with the Indians there. By the time Raleigh got interested in the area, there were plenty of sources of information and great tales of El Dorado there. The Spanish had heard of a ruler guilded with golddust and search for him. Soon it was decided that this great empire could only be in the Guinea Highlands. Don Antonio de Barrio had made search for fifteen years but he could not get pass the steep escarpment. He did gain the hostility of the Indians for the Spaniards.

The Raleigh expedition to Guinea set out with four vessels on February 6, 1595. Separated on the way from two vessels, Raleigh reached Trinidad on the twenty-second of March. On the continent, he spied out Spanish strength, established good relations with the Indians, and searched out the route to El Doraldo. Barrio's settlement on the island was captured and Berrio taken, which gained Raleigh the friendship of the natives and a base. The Indians helped him build a fort. While he was formally annexing Trinidad, Raleigh was preparing craft to ascend the Orinoco and learned that there was no channel deep enough for an ocean going vessel.

With a stripped galley and four boats containing himself and one hundred men and a month's provisions, Raleigh sailed a hard path up the river. They ran short of food because it took so long to make it up the delta. The explorer made friends with the Indians. In order to contrast the English with the Spanish, Raleigh took care to prevent plunder and punish those who managed to steal from the natives, and he hid the English interest in gold. He wanted to win over the people to England. The Indians, however told the English the stories of a rich and powerful people in the highlands that they have told the Spanish explorers. Then a heavy current and rains forced the English to return to the coast. Back there, he freed Barrio and fought in Cumana and plundered Rio de la Hacha and Santa Maria before returning to England.

Meanwhile, on March 12,1595, Dudley sailed forth from the island of Trinidad, near the coast of South America, and the next day took a small prize with its cargo of wine and other products. He tried to sell it to Spaniard at San Juan, Puerto Rico, but they would not purchase the vessel so he took aboard the goods and burned the ship. Not meeting with an English fleet to join against the Spanish fleet, he directed his course for England. Undermanned, he met one of the armada's ships of six hundred tons. They fought and the *Bear* got the better of a two day battle, but was unable to board the Spanish ship, so after expending all of his powder, Dudley continued on homeward. In the last days of May, he arrived at St. Ives in Cornwall though the fog of Silly. Meanwhile, another expedition had set out on the day of Robert Dudley's departure from Trinidad.

With two tall ships and a pinnace at their command, Captains Amias Preston and George Sommers awaited their consorts, Captain Jones and Captain William Prowse with their vessels in Plymouth for a full month. The fleet weighed anchor on March 12, 1595 (Preston and Sommers), and on the nineteenth (Jones and Prowse). Robert Davie wrote an account of the expedition that stated that at the close of March, Captain Preston was separated from Captain Sommers, and his pinnace when he chased a ship for plunder.

Captain Preston with his single ship tried to land at Puerto Santo, but with the old soldiers and such new ones as guards for the island were equal to the danger. The Spaniards stood behind the barricades and trenches. Seeing that the defenses were too formidable, Preston ordered his men into the two long boats to come aboard again. But the English captain had not given up yet. On the next morning some three or four hours before daybreak, Preston landed with 60 men to march against the enemy. Although they were then five hundred strong, the Spaniard s were caught by surprise and superior maneuvers and fled after a brief resistance to make successive stands without success. The English pillaged what little goods the Spanish had not conveyed away, burnt the town and the village, and returned to the ship to sail away.

Off the Canaries, Preston met with Captain Sommers and his pinnace and three other ships joined Preston. Because the wind blew so much, they did not land in Gomera but set course for the West Indies. They rested at the island of Dommica, stopping off place for so any privateers met with in the course of this book. There they refreshed their sick men and traded with the Indians. The hot springs they found there relieved the men of much of their sickness.

The privateers passed by Margarita because of the lack of something there to attack, but landed upon the island of Coche between the isle of Margarita and the mainland. There the English captured a few Spaniards, their slaves, and some pearls. They caught fish and a crocodile of four feet in length. After their success they sought bigger game and on May 21, 1595, they sailed to Cumona on the Spanish Main. Forewarned of Preston's presence, the authorities removed all goods and valuables into the mountains. In their parley with the

English, the Spanish told them that there was no plunder in the town. They would pay the privateer a ransom for not burning the town however. Preston received the ransom, boarded some ships on which they found a little food, and departed without a shot being fired.

Next, the English took a fort near Caracas without resistance. When they captured the governor, they asked him concerning the state of Santiago de Leon (Caracas) and found out that Spanish spies in England had betrayed their plans and the people of this city were prepared to defend themselves with a barricade and the top of a hill with a narrow passage at the head of a thick protective wood. Another way to the city was also fortified.

They found a guide who wished to secure his own release and reached the vicinity of Caracas, going through the mountains which discouraged many of the English privateers. An almost bloodless battle occurred near the city opening to the fall of the city stripped of its wealth by the defenders. The Spanish did not resist further, but there was no plunder worthy of the name. By their crossing of the protective mountains, the English had achieved momentary possession. The Spanish expected that no such passage would be successful. They would not pay the 30,000 ducat ransom demanded, so the English burnt the villages, towns, and the city and returned the front way to their ships, a shorter journey.

Between Caracas and Coro at Chichiriviche, the English found three ships whose sails had been taken ashore. Unable to use ships without sails, Preston had them burnt so the Spaniards could not use them. It was early June and on the eleventh, the privateers took the now empty town of Coro and burnt it. Next, they sailed to Hispaniola, but while there illness struck the fleet and eighty men died of dysentery. Three ships left and on July 2, 1595, they arrived at Jamaica. Sailing around Cuba, they met with Sir Walter Raleigh and his ships won their return from Guyana. They went by Newfoundland, fished, and returned to England. On September 10th, Preston and his men reached Milford Haven in Wales.

Diego de Ybarra, treasurer of Santo Domingo, wrote home to Spain on October 14, 1595, that during the last four years corsairs were numerous and were as bold as they would be in the ports of their own countries. They lay in wait on the sailing routes converging on Santo Domingo. None could get by them, the treasurer wrote. If all this continued, the Spanish domains in the Indies would either be depopulated or have to do their business with the English and French and not Spain.

The Spanish monarch had sent a special judge to deal with those captains who departed from their lawful course or with contrabandists. Ybarra wrote that this judge was upright and merciful, but could do nothing to prevent the illegal trade, because the land on the Caribbean was so sparsely settled and justice could not reach the pirates in the country with it a delinquents and its fugitive black hands. Ybarra told the king that he must send forth galleys to sweep the corsairs from the sea.

Before his death on November 24, 1595, Governor Domingo Martinez de Avendano, who had served in Florida for one year and five months, left his mark on the religious advancement of the colony. The governor was greatly aided by Father Francisco Marron, the Franciscan superior of the friar's contingent in the settlements in Florida. At the time there were five or six churchmen altogether for this much neglected outpost on the continent. They made good progress in Christianizing the Indians near St. Augustine and to the north in the province of Guale on the Georgian coast.

Avendano was a greatly enthusiastic official from Spain who was so eager to get to the New World that he made the long trip in about four months after he received the news at Cadiz of his appointment. Juan Menendez Marques de Marron accompanied him from

Havana to St. Augustine. Six days after their arrival, Marron discovered that ten soldiers were rebellious and planned to seize the fort. Avendano immediately sent them out of Florida, probably for punishment. The new governor early showed prudence and sagacity.

The few friars in Florida were diligent under the direction of the governor and the superior, but Father Marron recognized the need for many more priests and lay-brothers for the harvest of souls. Avendano petitioned the king for additional missionaries and this request was answered with a shipment of a large number of Spanish friars in late September of 1595. After appointment were made Governor Avendano, accompanied by a body of infantrymen took some of the new missionaries to their posts of duty. Because he knelt down in the installation ceremonies and kissed the hand of the religious, the assembled religious, the assembled Indians were impressed and henceforth held the friars in the highest esteem and called them "as gods in the land." Each house of worship and instruction was nine to twelve miles apart. According to the count of the governor there were 1,400 to 1,500 Christian Indians as counted by baptisms. A sick Avendano returned to his seat of government and during a trip to Guale (Georgia) hemorrhaged and returned to St. Augustine to die, truly a great loss to Florida.

Chapter XXVIII

AT CENTURY'S END

Following Avendano in Florida was an able seaman of thirty years named Gonzalo Mendez de Canzo whom Philip II appointed governor and captain-general of Florida on May 25, 1596. He set sail with a secular priest for the presidio, twenty-four soldiers and ten or twelve women of good reputation as prospective wives for the soldiers going with him. Canzo arranged that his entire salary be paid be paid from the subsidy, but the Council of the Indies, intent upon establishing agriculture in Florida, stipulated that this would last only two years, whereby the usual requirement that half of the governor's salary be paid in the land's produce, which in fact was insufficient. The constant difficulties with the Indians and the need to defend the coast from the English and French, as well as the lack of Spanish farmers prevented much cultivation. Elsewhere in the Empire the natives were made to work in the fields, but this was not possible in Florida, although the Indians had to pay taxes in maize.

The governors had not created a self-sustaining colony, and want and poverty added to the miseries and burdens of both missionaries and soldiers. Because of unfavorable weather Canzo had a hard time getting from Cuba to Florida and did not arrive until June 2, 1597. He discovered himself the penury of the people and the lack of quarters and vestments for the friars. Their church, for instance, was in need of a tile roof. A hospital was under construction but was already in debt.

Canzo recognized the need of good relations with the Indians and received twenty-two Indian chiefs, performing the usual rendering of obedience in the name of the king. Realizing the value of gifts, he gave them presents of flour, maize, clothing, and trinkets and lowered the tribute due from these poor Indians. He discovered the usefulness of two Indians in particular.

Indian princess Dona Maria, a leader of their people, was a very good Christian and married the Spanish soldier Clemente Vernal. She followed Spanish orders and made her house a rendezvous for chiefs and braves in St. Augustine, was liberal in giving gifts, and drew the natives into the faith. She also helped keep the soldiers from starving and in recognition, Canzo petitioned the king to remunerate her and send Maria a letter of appreciation. Her mother had also helped the Christians. Don Juan of San Pedro was also a faithful Indian ally, thoroughly Christian and Spanish, a supporter of religion in his territory. This man gave gifts to other chiefs to bring them to Christ. Canzo petitioned for recognition here too. King and Council gave him rations and salary like a Spanish soldier.

Soon after his arrival, the governor of Florida sent Gaspar de Sala, with two Franciscan friars to Tama in central Georgia to investigate a land said to be fertile. Thirty Indians went with them, some of whom were Christian. They discovered a good land with maize, beans, deer, fowl, fish, fruit, metals, and herbs. Beyond this at Ocute they heard rumors of Europeans four days distance on the other side of the mountains. The Indians of Ocute had been friendly to De Soto almost sixty years earlier and warned Salas about the next tribe who had killed Spaniards then and would kill Salas and his men now. The expedition turned back. Ocute's natives were to prove favorable to the Spanish faith. The expedition returned to Florida.

In a third marriage in 1595, Captain Christopher Newport made a most beneficial match. He married Elizabeth Glanville, a daughter of one of London's leading goldsmiths by the name of Francis Glanville. During the following months Newport found a fine and formidable man-of-war which he, his father-in-law, and Richard Glanville had major shares. Newport sailed forth in the ship for the West Indies six times in succession and the ship was taken other times for raids in the Caribbean. Unlike some larger expeditions, his returned laden with loot often, raiding the towns of Yaguana, Puerto de Caballos, and Tabasco among others. After hostilities ended, Newport sailed there twice to trade. Later, he took part in the Jamestown venture, helped secure the colony's foothold and harmonized the settlers and undertook three voyages to the East Indies, dying on the last in Bantam on August 15, 1617.

Another privateer was much like Newport. Michael Geare began his privateering career at the age of nineteen when the war broke out and made a succession of voyages. He helped pillage part of the West Indies, becoming a master in 1589 and sailing as master under Newport in 1590. Next year, he commanded the *Little John* and became known as a tough fighter and a none too scrupulous operator in pillage and smuggling. Following this he bought into an operation. Back in the West Indies in the year of Newport's third marriage, he lost his pinnace in a hard fight outnumbered but game, and returned with a profitable haul. With Newport in 1596 and 1602-3 and David Middleton in 1601-2, he did so well that he was knighted.

Meanwhile, along the coast of Florida and Georgia, the Indians were very unhappy with the Spanish and their Christian culture. The main conflict evolved around the attempt of the religious to replace polygamy with monogamy. Of all the Christian practices, this was the most hated by the Indians who saw such personal value in husbands with more than one wife. For the male natives there was the obvious physical and social advantages and for the female there were the benefits of shared task and the prestige of being married to a chief or leader of the tribe.

Men with the most personal possessions or power attracted plural wives. At Tolomato, Don Juanillo, the heir to the chief, had more than one wife and Father Corpa privately reprimanded him. When this did not work, the religious denounced Juanillo who he said must live a Christian since he was one. He should be content with a single wife. Not only did Juanillo resent this, but he was angered by friars meddling in tribal politics. Pedro Corpa acted with Father Blas Rodriquez in depriving Juanillo of his hereditary rights to be Chief of Guale after his father. Among other things the Indians disliked were Christian efforts to suppress witchcraft and the scolding and reprimand which were an affront to the strong sense of pride which the Indians felt.

Juanillo led two other polygamous natives from the mission town, without the permission the friars demanded, to join the pagan Indians and prepare for war. The band decorated themselves for battle. They reached Tolomato quietly by night. It was the morning of the 13th of September 1597 when the warriors opened the door and killed Corpa as he was in prayer. They placed the friars head on the end of the lance and set it up at the landing place. They hid his body in a forest grave. Juanillo and the two other leaders reestablished their rights to exchange wives.

    · Eager for blood, Juanillo gathered together many neighboring chiefs and spoke to them. He wanted the to wipe out all the friars, return to native customs, and defend themselves against the governor of Florida. Reeling off the complaints the Indians had of restrictive marriages in perpetuity, prohibited dances, banquets, feasts, celebrations, games, and wars which showed valor and skill, persecution of old men for witchcraft, Juanillo told the chiefs that their valor would impress the Spaniard if they would get the best of them, and the Spanish would have to treat the Indian better. They also disliked the prohibition of labor on certain days, reprimands, suppression of tribal happiness in hopes of Heaven, and their slavery.

The aroused chiefs followed Juanillo and the Indians killed the brave Father Blas de Rodriquez at Tupiqui after allowing the friar to celebrate Mass for one last time. They spared him for two days to prepare himself spiritually. Next the murderers demanded the dispatch of two more friars on a coastal island, but the chief there was sincere Christian and warned Brother Antonio de Badajoz, but he and Father Aunon stayed and were killed by the rebels. Other friars were now the targets. Father Francisco Avila was wounded and mocked on a horrible march to Tulafina through the mire. Then they tortured him, but did not kill the half-dead friar and he survived after ten months of abuse and ridicule in captivity. Avila was freed after the Spaniards threatened the Indians hiding him. Fray Francisco de Verascola was killed.

The rebels decided upon war against the enemy tribes. These had religious with them and would be unprepared for war. At dawn on the fourth of October, the hostile Indians attacked San Pedro, but the alarm was given and the chief Don Juan of San Pedro forced the rebels to flee. On the seventh, the governor received the news of the uprising and despite his illness prepared and led his soldiers to Georgia to defeat the Indian rebels

Once at San Pedro, Governor Canzo held an investigation into the causes of the Guale revolt and then marched his 150 men to Guale proper. The Spanish force met the Indians at Ospo. There the rebels fired their bows and then fled. Canzo's soldiers burnt the town and food stores, leaving the church alone. They marched forward, but the Indians had retreated further inland and Canzo returned to San Pedro on the eleventh of November.

A miserable life in the forests of Guale or Georgia brought upon the rebels contrition and futility. They were hungry and disgusted so they returned to the fold. Don Francisco of Tolomato and Don Juanillo, his heir, remained behind, while other rebels went forth to make their submissions to Governor Canzo of Florida. The two recalcitants eluded the Spanish in the swamps and woods, but the authorities managed Indian help and a chief attacked the fort of the rebels and killed Don Francisco and Don Juanillo and many of those who had gathered around them. Spanish Guale was now peaceful and the Spanish began its rehabilitation.

Canzo was concurrently faced with financial troubles, a fire in St. Augustine on March 14, 1599, an inundation on September 22, 1599, and the threat of a famine. The governor exhorted his soldiers to grow more crops for the families of Florida. Florida still provided no source of revenue for crown or subjects. Meanwhile, Canzo had waged war upon the Sorruque and his Indians along the coast of Cape Canaveral when they killed three envoys, one Spaniard and two Indians. The Indians of the cape then submitted. Friar missionaries Father Francisco Pareja and Father Baltasar Lopez blamed the governor for an unjust war.

Like Florida, New Mexico was a marginal colony. The usual imposition of encomiendas or estates with the attached labor of Indians did not work as well as they did in richer parts of New Spain or Mexico. Since the environment was semi-arid, the proceeds of rationing were limited, and the colonists would have starved without the labor force of Indians and the tribute and actual robbery of the few things the Indian owned. In New Mexico, there was as H. Allen Anderson wrote, "no large, organized native population, no productive land base, and none of the basic resources of central Mexico." There were other problems. The governor (political head and captain general) was faced with insubordination, mutiny, and desertions. Juan de Onate resigned as governor in 1607. In Mexico City, the viceroy talked about abandoning New Mexico and withdrawing the settlers. They finally decided to finance this losing proposition by making the province a royal colony and pay the costs with crown money. The chief reason for the action was the receipt of Franciscan missionary reports of great religious success with the natives.

Cumberland undertook still another expedition, one of 1598 for Hispanic America. True to form for the earl, this effort was well financed. It had also a very large, indeed a notable fleet, with fifteen large ships, a pinnace, two frigates, and two barges. A consortium of London merchants backed Cumberland with eleven large ships and a frigate. Excepting Sir John Hart, the leading backers were key men in privateering and shipping circles, and included Paul Bayning, John Watts, Thomas Cordell, William Garraway, and William Shute. Some of these men and others involved in the expedition had lent money to and or bought properties from the earl, Cumberland. James Lancaster, among those representing the City of London in the regulation for the voyages had earlier made the raid on Brazil's sugar coast, and the first objective was supposed to have been Recife on the coast.

Philip had learned of the expedition and had received rumors about its objective and when he strengthened Pernambuco's defense, Cumberland learned of this and took it as a warning. Setting sail in March of 1598, Cumberland decided to take the city of San Juan de Puerto Rico instead. He hoped to establish an English base on the island. He just missed the treasure fleet and the carracks outward bound from Lisbon. Portuguese and Spaniards took actions of caution that disrupted their fleets. The trip was undertaken without trouble and the town of San Juan was captured with ineffective opposition. Once they understood English determination, the Spanish defense effort folded.

Few Englishmen lost their lives in the attack, but two hundred died in the next three weeks from dysentery. San Juan could not be kept with these losses and sugar, hides, ginger, and ordnances were taken for the trip home. The expedition also brought in nine prizes for a disappointing total of L 16,000 in plunder. Because the attack was so easy, Cumberland dreamt of taking Panama and Havana, but this victory was the last of his maritime career. He ended his career heavily in debt, while the merchants in whose cause the earl had worked were glad to lend him money at interest.

In 1599, the Sieur Chauvin, de Ponthuiet, a captain in the Royal Marine and a Protestant was persuaded by his fellow Huguenot the Captain du Pont Grove of St. Malo to seek and received the privilege for ten years of founding a settlement in Canada. He managed to equip one. Du Pont Grave was given charge of one ship and they arrived with a majority of Catholics on the St. Lawrence. Unfortunately Chauvin obstinately chose a poor spot for settlement due to cold and rocky land. The winter was hard and many perished until neighboring tribes of Indians took them in.

George Weymouth undertook a voyage for the discovery of a northwest-passage. The East India Company took him up on his proposal and Weymouth sailed forth on May 2, 1602. On the eighteenth of the following month, he reached the south of Greenland and crossed Davis Straits and in ten days was off the American shore. At latitude 68 degrees 53 minutes, a meeting instigated by John Cartwright ended his advance. On July 25, 1602, he arrived at Hatto's Headland, the northern entrance to the Hudson Bay. John Knight also voyaged in the area in 1606 with no results.

Sir Ferdinando Gorges was born of ancient Somerset stock with a connection with both Elizabeth and the Howards, a great family filling up the sum total of Elizabethan achievements with a large proportion of talent and ties. A younger son with little inheritance, Ferdinando went off to fight in Flanders and in the nineties under Essex in Normandy. Henry of Navarre recommended Gorges to the queen for promotion, writing that Gorges made a reputation of valor in war. He was an able soldier. Rewarded by the English ruler with a command of the fort at Plymouth, he watched there the ships sail from and to America. Many were fishing boat for the Newfoundland fishery several hundred miles further southwest.

In 1602, there began the first serious attempt to establish a colony along the New England coast. Sailing from Falmouth, Captains Bartholomew Gosnold and Bartholomew Gilbert led their ships across the Atlantic and found the New England summer time climate to be healthful. The sailors on the voyage were so fortunate that no man was sick for more than one day, a different situation from so man voyages to the West Indies in the preceding century. Despite this encouragement, the captains left on settlement or plantation in the land, but they did name Cape Cod, Martha's Vineyard, and Elizabeth's Isle. They went up two broad rivers that they thought would lead to a Northwest Passage. Without going far they noted the good harbors and returned to England to report to Sir Walter Raleigh who had the concession or rights to New England settlement.

When Hakluyt was inspired and various Bristol merchants including Robert Aldworth backed the next venture, Raleigh gave his permission. This 1603 voyage was captained by Martin Pring, who made such a successful navigation and charting that Gorges was to testy that he made the most exact discovery of that coast. The result was that Pring's expedition greatly encouraged Gorges and the Lord Chief Justice Popham to persevere with their efforts despite the monetary losses of the trips westward. Pring was the first to enter and appreciate Massachusetts Bay, and his mastiffs frightened the natives like those of Cortes scared the men of Mexico, almost one century earlier.

Among the most important points in the struggle between Catholic and Huguenot was the Protestant stronghold of La Rochelle. Nearby there was the harbor of Brouage. Samuel de Champlain was born there in 1567 and saw Brouage several times taken and retaken by opposing armies in his youth. The future explorer loved the Catholic religion, but since was a strong royalist, he supported Henry IV and fought for him on land and sea in the years ahead. Of course Henry had turned Catholic in order to gain the throne of France. At the turn of the century Champlain was a sea captain and visited the Caribbean and its adjacent shores including Mexico off the gulf of that name. He went on the expedition sent by Aymar de Chastes in 1603.

The Sieur de Monts undertook to return to Canada with a plan of establishing a colony in which religious freedom would be allowed although the majority of the countryside would be populated by Catholics. De Monts fitted out three ships for all things needed for trading in furs at Tadoussac and to settle to the southward. Before leaving, de Monts asked Samuel de Champlain to go with him. Embarking at Dieppe in 1603, de Monts had his ships divided up. The first went to Tadoussac to trade. The second under Du Pont Garve went to Canzo and coasted towards the island of Cape Breton to search for interlopers in the territory claimed by the French king. The third led by de Monts with Champlain aboard went toe the coast of Acadia, where they discovered inlets suitable for ports and rivers. This was the promised land for de Monts. The settlement was made and Nova Scotia was founded.

Champlain spent a full three years to explore the area from the Cape la Heve in the north to the headland beyond Cape Cod. After a close inspection, he examined the land further north including Cape Canso and Cape Breton. In 1607, Champlain returned to France where there was a controversy over the ill treatment of certain Basque and Bretons in Canada by the ship crews. The trial led to the withdrawal of the lands from the control of de Monts. He had spent upwards of one hundred thousand lires of his own money for the operation and now lost the use of this sum and the profit he so richly deserved.

Meanwhile there was friction in paradise. The minister and the cure settled their differences with fistfights over points of theology. Indians took sides, but readily split and the diversity of religion in Canada caused trouble among people unused to such freedoms or for the necessary toleration.

In 1605, Captain George Weymouth of Torbay prepared a fishing expedition off North America with the backing of some Plymouth merchants, but when he actually sailed he went to Maine to prospect with the support of the earl of Southampton. Because the French had been making great profits in the fur trade, Weymouth took an interest in furs and collected some furs and skins eventually from the Indians in whom he took an interest. He reported back about the Indians and presented five natives to Englishmen on his return. Weymouth also reported back on sites for settlements in Maine.

Sir Ferdinando Gorges was by his own concept "a plain soldier and one that is no scholar." Still, he could write well and had a brief stay at Oxford. His chief interest was in problems of fortification and navigation and in the developments of the New World. At Plymouth Fort he was in touch with voyages and when Weymouth gave him three of his Indians, his interest in America was to grow.

Henry IV of France, better known as Henry of Navarre, was born on December 13, 1553, to be heir to the throne of Navarre held by his mother Jeanne d'Aibret, who educated him into the Calvinistic faith. He served under the Protestant Admiral Coligny, but escaped the admiral's bloody fate, marrying Margaret of Valois, sister of Charles IX. In marriage, he adopted the Roman Catholic creed, adjured it, and became a Catholic again to obtain the throne through the death of Henry III. He fought in the wars of religion and became king of France. Henry IV was descended from Robert, Count of Clermont, the sixth son of Louis IX. As king, Henry of Navarre secured religious freedom and prosperity for the nation. Looking outward for conquests and foreign revenue, he talked with Dutchmen of experience about establishing a French East India Company.

In 1606, in order to protect the Dutch company from rivalry from France, the Netherlands' state-general came up with a plan to turn French attention to the west. They suggested to Henry the establishment of a West India Company. Oldenbarnevelt, the political leader of the United Netherlands, told the French that Dutch capital and French support of a company in the Caribbean would inflict injury to Spain's America. Before November of that year, Archduke Albert informed Philip II of a scheme for an armada to attack Puerto Bello, Cartagena, and Cuba. The Dutch seizure of Havana would cripple Spanish colonial commerce, the planners believed.

However, in 1607, merchants were afraid to risk their capital. Dutch merchants were already having serious difficulties in East India. Further, there was such a possibility of peace with Spain that the armada idea was dropped. Despite this, Philip was still worried and warned Cuban governor Pedro de Valdes of Dutch desires. In 1609, there as a truce, allowing for mutual freedom of trade between Spanish and Netherlanders in America. More than two hundred ships sailed forth for the islands and coasts of Philip's empire.

Meanwhile, on May 1, 1607, Henry Hudson set sail from Gravesend to discover a short cut the China by the northwest. He sought to go by the North Pole but after reaching 67 degrees and 30 minutes, winds came up at northeast and blew him westward and he ran into a great fog with ice. Off the west, Hudson and his crew observed Greenland. Then on the fourteenth of June it began to snow, followed by wind and rain. The twentieth brought a summer's sunshine. Unable to move in a straight line, they reached 72 degrees 38 minutes and then reached 73 degrees; and then saw a small flock of birds.

On the twenty-sixth, they made observations and discovered themselves to be at 76 degrees 38 minutes coasting 'Greenland. Two days later, they had reached 78 degrees in a smooth sea. At this time, they began to see heavy ice lands. They had to steer between ice and land when they reached 78 degrees 42 minutes. Soon they had to turn about at head in a general southward direction before a second assault by which they arrived at 80 degrees 23 minutes and a sighting of many whales. They finally arrived at 82 degrees. Hudson took advantage of a rare, for his voyage, westerly wind to head for home.

In Hudson's second voyage, he went to the northeast and set out in that same direction and his third voyage, he had to turn back because the ice frightened the crew to mutiny. They reached the Banc des Sables off Mahone Bay. On the eighteenth of July 1609, the English ship sailed into a very good harbor. They then proceeded to coast along the North American Atlantic coast. They went on land near Cape Cod and brought back wild grapes and rose trees. Captain Bartholomew discovered this cape in 1602. Sailing southward, Hudson reached Virginia but did not go far enough to see the colony of Jamestown. Next, Hudson entered Delaware Bay, which some believed to be the all-water route to the Pacific. Going to the north, Hudson rediscovered Hudson River and its great bay. They traded with the Indians in places, but generally Hudson did not trust the Indians. Seeking a passage up Hudson River, the crew reached about the site of Albany. Soon, they were under way for England.

In late April of 1610, Henry Hudson and his crew went out on his fourth voyage to the west pass the isles of Orkney. They saw the northern part of Greenland and moved towards straits westward. They were soon in Hudson's Bay. Hudson made changes in his subordinates. He replaced Robert Just as mate and stayed on, iced in for the winter. There was a mutiny on board and Hudson and eight others were sent out on the bay in a shallop to die in the white wilderness.

Chapter XXIX

JOHN SMITH

John Smith, British born European mercenary and one of the important founders of Jamestown, Virginia, was born on January 9, 1580, in the parish of Willoughby, Lincolnshire, the eldest child of George Smith and his wife Alice. There were his brothers Francis and Richard, but the last lived only ten days. Located in rich farmland, the father successfully formed his segment of land and was a leading yeoman in the village settlement, where his grants with the obligations in the area were established. They had a nice home with its furniture, including a feather bed, and a nice farm with many farm animals. George was fined from time to time for minor infractions. One was for failing to keep animals from sown fields and from pastures at certain times. Authorities called upon George Smith to serve many times as juror in courts of law in the process of the years between 1584 and 1591. At various times, he showed his skills as a horseman and as bowler.

John grew up a farmer's boy having to do the needed chores, all the while dreaming of great adventure. He never liked farming, nor did he care for the settled life. Attending free schools at Alford and Louth, he began the process of learning to write which came in handy for his literary career and various subjects to guide him in his travels. Being a yeoman's son, he had opportunities in life associated with being educated with noble scions and dealing with them on a level above most tenants in England at the time.

His parents passed over his desire for one of the commissions created by Queen Elizabeth for England's Royal Navy. Because he had no training for the sea, they decided to apprentice John to a great merchant in Lynn named Thomas Sendall. John was soon disappointed with the work as a clerk for Sendall and seeking to go abroad, he talked Sendall and Lord Willoughby to allow him to go to Orleans, France, where the lord's son had just finished his education and were his younger son was headed.

The two boys dropped by London for a week taking in the sights of that glorious metroplex. John drank heavily and became sick, learning that heavy drinking would be a problem of serious dimensions. He never did overindulge again. Also there he developed a passion for gambling and women. Finally, the Willoughby son persuaded John that they were late and they headed for Orleans. When they arrived, the other son was off to Paris and they joyfully followed. Paris was even more fascinating than London with more inns, theaters, and dazzling architecture.

While in Paris, he met a friend of the Willoughby's, one David Hume who conned Smith out of his funds with promises of letters to officials and Scots court of James which were fictitious. Hume left with Smith's money in 1597 and Smith was left to his own devices. Deciding not to return home where he would have to work as a farmer or a merchant's clerk, Smith tried to enter the army of Henry IV. The recruiting sergeant turned him down but his coolness in this attempt kelp him there amid harassment or teasing by soldiers. An English speaking French captain suggested that he try one of the mercenary companies at the end of the bivouac. He went to the captain of one, Joseph Duxbury, and after proving some ability in a fight with the company's champion and surviving a fall at his hands, he was accepted.

The way was not easy since John was not a possessor of a full coat of armor, having no horse, no blanket, and no warm clothes. Quartermaster provided him with a steel helmet and a dangerous harquebus, a musket that was not safe for the man who fired it. Smith got food every day but no pay. At peace, the mercenaries had no pay nor had any for months. His pistol was stolen one night and so he was happy to find a job as a butcher's assistant for pay and a supper every night at the home of the butcher and his wife.

Soon, however, the mercenary companies ware sent to the Amiens region to defeat the Spaniards in that territory. The soldiers marched for eleven days with small rations of food and camped near Amiens. The local lord fled into the wall town with the Spaniards and the mercenaries looted his manor. Smith headed for the stables for a horse, two saddles, a thick wool cloak, and a sword. Now he could become a cavalryman. One of the saddles was traded for a pair of boots and a poniard. In addition, he received his one share of the proceeds.

In 1597, the Spanish had captured Amiens and the French besieged the walled town with its troops and their mercenaries. These later were set to patrol a wood and its environs to keep supplies from reaching the Spaniards. A part of that operation, Smith told of a time when they were ambushed by a platoon of armored Spaniards, upon which the mercenaries retreated. According to Smith, they took the offensive gaining his fellow soldiers' attention and winning the day. Later, he met Henry IV of France who went on night patrols with his men from time to time and by whom he was impressed and encouraged to continue his adventurous career. Amiens was to surrender and the war ended, leaving Smith unemployed for awhile.

Smith next went with Duxbury's company to the Netherlands to fight for the Dutch. There he exhibited his courage and was badly wounded. He required six months to get well losing his chance to gain further renown. Maurice of Nassau wrote him up in his reports noting his dealing death to the Spanish soldier in the advance and the demonstration of this to his fellow soldiers. By this time, he was a sergeant and soon Duxbury promoted him to ensign to be third in command; an officer and gentleman at last. John had proved a leader of men and a fighter deluxe. When peace came, Smith returned to England with gifts and money and also his ties with such great men as Peter Plancius, Richard Hakluyt, and Henry Hudson through fortune and introduction. While there, he visited his people and made time to study and read about exploration and colonization schemes and means.

The adventurer set out once more for the horizon and suffered great danger including a possible stay with Breton privateers and including a visit with Jesuits with whom he debated religion. Next, he found a position as aide to the earl of Voldam Meldritch and served against the Turks. Taking part in furious fighting on the front, John earned a captaincy. Among the towns of Transylvania was one Orastie, once a trade center and now the remnants of wars fought for its possession. When viewed by Smith, it was besieged by Sigismund who recognized its necessary capture for future campaigns, but who did not wish to shell it because the population was partially Christian. The Turks were strong to the south making the Christians wary.

While before Orastie, Sigismund received a challenge from a bored Turkish noble named Turbashaw who wished to meet any Christian in the army in personal combat. The fight would be on horseback with only a lance and a sword. Several of the Christian soldiers wanted to meet the challenge. John was insistent above al others. Sigismund agreed although he was hesitant. The two armies lined up to watch in great pageantry. The two men entered the lists and Smith quickly killed Turbashaw with the first trust of his lance, decapitated him and took the head to Sigismund. Another Turk challenged him. This time pistols were allowed and Smith failed in his first charge, but shot the Turk, and when the Turk reacted to his wound, had time to incapacitate him.

Next time, Smith made the challenge. A giant Turk accepted and the fight passed from firearms to battle ax. Smith did not have much experience using that weapon but did well for awhile. Having to guide his horse with his knees in order to wield the heavy weapon, John slipped and confident in victory, the giant headed for him, but finding an opening, Smith killed him with his scimitar and decapitated the giant. the siege was resumed, but the Turks soon surrendered.

Smith went with the vanguard of the army and they got too far advanced of the main army and were cut off. The Turks surrounded the Hungarians in the narrow valley picked out by them. Christian troopers fought until they were out of ammunition. Most were killed but some fifty officers were captured and stripped naked. When chained together, the men were marched in bitter winter weather in few clothes. At Tchernavoda, the Turks sold them at the slave market there. Pasha Timor bought John and took him to Adrianople and then Constantinople, where he bragged that he had defeated and taken the deadly champion of the Christian army. Soon John was taken to a farm, where when he was beaten, he gripped his heavy threshing bat and killed Timor. He escaped and made the difficult trip back to safety in Rostov.

The governor befriended him and Smith went to Moscow with his niece, to whom he proposed. Preferring to stay in Russia, she, the Lady Camallata turned John down. Taking his leave, John returned to Hungary where he learned a truce was in effect. He followed Prince Sigismund to Prague and to Leipzig and was reunited with his commander. The prince presented him with a coat of arms. Now Smith was a gentleman of noble pretense.

The prince and his count gave Smith a thousand five hundred ducats and a safe pass with which to travel Europe. He slept at the best inns and ate in the best taverns. In Siena, Italy, he met Henry Willoughby. In Spain, he learned that a Christian slave who had befriended him in captivity, was near at El Araish. With some mercenary soldiers with hidden armor and weapons under robes, he visited Mahonet ben Arif and asked to question the slave Elizabeth Rondee. She was brought forth and cried with joy at seeing him. Smith and his men fought and led her out to their ship and escaped.

On October 4, 1605, they were at London and soon afterwards Elizabeth married a squire. When his story was out, Smith was an instant English hero. He attracted friends who wanted to hear the tale of his violent life and met with explorers who wanted geographic information, especially about the closed society of Russia about which so little was known. His travels were well worth it and peaked with an audience with Queen Anne, wife of King James I.

Not slated to a life of talking only, Smith was probably soon interested in more adventures, such as would bring him profit and fame. There was talk about the New World across the Atlantic and in 1606 some gentlemen received a charter for colonizing in America. Other Englishmen had attempted to settle parts of America not colonized by Spaniards or Portuguese or French. Sir Walter Raleigh tried three times before getting imprisoned for seducing and marrying one of Queen Elizabeth's maids of honor. Many wanted to go to America in search for wealth. Smith was one who would join Charles Leigh's colony in Guyana, but it collapsed before he could ship out.

Smith sought out other groups of which there were many in London. Sitting there, he was not getting richer. Expenses were eating up his savings and he needed colonial employment. Hakluyt had advised Raleigh to settle in the Chesapeake Bay and the New London Company chose that bay. Accepted by the company, Smith was chosen to be a member of that group which would go to Virginia.

The time had come for this project. James I had signed a peace treaty with Spain in 1604, cutting off opportunities to privateers. Early in the following year of 1605, Captain George Weymouth probed the coast of North America and returned with some Indians. This voyage interested Sir John Popham, Lord Chief Justice of England, and he drew together those with an interest in colonizing Virginia. Sir Robert Cecil, chief official for James I and now the earl of Salisbury, joined in. Two plans were developed and a compromise was reached. Lord Arundell of Wardour advanced this settlement and a governmental plan was proposed by Popham. Three ships were obtained. These were the *Susan Constant, Godspeed*, and *Discovery*, and were soon underway with the hopes of the London group.

There were two sets of stockholders, a number of Plymouth merchants and a number of London merchants and each acted separately, each given a grant of land. The Plymouth group made its attempt in the summer of 1607. Its expedition landed where the Kennebec River empties into the ocean and there it built a fort. The winter of 1607/8 was a harsh one for the settlers. It was too much for them to endure on land, they were incapable of working, and they sailed back to England in the coming spring. After its unsuccessful attempt the Plymouth Company gave up settlement and began to finance fishing voyages to the coast of North America and trade with the Indians, bringing back furs to be sold in England.

The London group sent its one hundred and twenty emigrants by ship by way of the Canaries and the West Indies, landing them at the mouth of the Powhatan River, renamed the James River after the king. The peninsula, connected to land by a narrow neck of land, was thought to be a fine site, easily defended from the Indians and the Spaniards south along the shores of Florida. It was accessible to the three ships making up the settler's fleet and was advantageous for the anchorage of any other ships coming to the colony. On the other hand, the site was near a swamp with its malaria-breeding insects, a fact which did not bother the Englishmen when they selected their new home, since they knew nothing of the cause of malaria, and there was no level ground nearby which was uncovered by heavy forests. If land was to be cleared it would take much effort on the part of the settlers and most of them were unsuitable for this type of work.

Before they reach the settlement, antagonisms had developed. Winter gales hit them before they could reach the channel and the ships were anchored for six weeks and tempers were soon on edge. Smith was sure that his experience as a military man was so great that he could serve as a military chief in Virginia. Among the others there were many who wanted that honor too and they all got on each other's nerves with Smith in the lead with his assertions of high ability. He and Gabriel Archer shared a tiny cabin. Since both wished to be the sold leader, they became bitter enemies.

Someone told Captain John Ratcliffe that Smith was spreading the fact that Ratcliffe has served time in prison under the name Sicklemore. In time, Smith irritated everyone except George Percy, Captain John Martin, and Reverend Robert Hunt. He befriended the latter by supporting Hunt when others wanted him to go ashore because of his illness; Hunt stayed as he wished. When Smith drew his sword in a fracas, Archer and Captain George Kendal led a court presided by Edward Maria Wingfield and ordered him to be hanged. Smith laughed and no one was brave enough to try and seize Smith, although they built a gallows at one stop on the way to Virginia. The voyage leader Captain Christopher Newport and his officers would have nothing to do with the trial and persuaded them to get along on better terms with Smith. The incident was passed peaceably by.

The expedition visited several islands in the Caribbean, found food including fruit and got lost twice in gales. At one stop, Smith hunted with his friend Martin. They shot two boars that were butchered and then cooked in the waters of the hot springs of one island. Commoners enjoyed the pork and Smith was more popular among the common men of the expedition than before. He did not, however, win any favor from his enemies among the gentlemen by this success. When they could not find the continent in the following days, Ratcliffe tried to convince them to return to England. Smith opposed this. To give up would mean problems in refitting and the settles might lose heart or the investors might withdraw their financial support. His views won out. Newport seconded Smith, but again John proved too arrogant and earned more hatred. They continued westward and in the lull of a gale on April 25, 1607, a sailor in the crow's nest sighted land set out in Chesapeake Bay. Once again Smith proved right.

Ever eager for land, the shore party chose to spend the night on terra firme. They planned to explore the next day. The Indians attacked that night. Despite the achievement of surprise only a sailor was seriously wounded. Smith cried out for them to move away from the fire where they were targeted by the light. Newport fired his guns and the noise so unexpected frightened the Indians that they fled.

On the morrow, Captain Newport opened the box of instructions. Smith was named in the list of councilmen, but Smith was not allowed to sit upon the council until June 14, 1607. He did help explore before that however, taking command of one party on May fourth. Further, he and Percy stayed one night with Powhatan, the Indian chieftain whom the Englishmen had made friends with. Smith rapidly learned the Indian language and almost rapidly gained more control of the English expedition. Because of minor upsets and larger insults made by the English, not knowing their significance, the English except for Smith lost the friendship of Powhatan. The settlers soon had falling-outs among themselves. All in all, they were off to a bad start.

Smith continued his friendship with Powhatan, began preparing the settlers for an attack, and worked on defenses for the colony, covering all possibilities at hand. He made friends with the commoners who were numerous. President of the council, Wingfield was irritated because Smith was making friends with the mass of settlers, but Newport supported Smith.

While Smith and Newport were on an exploration expedition up the James River, some parties of Indian tribes not allied with Powhatan attacked the English. Wingfield had forbidden the carrying of arms by the colonists and the Indian caught them unarmed and undefended. They could only flee. They were lucky; only two lost their lives and only twelve had been wounded. Wingfield would allow no work to be done for defenses, hoping to pacify all Indians. This was unrealistic. The colonists ignored Wingfield and prepared for another attack. During third and fourth raids two others were killed. The English were better prepared now and even Smith's enemies were chastised. It was at this time that Smith was admitted into the council where he belonged by law and ability.

Once on the council, he undertook a more commanding role on colony affairs, increasingly giving commands and supervising the work necessary for the success of Jamestown. He showed fine abilities and was to rescue the colony from dire consequences in the near future. Smith was essential for existence and earned his standing in Virginia. Directing the men to prepare the settlements for defense, Smith had them strength the palisades, build new towers, and clear the bush for several hundred feet around the walls to deprive the Indians of cover for sneak attacks. Since the directors would want something to show for their expenses, he started a lumber industry of successful note. The colonists also collected beaver and fox furs for shipment home. Newport took the cargo loaded on the *Susan Constant* and in late June left for England.

With Newport gone, Wingfield setforth new rules. Smith and the other leaders outvoted the president and prepared the colony as best they could. Many settlers became ill including Smith and some lost their lives. Trouble was to continue, but Smith regained the friendship of Ratcliffe. Next, they brought back needed baskets of corn and venison. He bartered with other villages, and bought in more foodstuffs soon after the council deposed Wingfield. All was still troubled and Kendal arranged an alliance with Wingfield and the two gained the support of sailors and planned to flee in the remaining ship. Smith stopped him just in time. Kendal was tried, found guilty, and hung.

Smith escaped death twice in a short time. Arriving in Jamestown on January 7, 1608, free from Indian captivity, the arrival of Newport in the ship from England rescued him from a death sentence issued after trial by the council. Thirty-eight men had been left from the original 105 men, and now there was a transfusion of eighty new men. John set the workmen to build new dwellings and a church building for Hunt. When a fire burnt down part of the settlement, he had still more structures to supervise. Barely escaping death from the Indians and colonists alike, Smith survived to be of great service to the settlers.

One of the newcomers, a gentleman named Matthew Scrivener proved able and attracted Smith's notice; Archer and Ratcliffe thought his thin figure and reserved personality marked him a liability. Smith thought him able, dependable, honest, and well schooled in marksmanship and swordsmanship and made him one of his lieutenants. The London directors had made him a member of the ruling council.

Newport could not leave yet since it was too cold for the men to cut timber and furs were difficult to buy because of a scarcity. The sea captain loaded up when the cargo was ready in the spring. The council sent Wingfield and Archer back to England. Ratcliffe stayed but a day after they left, he accidentally blew his hand off, which broke his health and spirit. Smith now was in total control. A large group of new settlers told Smith they were out to seek gold, but when he told them they could leave, but were not to come back unless willing to work, they decided to stay. It was an eventful few days.

In the following weeks, Smith made two trips up the bay and some of the rivers of the Chesapeake area. He faced dangers large and small. There were almost no deaths and problems although the way was dangerous. Returning to Jamestown the first time, he found chaos with Ratcliffe causing trouble, but the second return found Matthew Scrivener well in successful command. The colonists insisted that Smith become president and Ratcliffe resigned. Smith was now in full charge once again. A ship came from England to the relief of the colonists and Smith wrote his first book, a good accurate account of the settlement. Martin took it back with him and got it published with the help of Prince Henry, son of James I, who was to die before his father.

Smith's directions brought Jamestown into a period of prosperity, but the way was still difficult and the colony needed so much support. Among them were the right type of settlers, carpenters, farmers, masons, a blacksmith, and others used to working with their hands. He wrote the London directors so. They still though the colony had gold and silver. Smith wrote him that this was not the case. The fort was changed from triangular sides to a five pointed fort which would have flank support. Farms were increased and a few women joined the colony on Newport's ship to Virginia. More of the colonists were making the land their own.,

Newport had brought gifts for Powhatan including a golden crown and was supposed to gain Powhatan's allegiance. The Indian chief acted as if the did not know what was being asked of him. Newcomers were trained and had their hands toughened for work. Newport took a loaded ship back to England but without the gold required. Ratcliffe was sent back to England with Newport and Scrivener died in a storm after having plotted against Smith.

Meanwhile, in France a most enthusiastic man, de Monts wished to make another attempt in Canada and consulted with Champlain who gave his good advise. Samuel wished de Monts to proceed directly to the St. Lawrence River. De Monts got another commission from the king. The French sailed in two vessels and reached Tadoussac. Sailing up the river, he found a good spot at a narrow part in the river and used the Indian name for the site of Quebec. The people in the two vessels established an agricultural colony and the land was cleared and sown. Champlain helped establish the French colony.

Once the fields were sown in the spring of 1609, Champlain sailed up river and met a body of Algonquins and Octatiquens who were on their way to ask French assistance against the enemies the Iroquois. This suited the French, but volunteers were hard to keep. However, two men stayed with Champlain and they set off with the Indians for a lake. There began a battle at Lake Champlain in which the firearms spoke, killing two Iroquois chiefs and wounding another. The startled Iroquois quickly abandoned the field. The murderous shot was a surprise to both friend and foe. The Algonquins took some ten or twelve prisoner. De Monts was stripped of all his venture once again and Champlain returned to France to help him with his problems.

Chapter XXX

VIRGINIA

In the winter of 1608/9, Smith opened up trading negotiations with Powhatan. The Indian chief increased his price. He asked for a house like the largest building in Jamestown for which he would supply 150 hogsheads of corn. Having to agree, Smith personally supervised the construction, driving the men hard and working twelve hours a day himself. This bred hostility. The Dutch carpenters were unhappy and hatched a plot to have the leader killed by the Indians, joined by some of the Englishmen. An Englishman told Smith of the plot, but he would not take the plot seriously. Some Indians attacked Smith and John Russell one morning with spears and knives and the two stood back to back, fired their guns and began to kill the attackers one after the other. When out of ammunition, they being unable to take time to load, fought with scimitar and sword until the climax when Smith went berserk. He whirled his scimitar, horrifying the Indians, killing one man and wounding another, and forcing them to flee. Smith and Russell survived and marched the workers to seize food and go back to Jamestown, where the guilty plotters and tried and sentenced to be punished. The house was left unfinished.

Smith cracked down upon the lazy in Jamestown and demonstrated his determination. The plotters were publicly whipped and treated by a doctor. Measures were undertaken to record work and many buildings were constructed, wells were dug, and fishnets were made. Defense was a top priority. With a pig and chicken population and hard working colonists, the settlement was successful.

Trouble was once again plaguing Smith. Captain Samuel Argal arrived with shocking news for Smith. He was to be replaced by a royal governor, Thomas West, Baron De La Warr, competent in administration and warfare. More settlers arrived with new officers of high position in England. Smith was to be a private citizen once again. Archer and Ratcliffe were back and were involved in more plotting. They were arrested and kept in their houses by a guard to the relief of veteran colonists.

For the large number of newcomers, Smith settled two plantations in the interior. While busy with important tasks waiting for the ship carrying the governor, Smith was badly burnt in an explosion and was persuaded to go to England for medical aid. Soon afterwards, Jamestown got into trouble known as the "starving time." The colony sure needed Smith, but when the lord arrived he did good for the colony and it began to climb again until the massacre which was also survived.

In the summer of 1610, Governor John Guy set sail with thirty-nine colonists from Bristol bound for Newfoundland. Once established the colony faced hostility from annual fishermen, but they found a good site in Conception Bay. The area was not fertile though and this was a setback for the Newfoundland colonists and their governor, but Guy had a positive view and set them to engage in the lumbering business. Glass was also manufactured there.

Smith had been burnt in a fire and headed home to England. John's voyage had been a difficult eight weeks when his burns were most painful. He was delirious for ten days and could take very little to eat once lucid. Back in England, he could barely walk and his recovery was still slow and painful although he had a doctor to help him. Three months were spent in isolation with a boy to bring him his meals from nearby taverns. The duchess of Richmond came to his rescue. She told him that his book *A True Relation* was the most popular book in the nation at that time. Visiting his printer, George Hall on Fleet Street, he learned that he had earned already over one thousand pounds. People were learning about Jamestown and more people were trying to join up. As the able writer Noel B. Gerson was to write centuries later, the directors of the London Company could treat him unjustly, but the common people loved his book.

The doors began to open for Smith. Frances arranged a meeting with Richard Hakluyt and Smith told his friend what the true situation in Virginia was and that there was no northwest sea passage in that part of North America he had explored. They met once again and Smith showed him his maps. Hakluyt arranged a meeting with Prince Henry and others interested in the matters of Virginia. The heir to the throne got his father James I to see Smith, but James seemed to have very little interest in the subject of colonization. Smith got a good chance to get over his views on Virginia and he became a widely used advisor in his areas of expertise and received a good pay. London Company directors listened to his advise to take advantage of Virginia's resources of timber and furs and forget gold, silver, and gems which he said were not there.

In the passage of months, he rested and kept up contact with such enthusiasts as Sir Fernando Gorges, leaving the capital for some months and early in the summer of 1611, returned to live in a more modest apartment. Seeing his printer, Smith learned that his first book had earned 780 more pounds. However, when he tried to get his next book published, he was up against a brick wall. A favorite of the king's Robert Carr, Lord Rochester, prevented it from being printed in London, but Smith went around the end and had it printed in Oxford. Had Henry lived he might have been able to counter Robert Carr, but Hakluyt probably used his influence with the university. The book was entitled *A Map of Virginia*. Rochester failed to stop its sales although he tried. It was a success and the sales of his first book picked up also.

In the midst of an expedition dispatched to gain gold which returned in failure, Smith decided to propose a voyage that he would command. Natives, who were kidnapped to England, told the English that they would lead them to gold in returning on English ships to America north of Jamestown. When they got back to America, they disappeared into the forests. The pioneers could not stay in the colony and returned to London. There, Smith learned of this trip and sent a letter to the earl of Southampton proposing to make a journey north of Hudson River and to chart the coastline and explore promising portions of the interior. Southampton was in favor of this and he and Sir Fernando encouraged Smith who went to one of the knight's estates to study the thing through. The lights lit up and Smith decided to take along fishing equipment and whale harpoons to fish while on the voyage. This would bring a good income for the trip whether or not they found gold.

Smith planned the voyage well and sought out two natives, eager to return to America and they a agreed to act as his guides if he took them with him. Hayluyt and the duke of Richmond gave their support and Smith had a free hand. Hiring two captains for the two ships, he prepared further. One was Captain George Langam and the other the cheerful extrovert Captain Marmaduke Royden. Next, he hired two soldiers, professional men, named William Skelton and John Buley. When bringing supplies, he looked carefully at what he was being sold.

The voyage was a good one and Smith sighted a "mermaid" on an iceberg. Off Newfoundland, they hunted and chased whales, but because of harpoons lacking in sturdiness they did not kill any. After this, he set his men to net fishing with great success. He drew accurate maps of the coastline from Nova Scotia to Rhode Island. Next, they landed at the site of Portsmouth, New Hampshire, and soon traded with the local sachems and established amiable relations. He discovered the Merrimack River that he charted for a distance and named the Charles River at the site of Boston. They returned a full-bodied success. After the cargo was sold and the crews and cost of the ships paid, there was an astonishing eight thousand dollars profit. They rewarded Smith with a fifteen hundred pound bonus. The success made Smith a popular and influential man in London when the news got around that second half of 1614.

He planned a second voyage for his original backers staying loyal with them because they had supported him when few would support him. He set forth to establish a small colony that would pay its own way from profits from such as fish and furs. Off he went but a storm in the Atlantic early in the voyage forced them back and they landed in Plymouth, England. The voyage frizzled, but Smith savaged what he could and went on fishing trips with his nets, sailors, and fishermen. They were chased by a pirate and caught but the men were old friends of Smith's from Transylvania days and joined him instead.

They were captured by French pirates, but escaped, all except Smith, who had to wait until he too made it to a French port. He turned in the French pirates and became a hero and got part of the prize money not long after the pirates were captured and/or killed. A widow who had befriended him and advised him was given by Smith the better part of the money, a large 2,000 English pounds. Returning to England, he settled down with his plans. It was January 12,1616.

Finding old friends cool, he published his third book *A Description of New England*. Because his last venture failed, he was to stir up no support for his hope of founding a colony in New England. Money was tight for Smith and he had to make promises to his creditors about funds from his book assigned for their payments. The book warmed up his friendships and he found money for his plans once again. He had bad success in gaining colonists, who had been frightened off by the realities of his book.

He dropped his plans for colonization for awhile and sent his ships on fishing expeditions. They left in March of 1617 without him. While the ships were gone, Smith visited towns in the north and was a guest of Sir Edward Eames, a baronet "who was one of Smith's more ardent advocates." The ships returned to Plymouth, England, with a rich haul returning two pounds and five shillings per pound invested.

When investors heard of Smith's fabulous profit, Smith was able to hold a large meeting in Plymouth, where enthused with his speech, the wealthy men made great promises that were not kept. But before this was discovered by Smith he believed himself able to colonize with twenty ships and over one thousand settlers as the first step. Meanwhile, Smith was made Admiral of New England. Learning of the investor's failure to live up to their word, Smith decided to write *New England Trials* to promote New England settlements. His aim was to convince Francis Bacon to support with government money his plans to settle New England. He failed. Working hard to promote his plans, Smith was treading water. Then came the Panic of 1618. Even the crown had to cut expenses. There was no fruit on that tree.

Elder Brewster of the Pilgrim colony in Holland saw him secretly at great danger to Brewster and wanted to colonize New England with his half. The two men were unable to see eye-to-eye and Brewster went back to Holland soon to help lead the Pilgrims to New England on their own. Instead of Smith, he hired Captain Miles Standish to be military leader. Smith was upset and held a grudge against Brewster. The adventurer began a period of writing and publishing in England that lasted until his death on June 21, 1631.

The English settlers abandoned the old English technique of broadcast seeding and adopted the Indian method of hill planting which turned agricultural failure into success. Hereafter the English would be able to feed themselves, but the primary effort of the English was tobacco planting. Due to the discoveries of John Rolfe in tobacco curing, tobacco became the standby of the colony and a profitable trade was developed in this expensive good which so exhausted the soil. In 1619, two events happened to foster tobacco cultivation: the first was the selling of black slaves by a Dutch merchant ship and the second was an English one also that forbade the planting of tobacco in England and Ireland and preserved a monopoly for Virginia. The first contributed to the use of slave labor that was so convenient to the plantation system and the second protected the plantation system of Virginia from competition.

The colony began to prosper, despite even an Indian massacre which saw one third of the settlers slaughtered, adding to the thirteen thousand who had already lost their lives by 1622. The result of this massacre was the end of a general policy of Christianizing the Indians and the beginning of a policy of extermination or driving west of the Indians from which the Americans were never to deviate for long, for the better part of three centuries.

The land of Virginia required hard work. Only those who put muscle and sweat in to the land were able to do well. Farmers and laborers made the land pay. The first community was a frontier settlement. Most of the gentlemen who came with the first ships were quickly weeded out, beginning with John Smith's dictum that only those who worked could eat. From the first only those who labored and made the effort were met with success. The redemptioners and convict servants generally fared better.

Large numbers of these laborers did well. There was plenty of land and freemen were entitled to fifty acres. Tobacco prices were rising and the great opportunities lay before the early settlers. Among the settlers was Adam Thoroughgood, who came over as an indentured servant and rose to become the greatest planter in Norfolk. Many others were rising fast into positions of colonial authority by dint of hard work.

Knowing about the settlement in Jamestown, Spanish authorities considered long to decide what to do. Finally the sixty-five year old Captain Francisco Fernandez de Ecija was given orders to spy on the settlement. In June of 1609, Fernandez left Florida and stopped at the Santee River in what was to become South Carolina. The Indians there told him that Jamestown was four days journey away, protected by a wood fort, and had given clothes and tools to Indians there, with whom they were in league. Fernandez set out northward. When he saw a ship in the vicinity of Jamestown, he retreated. Back at the mouth of the Santee, the Indians elaborated by telling him there were many women and children at Jamestown, a piece of news which was not true. Returning to Florida, this captain turned in his report. This report was read and a plan made to send English Jesuits to the English colony to spy and lead a plan to destroy Jamestown. Nothing was done, however.

The charter of 1609 was superseded by even more liberal 1612 and 1618 charters which given representative government a chance to take root in the new colony. When the liberals gained control of the colony over the court faction in Virginia, private landholdiing was sponsored, taxation was restricted, and martial law was forbidden in Virginia. A two-chambered provincial legislature was established and legislative government began to operate in 1619. Upon the company's bankruptcy in 1624, James I of England made the colony a royal colony by which action the governor was to be henceforth named by the king.

No diminishing of colonial rights was made, however, until Charles I ascended the throne in 1625 and decided that the governor should have more powers including that of an absolute veto over the laws of the legislature and his consent for the legislature to stay in session. The governor was also to appoint justices of the peace and county sheriffs who were to uphold the laws in the various counties of the colony and to appoint local officials who would serve at their pleasure.

Robert Harcourt went upon a voyage to Guyana on the northeast shoulder of South America, having furnished himself with a eighty ton burden ship called the *Rose*, a pinnace of thirty-five tons, and a shallop of nine tons. The pinnace was named the *Patience* and the shallop was named the *Lilly*. He had 31 landsmen, 23 mariners and sailors, and two Indians aboard his small mother ship. His brother Michael Harcourt captained the pinnace with twenty landsmen and eleven sailors and mariners. The master of the *Lilly* had one landsman and two sailors. They left Dartmouth on March 23,1609, but winds forced them back. On the next day, they made headway and steered for the Canaries. After a storm at sea, they made progress and rested at a barren and unpopulated island of Alegranza to exercise their legs on shore. They watered and then sailed westward reaching the currents of the Amazon River. The *Patience* was almost wrecked near the mouth of that great river when it was stranded for a time when the next flood came down.

They sailed north along the coast to the Bay of Wiapoco, where Indians came forth in two or three canoes to learn of their nationality and to trade with these white men. When they learned that they were Englishmen, they came aboard the ship, one of the natives speaking in English, having been in England at one time and had served Sir John Gilbert many years. The natives brought back food that was heartily welcomed to replace ship food. Harcourt had his men give these natives knives, beads, Jew's trumps, and such items that they coveted. One of the Indians aboard was from this country and the natives were delighted to know that he was still alive after four years.

On the next day, he moved up to the river and anchored over against the Sandy Bay. He found that Sir Walter Raleigh had been there the day before and a few of the Indians were attired in English clothes. Harcourt told them through their interpreter of the defeats the Indians had suffered from Raleigh, of the defeat of the Spanish at Trinidad and the burning of the town and capture of Governor Antonio de Berreo. Then he told them of the death of Queen Elizabeth I. When the Indians learned that the English would protect them and dwell among them, they expressed their satisfaction. The Indian Martin went ashore at this point. The English marched before the natives on the following day with arms and colors displayed.

Welcomed by each of the Indians, Harcourt settled his men in the village. He studied the country and noted the protection of the village with its narrow paths. Harcourt and his men then explored the rest of Guyana.

They were soon involved in warfare. The Indian Leonard Ragapo was a Yaio, who had seized upon the lightly inhabited country of Coosheberg. Harcourt sent four gentlemen of his company to remain with him. The Caribs marched upon the country to the number of 200. They were met with fifty well-organized Yaio Indians with the English musketeers. In front were the four Englishmen, followed by two ranks of Indians with wooden swords and targets, followed by two rows of archers and then of pikes. Surprised by the English in front, the Caribs made a sudden stand. Leonard went forward to parley, warning them to make peace. If the English were hurt in the assault, he could get more from Wiapoco. He instilled such a fear in them that they agreed to peace, met his conditions, and then returned home.

Robert Harcourt appointed his brother Michael to remain behind in the country as chief commander plus about twenty more. His pinnace had a leak and he left it there to be repaired and headed westward to learn about the coast of Guyana, passing several rivers and then went up one of the rivers until they reached a waterfall. He left three men at a friendly village to try and discover that great city of wealth that Raleigh talked about. Then he sailed away and arrived at Punto de Galea where they found three English ships at anchor. They signed at Port of Spain and then returned to Bristol by way of Ireland, on the second day of February of 1610.

William Baffin undertook the next series of voyages to the northwest, setting sail on Good Friday, the tenth of April 1612, with two small ships. This was James Hall's fourth voyage to Greenland. They sighted Cape Farewell, which Captain Davis had named. On May 17, 1612, the crew saw the part of the land of Greenland that had been called the Land of Desolation. They killed four seals. Sailing on they discovered two deep branches of Godthaab-Fjord and they named them Lancaster River and Ball River. On this voyage they searched out Greenland for scientific reasons, nothing being found that would make the voyage profitable, but there was hope for recompense.

When the crewman James Pullay tried to capture one of the natives, another cast a dart at him mortally wounding the Englishman, but the relations were generally friendly with the natives and they traded iron nails for the fresh fish the Eskimos brought them. At other times the natives threw stones at the English explorers along the coast of Greenland with their slings. There was some hunting. On one occasion one of the Englishmen killed a fox of which there were many. Hall had been along this coast before and the main features of the countryside were already names such as King Christian's Fjord, Cape Ann, and Cunninghams Mount. On the twenty-second day of July James Hall was also mortally wounded, a deliberate act which might have been revenge for the kidnapping on a previous voyage of Hall with the Danes. Soon afterward Baffin sailed his ships back home to England.

Baffin returned the following year to Greenland with six English ships and a pinnace, departing on the 13th of May of 1613. It was a swift journey, taking eighteen days to reach Greenland and find Horn Sound, discovered by James Poole on his voyage of discovery for the Muscovy Company in 1610. They were faced on this day by May snow. On the next day, they met with the fishing ship of 800 tons burden of Saint John de Luz, who was licensed by the Company to fish.

The master and pilot of the ship told Baffin that there were eight Spaniards on the coast, probably fishing, and a ship of French registry appeared with Allon Sailes the pilot. There were others in the vicinity. They met a small ship from Dunkirk. Four other ships were in Poppy Bay; two of which were Dutch, one was from Rochelle, and one was from Bordeaux. Baffin discussed their presence with the other ship's captain and got them to depart from the coast. Some of the ships had Englishmen aboard and Baffin took them and the Scotsman onboard his own ship. They got into a fight with Thomas Bonner's Dutch ship when Bonner would not come aboard. He had to give in because of superior firepower. Baffin kept the riddle Dutch ship. There was a great deal of whale killing by English and others, whales being in abundance in these waters. They returned to England and were back in the Thames on the sixth of September of 1613.

There were three more recorded voyages of William Baffin in succeeding years. On his third (1614) voyage, he discovered the end of Sir Thomas Smith's Inlet and its landlocked harbor. Baffin started early on his fourth voyage, leaving Blackwell in March of 1615. Next in 1616, he made another voyage, during which he had contacts with the Eskimos and saw a multitude of whales. Even at this late date there was still expectation of a northwest-passage which could provide a way to the Orient.

Back in France, Champlain made preparations for a new expedition and on April 24, 1615, he left Honfleur for Canada and shortly as time went in those days, was at Tadoussac, where he again promised to fight the Indian enemies of his friendly natives. He would help the natives kill other Indians to bring them to Christianity, despite the commandment of their Lord. Meanwhile, he explored to Lake Nipissing and then across land to Lake Huron. There Samuel de Champlain was involved with more warfare in defense of his allies. In one of several encounters Champlain was wounded. Noting geography and customs, the French made their way back to France. They arrived on September 10, 1616.

Sir Walter Raleigh was resting in prison when in 1614, Sir Ralph Winwood became secretary of state. Interested in Raleigh's Guyana project, he was to be promoter for the explorer's last effort to find the riches rumored to be in those highlands. Because the Parliament failed to provide James with appropriations for that year, the government was unusually desperate for money and thus sprung the hope that Raleigh could find gold mines in the highlands and provide the Crown with a fifth of the find and other loot plus custom dues.

In March of 1616, the king gave him a conditional release to prepare for a voyage. His preparations took him until June of 1617 and included a ship of 450 tons that he named *Destiny*. It was a large expedition of some one thousand men and stirred up great interest and speculation in Great Britain and on the continent. The alarmed Spaniards claimed that all Guyana belonged to Spain and put diplomatic pressure on James which prompted the king to promise that Raleigh should forfeit his life if he fought the Spanish or bothered their property and further gave Spain full information on the voyage and its destination. The king might well expect that there would be an armed conflict and that the would repudiate Raleigh and take his life. Raleigh still expected that he would get the gold and be forgiven. England and Spain would then war and Raleigh could build an empire in Guyana.

After serious delays and bad weather, Raleigh was able to sail on August 19, 1617. Instructions went out to all ships to avoid conflict with foreign vessels, but he impounded some French vessels off Cape St. Vincent and took goods which he paid for. He failed to get provisions from the Spanish along the wary. Fever struck and the trip became miserable. Because of Raleigh's illness and need to protect their rear, Lawrence Keymis led the party up the Orinoco to find the gold mine, on the tenth of December.

At the town of San Thome up the river, the Spaniards fired upon the English. Captain Walter Raleigh, the explorer's son, led an attack and was killed by a Spanish officer, but the small garrison and people of the town surrendered without a fight. One other Englishman was killed and Diego Palmomeque de Acuna and two other Spanish men were killed. At this point the guide Keymis became confused. Afire twenty-three years of asserting that he knew where the mine was, he now had no idea where to look. Keymis could not stand the strain and took no immediate action. He slipped away and brought back some ore, but when it was assayed it was discovered that there was no gold in the ore.

George Raleigh led a group up the river, but Keymis was afraid to go to Mount Iconuri to search for a mine because he was afraid of being cut off by the Spanish. With their patience worn, the soldiers and sailors insisted that they return to Raleigh. Keymis arrived and Raleigh was told about the bad news. The leader was unbalanced and Keymis committed suicide.

The expedition fell apart. Raleigh wanted to go up river again, but his disillusioned men would not follow, fearing the arrival of a Spanish army. He sailed to the Leeward Island where two ships were deserted and plundered by pirates. The least useful men he sent home in a ship. He suggested several plans, but his companions could not agree and he lost the rest of his ships. Faced with mutiny, he disembarked his mutineers in Ireland and returned home to his execution.

The population of Virginia in 1619 was about 2,400 people, but there was a mass movement coming into the colony at last. The annual addition at that time was about 1,200 people. There was a high natural increase subject to various changes of diet and climate. They suffered from malaria because of the conditions of the wooded land close to the shore. Because so many of the newcomers would die, the increase was less effective. It would be awhile before the land to the west would be opened to a healthier citizen. From the first to well within the colonial period, Virginia was settled by large numbers of settlers from the landed class of England. These were younger sons who sought estates that in England went to the oldest male. These men were able to establish themselves on plantations and gain a lifestyle like their older brothers had in England. Lower classes were present also in large number, but in the first century of Virginian life the numbers of gentlemen and sons of nobles and merchants were high. However, no peers emigrated to the English New World.

Chapter XXXI

BIBLIOGRAPHY

Aiton, Arthur Scold, *Antonio de Mendoza: First Viceroy of New Spain*, 1927, Rep. New York: Russell & Russell, 1967.

Alden, Daniel (ed), *Colonial Roots of Modern Brazil*, Berkley: University of California Press, 1973.

Anderson, Charles L.G., *Life and Letters of Vasco Nunez de Balboa*, New York: Fleming H. Revell, 1941.

Anderson, H. Allen, "The Encomienda in New Mexico, 1598-1680," *New Mexico Historical Review*, LX No. 4 (October 1985).

Andrews, Kenneth Richmond, *Elizabethan Privateering: English Privateering During the Spanish War, 1585-1603*, Cambridge: Cambridge University Press, 1966.

Andrews, Kenneth Richmond, (ed), *English Privateering Voyages to the West Indies, 1588-1595*, Cambridge: Hakluyt, 1959.

Asher, G.M. (ed), *Henry Hudson The Navigator*, 1860, New York: Burt Franklin.

Bandelier, Adolph F.A. & Bandelier, Fanny R., *Historical Documents Relating to New Mexico, Nueva Vizcaya and Approaches Thereby to 1773*, Hackett, Charles Hackett (ed), Washington DC: Carnegie Institution of Washington, 1923.

Beeching, Jack, *The Galleys at Lepanto*, New York: Charles Scribner's Sons, 1983.

Best, George, *The Three Voyages of Martin Frobisher*, 1967, New York: Burt Franklin.

Blom, Frans, *The Conquest of Yucatan*, 1936, New York: Cooper Square, 1971.

Boxer, Charles, *The Portuguese Seaborne Empire 1415-1825*, New York: Alfred A. Knopf, 1969.

Brading, D.A., *Miners and Merchants in Bourbon Mexico, 1763-1810*, Cambridge: Cambridge University Press, 1971.

Bruce, Philip Alexander, *Economic History of Virginia in the Seventeenth Century*, 1896, New York: Peter Smith, 1935.

Bruce, Philip Alexander, *Social Life of Virginia in the Seventeenth Century*, 1907, Williamtown, Mass: Corner House, 1968.

Burrage, Henry S, (ed), *Early English and French Voyages: Chiefly from Hakluyt, 1534-1608*, New York: Charles Scribner's Sons. 1906, Rep New York Barnes & Noble, 1952.

Cash, Wilbur J., *Mind of the South*, New York: Alfred A. Knopf, 1970.

Cell, Gillian T., *English Enterprise in Newfoundland, 1577-1660*, Toronto: University of Toronto Press, 1969.

Cieza de Leon, Pedro de, *The War of Chupas*, Markham, Sir Clements R. (ed), Hakluyt, 1917, Kraus, 1967.

Cieza de Leon, Pedro de, *The War of Las Salinas*, Markham, Sir Clements R. (trans), Hakluyt Society, 1923, Kraus, 1967.

Cieza de Leon, Pedro de, *The War of Quito*, Markham, Sir Clements R. (ed), Hakluyt, 1973, Kraus, 1967.

Chaplain, Samuel de, *Narrative of a Voyage to the West Indies and Mexico in the Texas 1599-1602*, Shaw, Norton (ed), Wilmuc, Alice (trans), 1859.

Columbus, Christopher, *The Journal of Christopher Columbus*, New York: Clarkson N. Potter, 1960.

Corbett, Julian S., *Papers Relating to the Navy During the Spanish War, 1585-1587*, New York: Burt Franklin, 1970.

Corbitt, David Leroy, *Explorations, Descriptions, and Attempted Settlements of Carolina, 1534-1590*, Raleigh, NC: State Dept of Archives and History, 1948.

Correa, Gaspar, *The Three Voyages of Vasco da Gama And His Viceroyalty*, Stanley, Henry E.J. (ed), New York: Burt Franklin.

Corwin, Arthur F., *Spain and the Abolition of Slavery in Cuba, 1817-1886*, Austin, Tx: University of Texas Press, 1967.

Davis, John, *The Voyages and Works of John Davis, The Navigator*, Albert Hastings Manhattan, New York: Burt Franklin, 1970.

Diez Del Castillo, Bernal, *The True Story of the Conquest of Mexico*, New York: Robert M. McBride, 1927.

Donck, Adriaen van der., *A Description of the New Netherlands*, 1655, English trans., Syracuse NY: Syracuse University Press, 1968.

Donworth, Albert B., *Why Columbus Sailed*, 2d ed., New York: Exposition Press, 1953.

Durant, David N., *Raleigh's Lost Colony*, New York: Atheneum, 1981.

Encyclopedia Americana (1954).

Encyclopedia Britannica (1911).

Encyclopedia of Latin America, Delpar, Helen (ed), New York: McGraw-Hill, 1974.

Fisher, Lillian Estelle, *Viceregal Administration in the Spanish-American Colonies*, University of California Press, 1926, New York: Russell & Russell, 1967.

Geiger, Maynard, *The Franciscan Conquest of Florida (1573-1618)*, Washington DC: Catholic University of America, 1937.

Gerson, Noel B., *The Glorious Scoundrel: A Biography of Captain John Smith*, New York: Dodd, Mead, 1978.

Graham, Robert Bontine Cunningham, *The Conquest of New Granada: Being the Life of Gonzalo Jimenez de Quesada*, London: William Hemematin, 1922.

Graham, Robert Bontine Cunningham, *The Conquest of the River Plate*, Garden City: Doubleday, Page, 1924..

Grant, W.L., *Voyages of Samuel de Champlain, 1604-1618*, 1907, New York: Barnes & Noble, 1952.

Greenlee, William Brooks, *The Voyage of Pedro Alvares Cabral to Brazil and India*, Hakluyt, 1938, Kraus, 1967.

Greenleaf, Richard E., *Zumarraga and the Mexican Inquisition, 1536-1543*, Washington DC: Academy of American Franciscan History, 1961.

Hanke, Lewis, *Aristotle and the American Indians*, Chicago: Henry Regency, 1959.

Hanke, Lewis, *The Spanish Struggle For Justice in the Conquest of America*, Boston: Little, Brown, 1949.

Harcourt, Robert, *A Voyage to Guiana*, London: 1613, Amsterdam: Da Capo Press, 1973.

Haring, Clarence Henry, *Trade and Navigation Between Spain and the Indies in the Time of the Hapsburgs*, Cambridge, Mass: Harvard University Press, 1918, Gloucester, Mass: Peter-Smith, 1964.

Helps, Sir Arthur, *The Life of Las Casas: The Apostle of the Indies*, London: Geo. Ball & Sons, 1896.

Helps, Sir Arthur, *The Spanish Conquest in America*, 4 vols., Rep New York: AMS Press, 1966.

Las Casas, Bartolome de, *Tears of the Indians*, Williamson, Mass: John Lulburne, 1970.

Lewis, Clifford M. and Loomie, Albert J., *The Spanish Jesuit Mission in Virginia, 1570-1572*, Chapel Hill: University of North Carolina Press, 1953.

Lizarraga, Reginaldo. *Descripcion de Las Indias*, Lima, Peru: Lo Pequenos Grandes Libros de Histories Americas, 1946.

Lord Stanley of Alderley, *The First Voyage Round the World, By Magellon*, New York: Burt Franklin.

Lowery, Woodbury, *The Spanish Settlements Within the Present Limits of the United States, 1513-1561*, 1901, New York: Russell & Russell, 1959.

Luke, Mary M., *Gloriana: The Years of Elizabeth I*, New York: Coward, McCann & Geoghegan, 1973.

Markham, Sir Clements, *The Conquest of New Granada*, New York: E.P. Dutton, 1912.

Markham, Sir Clements, *The Hawkins Voyages During the Reigns of Henry VIII, Queen Elizabeth, and James I*, 1840, New York: Burt Franklin, 1970.

Markham, Sir Clements, *The Voyages of Sir James Lancaster to the East Indies*, New York: Burt Franklin, 1970.

Markham, Sir Clements, (ed), *The Voyages of William Baffin, 1612-1622*, New York: Burt Franklin.

Means, Philip Ainsworth, *Fall of the Inca Empire and the Spanish in Peru, 1530-1780*, New York: Charles Scribner's Sons, 1932.

Merrien, Jean, *Christopher Columbus: The Mariner and the Man*, Michael, Maurice (trans), London: Odhams Press, 1958.

Merriman, Roger Bigelow, *The Rise of the Spanish Empire in the Old World and in the New*, 4 vols., vol. II (1918), New York: Cooper Square Pub., 1962.

Morison, Samuel Eliot, *Admiral of the Ocean Sea: A Life of Christopher Columbus*, Boston: Little, Brown, 1942.

Morison, Samuel Eliot, *Portuguese Voyages to America in the Fifteenth Century*, Cambridge: Harvard University Press, 1940.

"Narrative of the Expedition of Hernando De Soto, By the Gentleman of Elvas," Lewis, Theodore H. (ed), *Spanish Explorer in the Southern United States, 1528-1543*, New York: Barnes & Noble, 1946.

New Catholic Encyclopedia.

Newton, Arthur Percival, *The European Nations in the West Indies, 1493-1688*, London: A & C Blacks, 1933.

Nunn, George Emra, *The Geographical Conceptions of Columbus: A Critical Consideration of Four Problems*, New York: American Geographical Society, 1924.

Parry, John Horace, *The Age of Reconnaissance*, Cleveland: World, 1963.

Parry, John Horace, *The Spanish Theory of Empire in the Sixteenth Century*, 1940, New York: Octagon Books, 1974.

Prescott, William H., *The Conquest of Peru*, Various editions.

Prescott, William H., *History of the Conquest of Mexico*, New York: The Modern Library, n.d.

Prescott, William, *History of the Reign of Ferdinand and Isabella the Catholic*, Kirck, John Foster (ed), Philadelphia: J.B. Lippincott, 1872.

Quinn, David Beers, *England and the Discovery of America, 1481-1620*, New York: Alfred A. Knopf, 1974.

Quinn, David Beers, *The Lost Colonists: Their Fortune and Probable Fate*, Raleigh NC: North Carolina Dept. of Cultural Resource, 1984.

Quinn, David Beers, *Raleigh and the British Empire*, New York: Macmillan, 1949.

Quinn, David Beers, *The Roanoke Voyages 1584-1590*, London: Hakluyt Society, 1955.

Quinn, David Beers, *The Voyages and Colonising Enterprises of Sir Humphrey Gilbert*, Hakluyt Society, 1940, Kraus, 1967.

Richman, Irving Berdine, *California Under Spain and Mexico, 1535-1847*, 1911, New York: Cooper Square, 1969.

Rowse, A.L., "The Elizabethans and America," *American Heritage*, X No. 3 (April 1959).

Rowse,, A.L., "New England in the Earliest Days," *American Heritage*, X No. 5 (August 1959).

Sahagun, Bernardino de, *The War of Conquest: How It was Waged Here in Mexico*, Anderson, Arthur J.O. & Charles E. Dibble (trans), Salt Lake City: University of Utah Press, 1978.

Sancho, Pedro, *An Account of the Conquest of Peru*, Means, Philip Ainsworth (trans), 1917, Boston: Milford House, 1972.

Scisco, Louis Dow, "Discovery of the Chesapeake Bay 1525-1573," *Maryland Historical Magazine*, XL (1943).

Scisco, Louis Dow, "Voyage of Vicente Gonslez in 1588," *Maryland Historical Magazine*, XLII (1947).

Shiels, William Eugene, *King and Church: The Rise and Fall of the Patronato Real*, Chicago: Loyola University Press, 1961.

Smith, Bradford, *Captain John Smith: His Life & Legend*, Phila: J.R. Lippincott, 1953.

Smith, Judy Brant, *The Image of Guadalupe: Myth or Mirage*, Garden City, NY: Doubleday, 1983.

Solis de Meras, 'Gonzalo, *Pedro Menendez de Aviles*, Conner, Jeanette Thurbar (trans. and ed.), 1923, Gainesville: University of Florida Press, 1964.

Thomson, George Malcolm, *Sir Francis Drake*, New York: William Morrow, 1972.

Todorov, Tzvetan, *The Conquest of America*, Howard, Richard (trans), New York: Harpers Row, 1934.

Wait, Eugene M., *The March of the Teutons*, New York: Carlton Press, 1972.

Warner, George F. (ed), *The Voyage of Robert Dudley Afterwards Styled Earl of Warwick and Leicester and Duke of Northumberland to the West Indies, 1594-1595*, Hakluyt, 1899, Rep 1967.

Williamson, James A., *Hawkins of Plymouth*, 2d ed., New York: Barnes & Noble, 1969.

Wright, I.A., "The Dutch and Cuba: 1609-1643," *Hispanic American Historical Review*, IV No. 4 (November 1921).

Wright, Louis Booker, *Religion and Empire: The Alliance between Piety and Commerce in English Expansion 1558-1625*, Chapel Hill: University of North Carolina Press, 1943, Rep. New York: Octagon Books, 1973.

INDEX